MAROONED

ALSO BY PHIL FREEMAN

Running the Voodoo Down:
The Electric Music of Miles Davis

MAROONED

The Next Generation of
Desert Island Discs

PHIL FREEMAN

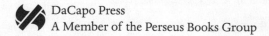
DaCapo Press
A Member of the Perseus Books Group

For Izalia

Designed by Timm Bryson
Set in 11 point Dante by The Perseus Books Group

Library of Congress Cataloging-in-Publication Data
Marooned : the next generation of desert island discs / edited by Phil Freeman.—
1st Da Capo Press ed.
   p. cm.
  ISBN-13: 978-0-306-81485-3
  ISBN-10: 0-306-81485-4
  1. Popular music--History and criticism. I. Freeman, Phil, 1971-
  ML3470.M345 2007
  781.64--dc22
                    2007011664

Published by Da Capo Press
A Member of the Perseus Books Group
http://www.dacapopress.com

Da Capo Press books are available at special discounts for bulk purchases in the U.S. by corporations, institutions, and other organizations. For more information, please contact the Special Markets Department at the Perseus Books Group, 2300 Chestnut St., Philadelphia, PA 19103, or e-mail special.markets@perseusbooks.com.

1 2 3 4 5 6 7 8 9

CONTENTS

      KILLERS
         by Ian Christe   267

21   RETURN TO TREASURE ISLAND   281

      ABOUT THE AUTHORS   323

      CREDITS   329

      ACKNOWLEDGMENTS   331

FOREWORD

BY GREIL MARCUS

You may be stranded if you stick around
And that's really, something!
—Roxy Music, "Street Life," 1973

THIS BOOK IS LIKELY FAR MORE EXPENSIVE THAN THE $17 OR SO YOU MAY PAY FOR IT. IF YOU DON'T KNOW THE RECORDS CELEBRATED HERE, YOU'LL WANT TO. IF you do know them, you'll hear them in new ways, under different skies. For that matter, you may find yourself driven to the record store or its ether equivalent in search of albums you discarded long ago—only to find you still can't hear a fraction of what Daphne Carr hears in *Ladies And Gentlemen We Are Floating In Space* by Spiritualized or what Michaelangelo Matos hears in *History of Our World Part 1: Breakbeat and Jungle Ultramix by DJ DB*. And you may nevertheless be convinced that what they hear is there for you to hear—if you hold your breath, care enough, live that long.

Again and again, the albums taken up by Douglas Wolk (Stereolab's *Transient Random Noise Bursts With Announcements*—Amoeba

Records in Berkeley had a dozen Stereolab discs, but not this one;
the manuscript of this book must have had other readers before
me), Simon Reynolds (John Martyn's *Solid Air*—bought it again,
again found a swamp), Ned Raggett (My Bloody Valentine's
Loveless—his piece is a treasure map to a treasure that may have
never been buried), and a dozen others are liberated from cliché.
Particular records are liberated from the clichés that have surrounded them since they first appeared, and pop music as such is
liberated from the clichés of pop writing, even—or especially—
when those clichés are wheeled onstage and faced head-on. "Art
stands alone and free of the breath that expels it," says Scott Seward of Divine Styler's *Spiral Walls Containing Autumns Of Light*.
The idea may be trite. But there's a desperation in the words Seward chooses—from the airy "alone and free" to "expels it," which
is brutal by comparison—that opens doors into a world where
nothing is trite. Seward is in fact talking about the tenth track on
the album, "The Next," or rather a single couplet from the song—
"as if it explained everything," he explains. "It doesn't. It couldn't.
It never will. Art stands alone and free of the breath that expels it.
All music and words belong to the universe once released from
our mortal grasp. Many people who hear that line don't even
speak English. To them it is simply a disembodied voice's assertion
of existence."

As I read Seward, he is saying that the challenge is to hear lines
from an English-language pop composition as if they are not in
English—to hear them as the desperate attempt to communicate,
to hear the desperate attempt to connect ("I wanted to know
everything that Rakim knew," he says), and, in that abstraction, to
begin again, from the beginning.

Whatever pop music might be between the covers of this book, it isn't lingua franca. In the fifties, young people woke up to find that, somehow, they'd been born knowing the pop language that was taking shape all around them. How was it that, for a white, teenage girl on a farm in Iowa no less than for an eight-year-old African-American boy in Tulsa, Little Richard needed no translator? That was the pop world; it isn't any longer. Over the last twenty years some of the most interesting and many of the most radical pop artists have worked as if to erect barriers between themselves and any version of a so-conceived mass audience, if only to ensure that whoever made it to the other side really wanted to be there. Again and again, writers here find themselves speaking not of how a record or a musician or a singer changed their lives, or the world, or the-face-of-pop—but rather "invented a language," or tried to. The metaphor of the desert island—where there may be no one to talk to, where, after a time, even your own words, as you talk to yourself or your imaginary friends and enemies, begin to sound foreign, empty, backwards—moves through the pages like a bug, buzzing here, disappearing there, but getting bigger and bigger as the story collages itself together, the bug changing colors, until, with Ian Christe on Iron Maiden's *Killers*, the themes of reinventing language and the desert island turn into a single all-consuming image, with Christe, stranded on an ice floe, certain "The Western world could rebuild itself pretty well on the blueprint of Iron Maiden's second album. Sure, you could say there's too great an emphasis on *killing*, but what's so unusual about that?"

I like the way, again and again, people find themselves fetishizing their records—describing labels, lettering, coloring, pictures

hidden in sleeve art. I like the way, again and again, the writers
here blindside the reader, if not themselves. "The flyer implied a
subculture," Matos writes of a rave throwaway, "—not the only
one, but one that drew me in, suburban in nature but without the
studied casualness that typified indie rock, an indifference I
couldn't have faked at that point if you'd force-fed me 'ludes and
strapped me to a chair at a Warhol retrospective." "This is all textbook stuff," Seward says. "I have no idea which textbook, but one
of them." The cover of *Force It*, "the most successful album" by
UFO, Dave Queen notes, "depicts couple—rumored to be Genesis
P. Orridge and Cosey Fanni Tutti of Throbbing Gristle of 'Zyklon
B Zombie' fame—'forcing it' while surrounded by faucets. This
was around the time Farrah Fawcett . . . "

> *Not present in the present, overboard with limited future*
> *And I'm standing alone still getting a thrill*
> —Wire, "Marooned," 1978

There may be a more delicate sense of how people listen to
music, and of how music crosses borders—borders of its own
composition, or those the world sets between forms, styles, eras,
and people—here than in any other book on pop music. "This
year, Dionne Warwick is hosting the American Music Awards,"
John Darnielle writes in his piece on Warwick's *Legends*; he's back
in 1977. "That's all I remember; I don't know whether this was the
first time I heard her sing or not. I just remember seeing her, feeling both confused by and attracted to her languor, her sense of
self-assurance, her easy manner. Something in her approach suggested to me that there was a separate reality somewhere, one in

which emotions were much subtler and less raw than they were in my reality." As Lou Reed said when he inducted Dion into the Rock & Roll Hall of Fame, speaking of the lingua franca of "I Wonder Why," "it was the sound of another life," or as Darnielle puts it, "The connection between moments; all we can really ask of pop music."

But it's not all we do ask. "I wanted to know everything Rakim knew": we ask pop music for everything. We ask it to inform our lives, shake them up, call them into question, save them, end them, and for that matter raise the dead. On *The History of Our World Part 1*, a sample from Touch's 1971 "Once You Understand" has cops telling one Mr. Kirk that his son is dead from an overdose. But then an Isley Brothers sample "turned into chipmunk talk . . . exposes the opening sample's pathos as a sick joke—on Mr. Kirk, on his foolish son, on the hopelessly square 'Once You Understand,' on the drug faddism and generation gaps that play out in more or less the same manner every few years, and on you the raver, who by hearing and ostensibly dancing to this new song, is implicated as a potential overdose." In other words, you have no idea what you're getting into when you listen. It may be, as Matos says, merely "weirdly inviting": "If these guys can laugh at something that harrowing, maybe we can have some of what they are taking, or at least watch from a relatively safe distance while they skirt the edge." But it may be much more than that.

Scott Seward's chapter on Divine Styler is about a breakdown— a personal breakdown, an aesthetic end-of-the-world-out-of-which-a-new-world-may-be-born breakdown, and a social breakdown. It's the early nineties; the writer has reached a dead end, a whole nation of dead ends, and time stops. He finds an

American nowhere, one place as good as another, in this case, Philadelphia:

> They said that cities were a lost cause. Blow them up and start over. Dirty, rotting husks filled with crime and insanity, which was kind of true at the time. A trip of a few blocks to the store could mean running a gauntlet of illness, need, and menace. . . . I can't help but feel that this country went through some sort of brutal senseless war during that period and that nobody wants to talk about it. It's like it never happened. So many dead and lost and gone and locked up for life. Entire neighborhoods . . . poof! And yes, you guessed it, despite the neglect and misery there was vibrancy and life and the radio was rocking with yet another generation of craftsmen fashioning art out of the bare minimum.

It's a manifesto by hindsight; at the time, Seward is working the graveyard shift in a supermarket. In his pages, time slows, until you are with him minute by minute, inch by inch. Everything becomes clear, as if there's a fluorescent glare coming right through words. The music he's trying to enshrine, to set free, to bring to you, establishes a different dimension of time; that's its gift. And it redeems, or calls into question, the sense of time in which Seward is actually living his life—and the result is that meaninglessness becomes impossible. You are always hearing. You are always anticipating the next turn, the next surprise, the next note, the next confirmation that affirms what went before, the life already lived, gained, wasted, but is not quite the same.

That sense, shared by many of the writers brought together here, creates moments in which each reader of this book will find his or her epiphany, one that says, *yes, this is how it is, this is what I've always felt*—or that says, *no, I didn't know that, I never understood that, I may never understand it, but now I know it's there, and maybe, when the time comes, in my own life, I'll recognize this moment for what it is.* For me it is the satisfaction Seward takes in blocking his store, going "through the aisles one by one stacking cans and jars and boxes until every shelf was a solid wall of products." For you it might be Daphne Carr on the wrong end of a telephone call, or Ian Christe laying waste to the entire heritage of Western pop music until only one squawk is left. You may be stranded if you stick around, all alone but still getting a thrill, and, as the man said, handing you an ice-cream cone after squealing and jerking and otherwise turning words into hiccups, that's really—just the barest pause—something: that you're hearing not what anyone else is hearing, but nevertheless hearing in the same way, wanting everything, taking what you can get, knowing that there are times when you know you've gotten more than you deserve.

INTRODUCTION

By Phil Freeman

B ECAUSE THE DAMN THING WAS MY IDEA, I'VE PROBA-
BLY SPENT MORE TIME THAN ANY OF MY CHOSEN
CONTRIBUTORS THINKING ABOUT THIS PROJECT. I
hope I have, anyway. Make no mistake, I don't wonder whether
the idea of picking a single album is in any way irrelevant in the
iPod era. In fact, I think the opposite is true. I believe that anyone
who thinks seriously about music (as the writers I chose for this
project certainly do) must recognize that the album remains the
artists' chosen mode of expression. And artistic intent, as mani-
fested in track running order and selection (what makes the album
vs. what is relegated to a B-side or tossed with a shrug to the producers of a charity compilation), is still something to be honored.
The shuffle function is fun, but ultimately, albums continue to
matter.

That's one reason for putting this book together—to remind
readers and writers of my generation that albums remain important. Another is to document all the ways music has changed since
the 1979 release of *Stranded*, the anthology that first tried this

trick. While that book was and remains an entertaining read, its vision of pop music is almost unrecognizable today. Let's tick off the examples: First of all, there was no drum 'n' bass then. By now, though, it's gone from cult sub-subgenre to car-commercial soundtrack, and Michaelangelo Matos chose the d'n'b comp *History Of Our World, Part 1* for his personal island.

Hip-hop was the soundtrack to parties in the Bronx, but had yet to migrate down to the Lower East Side and the art scene. Soon, the Clash's "This Is Radio Clash" would appear, followed eventually by Blondie's "Rapture" and eventually the wholesale colonization of the pop landscape by hip-hop. But nobody was talking about rap in *Stranded*, and again, that's redressed in this volume with Scott Seward's look at Divine Styler's *Spiral Walls Containing Autumns Of Light*, and Tom Breihan's discussion of Brand Nubian's *One For All*.

Some would say jazz was already dead by 1979, so it's no surprise that it wasn't mentioned back then. But this time out, Geeta Dayal pays tribute to Alice Coltrane; Derek Taylor conducts a detailed exegesis on Sonny Rollins's *A Night At The Village Vanguard* (an album that was already twenty years old in 1979); and Greg Tate, a personal hero of mine, discusses Miles Davis's *Bitches Brew*.

In 1979, metal was Black Sabbath, Alice Cooper, Deep Purple, Led Zeppelin, AC/DC, and maybe Van Halen—all targets of critical spitballs. In 2007, as this book goes to press, metal is commercially huge, and five *Marooned* essays discuss works in the genre—Ian Christe's take on Iron Maiden's *Killers*, Laina Dawes's explication of Skunk Anansie's *Stoosh*, Anthony Miccio's look at Dio, Dave Queen's bent take on the Scorpions, and my own piece.

Punk was either an English thing that had burned itself out two summers earlier, or a New York art students' circle jerk—the genuinely proletarian hardcore movement (for the most part, just as critically reviled as its equally populist cousin, metal) hadn't yet gotten off the ground. Hardcore came and went, and spawned—for good or ill—indie rock, which gives us subject matter for several more essays in this volume, like Ned Raggett's take on My Bloody Valentine's *Loveless*, Daphne Carr's investigation of Spiritualized's *Ladies And Gentlemen We Are Floating In Space*, and Douglas Wolk's look at Stereolab's *Transient Random Noise Bursts With Announcements*.

So the point is, *Stranded* is no longer anything like an accurate representation of the pop music universe. It was never intended to be, of course—it was only ever meant to semi-accurately reflect the tastes of the selected batch of critics, and it probably didn't even do that. If Greil Marcus's pile o' scribes were anything like the folks I invited to my party, they second-guessed themselves like mad, chose new albums at least three times before writing, and . . . you get the idea. *Stranded's* vision of history—heavy on '50s and '60s rock, with some acts only a few years old thrown in, plus one bizarre defense of Linda Ronstadt that somehow has more passion than any of the pieces lionizing more canonical picks—probably bears some resemblance to what the surviving contributors are still listening to, but I gotta be honest and say that I don't personally know a single person who listens to a lot of the *Stranded* artists with any kind of regularity. Sure, the Ramones and the Velvet Underground still have an audience, but Van Morrison and the Ronettes and, yes, even the recently sorta-reunited New

York Dolls are more frequently mentioned in passing than played for pleasure.

But by doing this, I've learned that asking people to pick just one album generates unpredictable answers. For example, John Darnielle, who I half expected to pick something by Mastodon or Pig Destroyer, turned out to be a Dionne Warwick fan. Scott Seward, another guy I know as a metalhead, picked the aforementioned Divine Styler, a rapper I haven't even thought about in over a decade. What really astonishes me, though, is how personal everyone's choices were. Nobody said, "This is a really good album, deserving of wider attention." They all said something like, "When I was [ten, or thirteen, or twenty-one], this album ate its way into my brain, and it hasn't departed since. Here's why I don't ever want it to leave." So in reading these essays, you're going to learn as much about the writers as the records.

I've read all these pieces repeatedly, first as a proofreader and then as a fan of language well used. Not only did these folks choose records I was unfamiliar with (in some cases, albums I wouldn't listen to on a dare), they talked about them in ways I would never have thought to do. It's been a hell of a lot of fun for me to watch them think, and work. I hope you enjoy the journeys you're about to take, accompanied by some fine, talented people.

MOTÖRHEAD
No Remorse
Bronze, 1985

By Phil Freeman

WHEN I STARTED THINKING ABOUT WHAT RECORD I WOULD WANT TO TALK ABOUT IN THIS BOOK, I WHO HAVE BEEN LISTENING PRIMARILY TO METAL for almost the last twenty-five years (one of the first albums I ever bought, or talked my dad into buying for me, was Judas Priest's *Screaming For Vengeance*, in 1982), one somehow kept coming back as an obvious candidate—Steely Dan's *Gaucho*. I've listened to *Gaucho* dozens of times over the past few years, and the older I get, the more its bitterness seems to match my own, for reasons I'm not going to get into here. It's more like a collection of ultra-pared-down short stories about the death of love and the hollowness of American culture than an album. But that's only if you don't take the brilliant musicianship into account, something that seems to happen a lot when critics discuss Steely Dan. Their music fades into the background and becomes a mere platform for the lyrics. That's understandable—critics are writers, and they'll go for the familiar territory of words first. But when I focus on the way the instruments bounce off each other and then come together, everyone working in service of a collective goal with little or no showboating, even during solos, I love the disc even more. "Babylon Sisters," the title track, and "Third World Man" in particular are just impeccably performed pieces of *music*.

Of course, I love the lyrics. The song "Gaucho" may be the most perfect exploration of cuckolding I've ever heard, from any songwriter. "Can't you see they're laughing at me?" Nobody's ever put the raw pain of watching the person you love (whether straight or, as has often been claimed about the song's characters, gay, though I'm not so sure about that theory, if only because the Becker/Fagen song-universe is so thoroughly heteronormative about 99.9 percent of the time) publicly burn you into such gleaming relief. But I've only been seriously listening to *Gaucho* for a few years, and though I'm sure as I type these words that its impact on me will only grow as time goes on, I could be wrong. After all, *Gaucho* didn't start to really mean anything to me until I was thirty. Perhaps when I'm fifty or so, it will lose its significance, and seem like an emotional relic of times past. So it's not The One.

Neither is the disc that seemed like an obvious second-place candidate, the Minutemen's *Double Nickels On The Dime*. I'm too young (and not by much, either, which makes it doubly irritating) to have seen Black Flag or the Minutemen live. Their singer and guitarist, D. Boon, died before I'd heard of the group. But not long after his van crash, I read his obituary in *Rolling Stone* and decided they were a band I needed to hear.

When *Ballot Result*, a posthumous live compilation, was released, I had my local record store order me a copy. They did, but the guy I knew who worked there, the guy every budding rock geek has in his life who's just a few years older, and yet (in the perceptions of said budding rock geek) immeasurably cooler and more knowledgeable, got in a copy of *Double Nickels* a few weeks later, and when I stopped by for something else, he pushed it across the counter, saying only, "I got this in for you. Just buy it." I did, and my head pretty much exploded.

I admit it—I hadn't listened to *Ballot Result* very much. The songs were poorly recorded, and seemed like herky-jerky and formless blurts to my hard rock–trained ear. But *Double Nickels* sounded like a real album, not just a collection of lo-fi live tapes. All three instruments were crystal clear, and D. Boon's and Mike Watt's lyrics were perfectly audible and—at least in terms of knowing what the words were, if not exactly parsing out meaning yet—comprehensible. So those trebly guitar riffs and throbbing, minimal yet totally active and compelling basslines (and the ridiculous beats George Hurley was laying down behind) all drilled their way into my brain from the first seconds of "Anxious Mo-Fo" all the way to the fade-out of "Love Dance" on first listen. That tape stayed in my Walkman for almost all of high school.

And unlike with Steely Dan, the lyrics weren't very important to me at all. I was fascinated by the instrumental interaction—the way Boon's guitar and Watt's bass occupied almost entirely separate spaces, with Hurley's drums in between and all around. A couple of songs leapt out, lyrically: "History Lesson, Part 2," which told the story of the band's beginnings; "Political Song For Michael Jackson To Sing," with its words to live by: "If we heard mortar shells / We'd cuss more in our songs / And cut down the guitar solos" (coming, of course, right before the guitar solo);

"Corona," a bittersweet story of disillusioned patriotism. Oh, and there were cover tunes. Van Halen's "Ain't Talkin' 'Bout Love," Creedence Clearwater Revival's "Don't Look Now," and Steely Dan's "Doctor Wu," all stripped down and transformed.

But I didn't choose *Double Nickels On The Dime* for my desert island album, precisely because I know it so well. It exists in my mind in almost perfect recall. If I want to, I can hear it anytime by turning off whatever's playing through speakers or headphones and just thinking about it. And yet, my actual selection is an album I know nearly as well—it's one I've had, and have been listening to, since junior high school.

I don't have rock heroes anymore. I've met enough musicians, especially front men (who are the most frequently idolized members of their bands), to know they're just people, and frequently subpar people at that. I'm not gonna name names, but there are a lot of real assholes out there, and by now, nobody should be learning that from this essay. There was a time, though. . . .

When I was a teenager, thirteen or fourteen at most, one of my friends told me about two bands. One was Black Flag, and the other was Motörhead. At that point, I was primarily a Judas Priest fan. I loved *Screaming For Vengeance, British Steel, Hell Bent For Leather*, and the latest disc, *Defenders Of The Faith*. That kind of high-gloss, utterly produced sound was my dominant paradigm for hard, heavy music. But that had exactly nothing to do with what I heard on *My War, Slip It In* (both released the previous year), and *No Remorse*.

Henry Rollins was the best vocalist Black Flag ever had. Nobody believes that but me, it seems, but I'll stick by my opinion. Keith Morris was fun, but Chavo Pederast and Dez Cadena were just ranters. It wasn't until Rollins came along that guitarist/bandleader Greg Ginn found his ideal foil. Rollins' intensity and rage matched the nihilistic obsessiveness of the music. And as Ginn expanded the parameters of Black Flag's sound beyond punk and into metal and even something close to jazz-rock fusion or progressive rock (on *In My Head* and the instrumental records), Rollins became a more compelling front man, mustering an almost Jim Morrison–like intensity, without the florid phallic imagery. When the band broke up, he was just beginning to come into his own as a performer.

Slip It In and *My War*, companion albums recorded and released in 1984 after three years of court-mandated absence from the studio, shocked the hardcore community. Black Flag, whose *Damaged* album and the relentless touring that followed built a nationwide punk scene where none had been before, had ignored almost all the harder-faster developments of their time away. Instead, they'd blossomed into a crushing rock force, influenced as much by Black Sabbath as the Ramones. And the evolution didn't stop; by the time they recorded their final studio album, *In My Head*, a year later, they sounded like King Crimson raging on crank.

As a solo artist, Rollins blossomed as a writer while surrounding himself with musicians who were arguably even more talented than those in Black Flag. I got to interview him twice in the mid-90s and again in 2006. All three times, he was a smart, funny guy who was happy to talk at length not only about his own music, but about jazz or metal or anything else. The journalist half of me appreciated the great quotes for publication; the geeky fan half of me lapped up the chance to spend an hour or two monopolizing the attention of someone I admired.

But that was years in the future. What Black Flag and Motörhead offered the teenaged me, on initial encounter, was raw ag-
gression. Volume, speed, power (and power chords)—these were
the greatest sounds I'd ever heard. They were very different from
each other, of course. Black Flag were one of the first bands to
help divorce metal from the blues and rock 'n' roll through their
embrace of dissonance and un-swinging rhythms—most evident,
ironically, on the *My War* song "Swinging Man"—while Motörhead were very much rooted in both. (Lemmy's even made a solo
album of rockabilly covers alongside former members of the
Stray Cats and the Rockats.)

At no time since first hearing *My War, Slip It In*, and *No Remorse*
have I not owned all three. First, tapes of the vinyl albums from
the guy who introduced me to both bands; then, my own copies
(Black Flag on cassette, Motörhead on double vinyl, though I
didn't spring for the fancy leather sleeve). I never upgraded to CD
with Black Flag, though both albums and a bunch of their other
stuff sit in my iPod, transferred from a coworker's hard drive to
my own. I do have *No Remorse* on CD—a recent remastered reissue with a few bonus tracks, none of which add much to the experience as I've known it for twenty-one years.

"Ace Of Spades," which starts the first disc off just as it did the
album that shares its title, is the one Motörhead song that people
who don't own a single Motörhead record might have heard. It's a
great rock single, starting with an undeniable riff and a chorus any
fool can remember and punch their fist to the second time it
comes around. It also encapsulates Motörhead's sound, all headlong speed and minimalism. They were embraced by punk audiences for exactly this kind of head-bashing mayhem, the guitar

solo rising as organically out of the core riff as any rockabilly or garage-rock classic, with none of the "Hey, look at me!" pomp of 1970s stadium rock. Motörhead didn't change their style in an attempt to get a hit. The song was the lead single (and title track) from the best-selling album of their career, but it was a play straight for the then-underground metal audience. There was no thought of ascending the pop charts. Just slam it at 'em, was the strategy, and it worked beautifully. Three minutes of pure energy, with lyrics about playing cards—and *only* about playing cards. For a lyricist of frequently biting wit, Lemmy kept it simple this time.

The next track is a live version of the song "Motorhead." Lemmy wrote it as a B-side for Hawkwind just before he left, and wound up playing it harder, faster, and louder than those cosmic stoners (who had undeniable merits of their own) ever could. That's followed by another pummeling cut from the *Ace Of Spades* album, "Jailbait." Lemmy's got a ravenous and well-documented sexual appetite, which is not all that surprising in a rock star but somewhat unnerving, considering the sheer physical ugliness of the man. He's got warts the size of garbanzo beans on his face, so he covers them with a Civil War mustache, one of those things that comes down on both sides and runs up to reconnect with the sideburns, but leaves the chin bare. The idea of a guy like that chasing after teenaged pussy is more than a little upsetting. Sex vanishes from the next two songs, though—"Stay Clean" and "Too Late, Too Late" are punky anthems about self-sufficiency and rejecting idiots, respectively. The latter works as a sort of hyperaggressive "Positively 4th Street," if you will.

"Killed By Death," which closes out side one of the vinyl version of *No Remorse*, is one of four new songs on the disc meant to entice longtime fans with a taste of the band's recently overhauled lineup. For everyone else, it was still a best-of, since at least two of these new tracks were absolute monsters, and "Killed By Death" was surely one of those. The new guitarists, Phil Campbell (who's still with the band) and Wurzel (who departed after the band's very next full-length studio effort, 1986's *Orgasmatron*) hammer out a heavy blues-metal riff that's slower than most early Motörhead cuts and closer in spirit to the work of Black Sabbath or Brian Johnson–era AC/DC. Lemmy's lyrics turn blues clichés on their sides—"If you squeeze my lizard/I'll put my snake on you" is a lead-in to the chorus, which is a raw-throated boast of his, and by extension the band's, immortality. When one considers that *No Remorse* was a tenth-anniversary release for Motörhead, and they're now into their fourth decade as a unit, its resonance only seems stronger.

Side two of the vinyl commences with "Bomber," the title track from the band's third album (and second of 1979). It's as aggressive as anything that's come so far, a perfect side-opener, with lyrics describing the band as an invading air force, here to devastate the unwary. Not all that hyperbolic, considering the legendary levels of volume Motörhead pumped out in those days. I remember reading a review of one of their shows in an issue of the British metal magazine *Kerrang!!!* (punctuation in original) from about 1985, wherein the writer described audience members dissolving into puddles of liquid flesh from the noise. When I saw Motörhead opening for Iron Maiden at Madison Square Garden in 2004, the arena was still half-empty during their set (Dio was also on the bill) and the waves of sound crashing off the steel and concrete nearly brought tears to my eyes. Motörhead liked to punish their listeners, that's for sure.

The next few songs demonstrate how much difference changing one member of the band can make. "Iron Fist" is a punky, grinding track driven by a riff not all that different from what would be heard on early, primitive thrash metal records from the likes of Voivod and Slayer a few years later. "Shine" and "Dancing On Your Grave," by contrast, are radio-ready, with soaring lead lines and a previously unprecedented emphasis on melody and guitar solos. These two tracks are a snapshot of the short year that Brian Robertson, formerly of Thin Lizzy, was the lead guitarist. For all the technical flash and beauty of his playing, though, his short curly hair and penchant for wearing shorts onstage made him almost comically ill-suited to life with Motörhead—never mind that he refused to play some of the band's most-requested tracks.

Side two ends with the slightly slower-than-usual "Metropolis," based on Lemmy's vague memories of the film of the same name, and another new song, "Snaggletooth." The latter is both fast and crushing, and lyrically it pokes fun at Lemmy's speed-ravaged teeth (later replaced with dentures).

The second disc begins with a rumble and a roar—"Overkill," the title track of their first album on Bronze Records. The lyrics are probably their most anthemic and self-defining: "Only way to feel the noise is when it's good and loud/So good I can't believe it, screaming with the crowd," it begins, Lemmy barking over Philthy Animal Taylor's double bass drums as they somehow manage to combine primitive thrash with swing. This song has a rocking beat second to nothing short of Elvis's "All Shook Up," and really demonstrates Motörhead's commitment to classic rock 'n' roll aesthetics.

Motörhead's earliest studio recordings, *On Parole* (only released once "Ace Of Spades" proved their commercial viability) and a self-titled disc that includes their cover of ZZ Top's "Beer Drinkers and Hell Raisers," are not represented on *No Remorse* for the obvious reason that both those discs preceded their contract with Bronze Records. Instead, things pick up with 1979's *Overkill*, the single most heavily represented release, with four cuts ("Overkill," "Stay Clean," "No Class," and "Metropolis"), two B-sides ("Too Late, Too Late" and "Like A Nightmare") and their contemporaneous single version of "Louie Louie." By contrast, only two cuts are culled from the same year's *Bomber*—its title track and "Stone Dead Forever." A live version of "Leaving Here," from the *Golden Years* EP, is also incorporated into the *No Remorse* package, and then it's on to *Ace Of Spades*, which offers the convenience-minded its title track, "(We Are) The Road Crew," and "Jailbait." Both of Motörhead's collaborations with their all-female contemporaries and sorta counterparts Girlschool (a bunch of ugly hard-rocking chicks, indeed), "Please Don't Touch" and "Emergency," are included, too, and the trio's utterly crushing live album *No Sleep Till Hammersmith* offers "Motorhead" and "Iron Horse." The latter inclusion saves them from plucking anything but the title track from *Iron Fist*, an album many fans think of as substandard. And the group's final pre–*No Remorse* offering, 1983's *Another Perfect Day*, yields "Shine" and "Dancing On Your Grave," both solid cuts, even if I'd probably have tried pretty hard to make room for "Back At The Funny Farm," one of Motörhead's greatest songs ever, from any lineup.

No Remorse isn't the best of Motörhead. They've continued to make good-to-great records in the twenty-two years (at this writing) since its release. In fact, it's arguable that the current lineup of band members, who have been together since 1992, is the best one they've ever had, and some of the albums with current players, like 1996's *Overnight Sensation* and 2002's *Hammered*, are among their most consistent and powerful. Certainly, the Motörhead of 1985 would never have been able to write songs as musically expressive and lyrically punishing as "I Don't Believe A Word" or "Brave New World." Lemmy's worldview was just as cynical in 1975, when he formed the band, as it is today, but he's grown wiser in his old age—he's sixty now—and his perspective has broadened beyond pussy.

The thing is, though, I've been paying close attention to the band for over twenty years and have given each album—from 1986's *Orgasmatron* to 2006's *Kiss Of Death*—at least a careful listen, if not a permanent place in my collection. (I admit it, I didn't find *1916, March Or Die, Bastards, Snake Bite Love,* or *We Are Motörhead* to be keepers.) So for me, *No Remorse* is as much a signpost as it is a stand-alone album. While I love the majority of its tracks, even the ones I don't like remind me of all the other Motörhead songs on albums I couldn't haul with me to my figurative desert island. And it also reminds me of how many years Motörhead's music has been an important part of my life. How long I've felt the adrenalin rush that only "Ace Of Spades" and "Overkill" and that incredible wall-of-noise live version of the song "Motorhead" can provide. How long I've admired Lemmy, as a musician, a writer, and a thinker. (Check out his autobiography, *White Line Fever*; it's almost as funny as David Lee Roth's book, *Crazy From The Heat*, and is as

utterly clear-eyed a look at the quotidian reality of life as a professional musician as you're ever likely to find.)

I got to interview Lemmy once, in 2002. He drank from a massive glass of Jack Daniel's and Coke throughout, but it never
seemed to affect his clear-eyed logic or his self-deprecating sense
of humor. Like Rollins, he was everything I could have hoped for,
as a journalist and as a fan. So I've got that memory, as well as
memories of the shows I've seen them play—from headliners on a
small nightclub stage to headliners opening for Iron Maiden in a
vast arena—and all the songs that have burned themselves into my
brain over the decades. And it all started with *No Remorse*. In many
ways, *No Remorse* and its leader/figurehead/visionary helped
make me the person I am: Motörhead taught me the values of
skepticism and self-reliance; sharpened my wit; convinced me beyond any doubt that simplicity and crudity are cardinal virtues, especially when accompanied by a sense of humor; and gave me the
firm knowledge that louder is *always* better.

2

SKUNK ANANSIE
Stoosh
Epic, 1996

By Laina Dawes

WHEN I WOKE UP, I WAS LYING FACEDOWN AT THE EDGE OF THE BEACH, GRIPPING ONTO WHAT LOOKED LIKE THE WING OF AN AIRPLANE. I TURNED my head to the side, wiping sand out of my eyes and trying to figure out exactly where I was. My waterproof backpack was miraculously at my side and I painfully hoisted myself up until I was standing in the sand. Pebbles filled my pants, T-shirt, and bra. Alone in the dark, I grabbed my knapsack, peeled off my water-soaked clothes and tried to remember what happened.

After remembering the plane nose-diving into the ocean and the muted screams, I realized what had happened. I tried to yell for help, but my sore sand-filled throat wouldn't let me. After staggering naked along the shoreline in the dark, hoping to find another survivor, I realized that at least for now, I was alone. Walking inland, I found a tree whose branches made for a decent emergency shelter and, using my knapsack as a pillow, passed out.

The next day, I reached into the bag to see what had survived the water. My MP3 player was there, sheathed in a leather case. I also found some chocolate bars, packed in case I tired of the crappy airline food, and a book. After inhaling one of the bars, I put on my player, got dressed, and started walking along the coastline. I prayed, thanking a higher power that I'd survived with nothing more than just a few cuts and scrapes. Most importantly, I thanked the now crystal-clear sunny skies that I had been listening to *Stoosh* before the plane crashed. I stopped for a minute, breathing in the salty air and feeling the blinding sun warm my body, and realized that for at least a little while I should sit and reflect on what had just happened. The familiar music coursing through my headphones seemed to automatically energize my mind enough to think about the life that I had unwittingly left behind—and might never see again.

During the grunge era (1989–1996), it seemed like there was a major concert happening in Toronto every week. With my Doc Marten boots, shaved head, nose piercing, and new tattoo, I was there. One of my first ventures into this new world was to check out Soundgarden at the now-defunct Concert Hall, a historic and once elegant building on the outside but a cavernous sweat den within. If you wanted to sit in the balcony (advisable unless you wanted to get swarmed in the huge mosh pit that took over the entire lower floor), it was guaranteed that halfway through the headliner's set it would start raining.

And no, there wasn't a leak in the roof. It was sweat, intermixed with beer and cigarette smoke, that rose to the ceiling and came back down in a viscous liquid form. Many concertgoers would use their hands to shield their permed hair from the noxious substance and run downstairs. But a true fan would stay put and continue rocking out, leering at a shirtless Chris Cornell, whose long, wavy hair caused men to reexamine their sexual preference and women to throw their bras onto the stage.

In one year, I must have seen about twenty concerts. While I always went with an odd mixture of friends, from pot-smoking doctoral candidates to my long-suffering best friend, who dug bands like Alice in Chains and Metallica but hated the scene, I couldn't shake the fact that more often than not, there were only one or two other black people in the crowd. With youthful ignorance, I dismissed the stares and stifled guffaws at first, but after a couple of years, it got real tiring. Grunge opened the door to millions of teenagers, and for folks like me, that grew up listening to their neighbors blast Deep Purple's "Smoke on the Water" over the rural country fields that surrounded my childhood home; grunge took us back to a place where we could openly enjoy music that successfully merged classic metal and punk together in a tight package with a grimy new veneer.

I grew up feeling like an outsider, and most bands that emerged during the grunge heyday sang about being alone and lonely in a miserable world. So during that era, in my early twenties and watching my professional aspirations to be a pastry chef go down the tubes, I wallowed in Eddie Vedder's angst-filled lyrics that served as partial solace for my inner turmoil. But while my heart understood, my head didn't. What did these white boys have to complain about? But American heavy metal was—and to many, still is—the bastion of young and angry white men; white men who (like black, female me) had bought into a capitalist society and then became angry when their dreams didn't pan out. The women on the scene were simply window-dressing on the arms of their boyfriends. Those who wanted to rock, like the Runaways, Vixen, and later Lita Ford and Joan Jett as solo artists, were forced to sexualize their live performances, or be labeled as dykes or dismissed as amateurs.

Growing up black in the backwoods of Eastern Ontario in the '70s and '80s was not particularly fun. Not only was I always one of a very small handful of brown faces in my public and high schools, but the fact that I had been into metal since receiving my first KISS album (at eight) didn't help. I wanted to hang out with the "greasers," the guys who took shop class and had fashioned their hair like a post-Metallica Dave Mustaine. They wore skintight jeans tucked into Adidas high-tops, because they were also into Judas Priest and Iron Maiden. But after being called a nigger on numerous occasions by the same group of guys, the potential for any semblance of a friendship quickly faded. At least they were nondiscriminatory in one sense—they pretty much hated and feared every ethnic and class group that didn't sport mullets.

I started reading Toni Morrison, bell hooks, and later Malcolm X, Eldridge Cleaver, and Franz Fanon—with that came a newfound political awareness about race and feminism that my black girlfriends would eventually call "militant," and later, "scary." But back then, always being outnumbered and outgunned, it was best to try and conform to the masses with their blonde hair and Roots sweaters, as anyone that rejected our upper-middle-class existence was perceived as a threat. That, and my girlfriends couldn't understand how I could get down with Salt-N-Pepa and Queensrÿche within the same ten minutes. So my quest to find a community of like-minded freaks led me to hanging out in front of crumbling music venues in Toronto, waiting for the doors to open so I could run down into the pit and mosh.

It was when I was living on my own and finally able to afford cable TV that I first saw the video for "Selling Jesus" by Skunk Anansie, a band whose name comes from a creature in Jamaican folklore who is half man, half spider, and always a prankster. Skunk refers to either good marijuana or the smelly little black-and-white animals. I had never heard of the English quartet, but the sight of the singer, Skin (Deborah Anne Dyer), a beautiful tall sexually ambiguous woman with a shaved head and heavy-duty eyeliner, made me sit up and notice. She was mysterious, not revealing anything about herself to the public unless the other members were included, and she only discussed her personal background through her lyrics. All the other members of the band also went by one-word monikers: Guitarist Ace (Martin Ivor Kent), bassist Cass (Richard Keith Lewis), and drummer Mark (Mark Richardson).

So why did Deborah choose Skin as her introduction to the metal world? I discussed that with some knowledgable fans who offered several possibilities. One was that skin color is the first thing we notice when approaching a stranger, and the color (or lack of color) of one's skin can define social and cultural status. As a black woman, choosing to be known as Skin could be in defiance of what people thought of her, devoid of personality and only judged by her skin. Another suggestion was that because she was once a skinhead—in England, skinheads were initially non-racist and were once regarded as people who were involved not only in the punk scene but also ska and reggae—so perhaps it was an abbreviation recalling her rebellious teenage years? Or maybe it was the residue of a childhood nickname—perhaps she was a skinny kid?

Anyway, the reason hardly mattered: if Madonna and Sting did it, why couldn't she?

But her choice to be referred to by one name served as both a blessing and a curse. A curse because her name conjured up a mysterious, yet sexual, fear among interviewers and critics, many of whom were afraid to speak to her alone after witnessing the band's early gigs and watching her thrash around the stage. And a blessing because it took the attention away from the individuals in the band and brought them together as a cohesive unit, putting the spotlight on the band as a whole instead of just the lead singer. And while the imagery of Skin slowly became the focus of the music media's attention, Skin herself was more concerned about the media's attention to the band.

The lyrics to "Selling Jesus" hit me smack in the face. It was the first time (aside from Tina Turner, who perhaps from a need to break back into the mainstream music market, took the edge off her rough, soulful delivery by turning more to the pop-rock genre) that I had heard a black woman singing in such a raw and aggressive manner. "You're givin' money to the white men in the white limo/That kind of god is always man-made/They made him up then wrote a book to keep you on your knees/They get their theories from the same place/Then build a church if there's some money left/From lying on the beach."

And a black chick was singing this? I don't know if it was the visual reaction to seeing Skin—who, unlike myself, was bold, arrogant, and had an I-don't-give-a-fuck attitude—sing lyrics putting

The Man in his place, or the fact that some way, somehow, she was actually allowed to sing those words in a public forum, but I was excited—and slightly stunned.

On Skunk Anansie's debut album, 1995's *Paranoid and Sunburnt*, Skin sings about racism, lost love, and her feelings of being an outsider in a world that ignores her, with a viciousness not heard in music since the Sex Pistols' *Never Mind the Bollocks*. "Selling Jesus" was part of the soundtrack for the 1995 movie *Strange Days*, and the band appears in one of the final scenes, taking over a crowded downtown concert in futuristic Los Angeles on New Year's Eve. While Skin, dressed as a renegade warrior à la Mad Max, barely has any screen time in the movie, she blends in with the crazed audience, which is either happily waiting for the next year to begin or is ready to start a riot.

Within the week, I had tracked down and bought *Paranoid*, which was a miracle in itself. Since Skunk had been more popular in their homeland and across Europe than in North America, Europeans had been privileged to hear several singles from the record well before Skunk's full-length album was available as an import in other countries. Buying anything other than a past or present Top 40 album in those years meant that you were forced to pay import prices or spend countless hours searching through the then-popular alternative record shops, or both. And that meant lots of dirty looks and an "Are you sure you want *that*?" attitude from sales clerks, who treated their rare discs as if they were gold that should only be in the collections of *real* music fans.

But if I were to be marooned on a desert island, could *Paranoid and Sunburnt* quell my initial feelings of fear and panic? More likely the opposite, as the album consists of a storm of metal guitar licks and an aggressive rhythm section that is so hard and so full of fury that with repeated listening, it could permanently shatter your eardrums. With Skin's unique soprano, which ranged from a high-pitched wail of unwavering anger to a soft, seductive purr, I believe that I would be driven to slay anything in sight. I would rip though the island in a rage, not interested in finding ways to survive. Skin's lyrics revealed why hard rock, race, and class are a perfect match, because the pain of racism and the personal stigma that the poor and working-class feel are as frustrating as the music itself. But it would be too personal, too real. While I think it would be perfectly reasonable to pine for the past, it would only provide me with bad memories. So while *Paranoid and Sunburnt* is an excellent album, one has to be practical; to survive on this island I would have to retain some semblance of sanity.

As my introduction to both Skunk Anansie and their debut album was an eye-opening and liberating experience, I wanted more, but couldn't articulate why. The release of 1996's *Stoosh* (pronounced "stush" by our English neighbors, meaning posh, or a classy dresser) was a silent celebration, one I found on a boring summer day when I was exploring for new releases at my favorite record store. Even if I hadn't been turned on by the debut, the album cover would have still stopped me in my tracks. Skin's contorted face takes up the majority of the cover, with her arms raised over her head looking like a woman who is on the brink of insanity, while the other three members stand stoically in the background.

With other metal bands, like Slayer and Metallica, the lyrics were of secondary importance—the first thing was simply the sound that unconsciously shook your core, making your head furiously nod and your body shake with aggressive force. But being a little older and getting tired of the nonstop clubbing and concerts, I started to pay more attention to what Skin was saying (perhaps in the pursuit of finding something that would explain my growing disillusionment with society). And I was surprised at how the relevance of her lyrics—while sometimes confusing and needing several listens to decipher—fit so closely with my life experiences. And while the title was actually a nickname for the band's manager, it also describes the record, a bit more full and polished than *Paranoid*.

Complex people make complex music. *Stoosh*, like *Paranoid and Sunburnt*, is an uneven album—no beginning and no definitive ending. It consists of fragmented pieces of blurred perfection, as the music conjures up cloudy imagery akin to looking through a dirty window. Yet life is sometimes blurry. Even though Skin sings about the usual human emotions on the band's sophomore album, she delves into the messy, complicated parts, singing about the nebulous divisions between love and obsession, lost love, and using others to fill what is missing inside her. While *Stoosh* isn't necessarily a confessional album, one might argue that the band's philosophy centers on evaluating the reality of human relationships, stripping away the imagery of hearts and flowers and replacing them with dead bouquets. But this album includes much softer songs that showcase the musicianship of the band, proving that they are not a three-hit wonder, but are in fact willing to experiment with a variety of genres and emotions. Perhaps Skin's writing was designed to purposely destroy idealistic notions about relationships, calling out the seedy underbelly of humanity.

The album is a puzzle, not created for easy listening. But instead of begging the listener to interpret it, *Stoosh* gives you the proud middle finger of defiance, and for a sophomore album, presents a level of arrogance (confidence?) in the band's philosophy of doing what they want. Skunk Anansie still provided classic riffs, but delved more into sampling, providing a futuristic atmosphere by exploring electronica, dub reggae, and drum samples in the rhythm section and adding string arrangements to the surprisingly delicate ballads. But there is a catch: while the music tricks you into a smooth comforting lull, Skin's lyrics continue to surprise, as her vocals play with you, tease you into submission and then attack.

But the album, despite the unique sound of the lead singer and the experimentation of the band, still had difficulties creating a large fan base in North America. Barbara Beebe, reviewing *Stoosh* in the *Music Monitor* in 1997, proclaimed that "upon a thorough investigation of the music and lyrics of this album, I have come to the conclusion that Skunk Anansie is faking the heavy metal funk," and "however, one good song cannot compensate for the damage which has been done. I have concluded that Skunk Anansie, like hundreds of bands which have surfaced in the '90s, had only one album under their belt, the first one." The not-so-subtle references in *Stoosh*, especially "Yes, It's Fucking Political," is a response to the critics after the release of *Paranoid and Sunburnt*, where the legitimacy of the politically inspired lyrics offended seasoned music critics.

But is this simply rockism? That measuring stick, first conceived by British journalists in the '80s, judges music on its relationship with what is perceived as "legitimate" rock 'n' roll, and dictates that:

- Rock music should be bass, drums, guitars.
- It's about artists and songs, not about production.
- A good artist "keeps it real."
- Some artists are more "real" than others.
- Good songs are timeless.
- At some point in the past they "got music right."
- Music has value to the extent that it's one person emoting sincerely.
- Although the real is very important, the real is today absent (metaphysics).

According to these rules, it could be implied that the sampling techniques and the politicized lyrics poisoned the legitimacy of the band to "rockist" music critics, but also conveniently ignores the artistic merit of infusing several musical genres and creating one's own unique style.

Beebe's dismissive comments imply that within her reviews she uses the rockist paradigm in order to separate what she believes is the bad from the good. Is this fair to the music listener who searches the Internet for music reviews before purchasing a CD? No, it isn't, and it also dismisses other genres of music, especially hip-hop, which is now referred to as the most dominant form of music entertainment in the world.

While conveniently ignoring veteran musicians like Bob Dylan and Woody Guthrie and more contemporary artists like Corrosion of Conformity (all of whom wear their politics on their sleeve), Beebe also "took offence at their pathetic attempt to be radical," labeling the band simply a rip-off of Rage Against the

Machine, as though only one band was allowed to tackle weighty political issues at a time. But having the dubious distinction of being the only black woman singing "Clit Rock," the band's definition of merging heavy metal with black feminist rage, meant that they were begging for controversy. As Skin herself mentioned after the band's demise, being the first black female fronting a metal band meant that she was susceptible to a myriad of opinions—both as a female front person and as a black woman.

Maybe unwittingly, Skin is a symbol of the opportunities that women of color can achieve, even though the larger society might disagree. And as rockism first emerged over two decades ago and the political climate has changed since then, perhaps people are looking for music that speaks about today. Instead of dismissing an album as the narcissistic ramblings of a social outsider, I argue that it serves as the pseudo-documentation of the era that reminds people of an aspect of their past lives.

In the previously mentioned track, "Yes It's Fucking Political," Skin coos the verses, playing coy and sweet, singing, "The wild ones like to hide/As the dirty priest confides/In the love of baby whores/Political." With a burst of a guitar riff and tribal percussion, the track is one of the more fervent and passionate on the album and unleashes a venomous snarl that lets you know that the band is undeterred by criticism.

The band then quickly switches emotions with the soft, sensual ballad "She's My Heroine." The song begs for interpretation. Is she singing about a part of her that she hides? Is she afraid of her emerging sexuality thereby fantasizing about a woman, perhaps a potential lover who embodies all the strengths she wishes she had? Or is it a song about an obsession with a mysterious stranger?

According to an interview Skin gave in 1994 before *Paranoid and Sunburnt* was released, she said that the band made a point of not writing about specific issues, but only what affects the band members on an everyday basis. So their songs are not specifically political in a structural sense; they are both a reflection of their observances about life and questioning human nature.

Skin's lyrics draw heavily from her upbringing and the two riots she witnessed on the streets as a child, growing up in a racially charged neighborhood in South London in the '80s. In a single-parent home in Brixton, a community that primarily consisted of Jamaican immigrants, she witnessed several of her neighbors being beaten up by the police. Her family life was also dysfunctional. In particular, she had two older brothers, one who eventually died of AIDS, the other with severe mental problems. These experiences most likely led to her honest and sometimes brutal lyrics. Perhaps having some unfortunate relationships with men at an early age led her to write about the seedy underbelly of love and loss. After dropping out of college, where she had been studying interior design, she met Cass, and then added Ace and Mark to the band.

Unlike other British singers who hid their accents in order to gain credibility across the pond, her heavy Brixton dialect adds flavor to the tracks, accentuating and spitting out lyrics, punctuating her points and legitimizing her delivery. When she sings a ballad like "Infidelity": "In my mind nothing makes sense/I'm nothing you can't have/Cracked up to disagree/That's all we ever had," it is with vulnerability, and her sometimes scratchy delivery belies a sense of frailty and fear.

From *Their Eyes Were Watching God* by Zora Neale Hurston to "Four Women" by Nina Simone, many experiences associated with growing up as a black girl in post-slavery days have been documented. In a similar fashion, but manipulating a different art form, Skin sings about her rage, delving even more into the murky waters of racism, sexuality, and political corruption, the first time in my generation that such ideas have been addressed musically in front of a worldwide audience.

For me, Skunk Anansie's music provided a solace for my mid-twenties angst, yet I wish the band had been around when I was a teenager. For all the times I cried in silence so my parents couldn't hear, I wondered what it would be like to scream, to shout in outrage and anger. There was no one in my life at that time who could fully understand my feelings of being hated over physical features beyond my control, and of not being able to do what I wanted in a society where I was expected to be quiet and simply obey orders.

So you go up to your room, put on Judas Priest, and scream along with the bordering-on-insane screeching of Metal God Rob Halford, channeling your anger though the hypermasculine, slightly sadomasochistic music. It is cathartic to scream, to feel the physical rush that makes you want to punch someone out—in a manner where you don't have the cops pounding on your door. So while *Stoosh* might not be comforting for everyone, forcing you to reevaluate your belief system and then striking your senses with the voice of the voiceless, it still feels right, and legitimized the confusion in my head, making me feel that my childhood anger was justified. Because of that, I use *Stoosh*'s energy to face the fact that potentially, I am alone on this island.

But what about those sunny days, sitting on a beach with flags made from tattered clothing, and a fire sparked by rubbing two rocks together? Shouldn't one have a song that celebrates the sun and flame, yet keeps the mind off the wait for a rescue that might never come? Well, while *Stoosh* is appropriate for some self-reflection and energy, perhaps the Beach Boys would be a better match for those quieter moments.

"Glorious Pop Song," the final track on the album, sounds exactly like what it is: A light, breezy pop song, dominated by acoustic guitar, with the band providing almost sing-along backup vocals. But in true Skunk Anansie fashion, while the music would be the perfect soundtrack for an idyllic day at the beach, the song is deceptive. The lyrics are about people's reactions to Skin's appearance and perceived offensive behavior: "How can you be so angry/When all you're doing is looking at me/You chastise me for my behaviour/It's gonna last too long/And what I am now but your reaction/I'm all those memories you tried to steal/This war will never be over." And to further press the point, the chorus breaks it down as she sweetly taunts, "You're still a fucker (x3) to me." Now, these are lyrics I could recite every day. Of course, with only me on the island, there wouldn't be much point.

Never quite breaking the American music market, the band nevertheless continued to command a large following in Europe, until it disbanded in 2001. Ace, Cass, and Mark all went on to start their own music and writing projects in England, and Cass later supported Skin as a session musician for her 2003 solo debut, *Fleshwounds*. Skin went on to grow her hair and develop a taste for fashion—to a lot of complaints. Followers of Skunk Anansie were disappointed with the soulful R&B sound, wanting more of the aggro feel of the band's three full-length albums. But wanting to experiment and complaining that the creativity of Skunk Anansie was over and done, the band members all felt compelled to explore their musical options.

Over the years since I first entered the grunge scene, I have also grown my hair out, traded my Docs for conservative heels, and after a nasty infection, was forced to remove my nose ring. I witnessed the slow demise of grunge, sucking my teeth in disgust at the genres that rose from its ashes. I was suddenly too old to understand the relevance of the screaming and wailing of emo, and way too old to believe that bands like Good Charlotte and Simple Plan are considered the saviors of this latest emergence of so-called punk.

I have walked by the Concert Hall, where I first saw Soundgarden, several times over the years, watching in dismay as the place that for so many years was a second home to thousands of dirty kids slowly converted back to its original facade and was then bought by a national television station. The inside of the hall has been modernized into a state-of-the-art interactive studio, no longer open to the general public. Perhaps, like Skin, it was time to move on and flourish.

And like my fond memories of attending concerts at the now-refurbished building, Skin's fiery attitude hasn't dissipated, as *Fleshwounds*, with its softer ballads and R&B soul, still is a backdrop to Skin's sometimes uncomfortable tales, but sung by somebody who has found personal if not political satisfaction and has perhaps tired of living the rock 'n' roll lifestyle. I wonder if the desire for commercial success has overridden the tormented sounds of a woman and a band that thrived—while probably hungry—in the underground scene.

The time has passed, yet I don't have a watch to determine how long I have been sitting here. But the sun has moved from the east to the west, and a brisk wind has awakened me from my thoughts.

I'll play *Stoosh* on my MP3 player on my desert island—in spurts, so my batteries won't run out—for awhile, anyway. The music will not only serve to conjure up both good and difficult memories, but will instill grit, determination, and the will to survive. The energy will always be in *Stoosh*. When I need an emotional release, I will turn to that album for enjoyment, energy, and the comforting knowledge that yes, there are other angry, fierce, and sexy black women out there. I just wish I could have one on my island to commiserate with.

3

MY BLOODY VALENTINE
Loveless
Creation, 1991

BY NED RAGGETT

F I AM GOING TO BE STUCK ON A DESERT ISLAND, THEN
MAKE NO MISTAKE ABOUT IT, I INTEND TO BE THERE IN
COMFORT. I MAY ONLY HAVE ONE ALBUM, BUT DARN IT,
my other creature comforts will not be denied. Right now, this
means I'll at least have the help of a friendly genie in a sriracha
sauce bottle that I'll stumble across shortly after landing on said island. The genie will ensure that I can at least play an album on a
stereo system made of coconuts and palm oil, or whatever else is
necessary. The system will be located next to a mysterious cache
of Moët & Chandon White Star champagne (perfectly chilled at
all times), along with alternating meals of exquisite Vietnamese
soups and Genoese seafood cuisine.

But only one album. *That* album. The one whose cover I use as
my icon for online chats, and which I had as a backdrop on my
computer screen for the longest time. In a way, My Bloody Valentine's *Loveless* is a cartoonish representation of myself in general

parlance, an intentional oversimplification on the face of it. It can't represent *everything* about life, no one thing ever does, whether we're talking about romantic love or working in an organic garden that grows some of the best basil I've ever tasted. (Say what you will about love, basil's easier to keep in one's fridge for a bit, at least.)

Whenever I'm asked what my favorite album is, *Loveless* is the answer. In a couple of online boards I participate in, if MBV comes up, someone usually asks where I am (and I usually appear reasonably quickly if I catch the discussion in progress, moth to the flame). I've heard it more times than I can count. Now, finally, I'm actually going to talk about it.

That may seem strange to say, but I can't *not* say this: I have done so much to avoid talking in depth about this album. I have evaded, dodged, weaved, ducked. Years ago, as part of a running project on the Freaky Trigger website, I indulged myself in the memorably ridiculous but fun project of talking about my favorite 136 albums of the '90s. When *Loveless*'s entry at number one came along, the final one I wrote and the shortest, my key sentence began, "What more can I say that I haven't said already?" Except that really I had said nothing.

So I deferred quite a bit, until now, because *Loveless* is crucial, central, necessary to my life, as memory, as signpost, as signifier. Its importance has been that hard to capture in words that seem so tame and limited. This is more than a "desert island disc," this is something far greater than what it is physically.

A book can be a central text for the living of one's life, moral teachings the foundation of so much that follows. A memory of a certain day, a random meeting with someone, can change and define a person's personal history. We can treasure the family heirlooms passed down over generations, we look to the example of someone in our own time as providing a new direction towards how we deal with the many complexities of life. Why *not* a record, having this kind of mark on a person? There is no irony in this question: what about when music, a band, a song changes who you are, in a moment of sudden shock?

That moment is something I still think about every time I dig out the album to give it a listen. I've never ripped it to MP3, I don't want it playing out of my computer for heaven's sake, I want it out of the stereo speakers, the great old ones from the '60s, that my dad got as a young sailor and which I now own. They're monstrous and clunky, but dang if they don't make everything I play through them sound great. *Loveless* is playing now as I type, the grinding beauty overload of "I Only Said" becoming a smile and snarl through clenched teeth at the same time.

The CD case has held up well all these years, there's a small crack in the back cover but no matter. It's the American issue of the album, so on the back is the Sire logo, the Warner Bros. logo, one of the many Creation logos, and one of those 'AAD' codes from the time when labels were proud to tell you how everything was recorded, mixed, and mastered. This is what constituted amusement for record packagers before it became necessary to list endless, mostly useless websites. There's a hole punched in the cover booklet, another in the UPC code in the back cover art; mine was a promo copy, found used at a record store near UCLA that always seemed to get advances to sell before the official

release date. Same as always, same as it ever was, pink on the outside, pink on the disc, blue on the inside art, everywhere blurred
bits of guitar.

So far, so universal. Not for *Loveless* but for so many different
people and "their" album or "their" song—or "their" movie or
whatever example of an artistic medium is to hand—and how we
can obsess and observe over the details. I love the fact that we can
fetishize the containing of the experience so readily, that we love a
beloved book for its creases in the spine, that the cutting board
used so often to prepare a meal has hundreds if not thousands of
knife slices patterned across the top, that the backpack hauled
across the world from Port Chalmers to the Isle of Skye has a zip-
per that always jams. So too, then, with the crack on the case of
Loveless, those holes in the booklet.

But beyond that what does *Loveless* mean to me? I can describe
it in no other fashion but as it was when I first heard it, the impact
it had and what was left in its wake. I am not religious—instead,
agnostic at heart—but I have felt the force of what others must
consider revelation.

I do not choose the word lightly.

In late 1990 I was nineteen years old, doing what many a music
fiend does at college—working at the campus radio station. At
the time, UCLA's station was pretty low-key, broadcasting only
over a cable radio system, barely audible beyond pockets of appreciation here and there on and just off campus. As a result, anyone who DJed there did so mostly for themselves, and so it was
with me.

I was working my shift and scrounging through the new
records, a mix of vinyl and CD. One light-colored vinyl cover

caught my attention—a seemingly abstract geometric design I couldn't make head or tail of (only later did I realize it was two people in an open-mouthed French kiss)—announcing the name of the group to be My Bloody Valentine and the name of this EP, as it was, to be *Glider*.

Standard rule of thumb for college DJs confronted with something new—seeing if anyone else has recommended a particular song on it, scrawled somewhere on the sleeve. And sure enough on the back was a listing of the songs, the first one being "Soon," some DJ notes next to it. What was said specifically I can't recall, but it was attention-grabbing enough, something along the lines about how this song was showing why MBV was "reinventing modern music along with Sonic Youth."

Now personally I respect Sonic Youth, then and now, more than I ever actually loved them—they were received wisdom in a way, something already established as worthy. Still, I liked them enough to think, "Hm, I suppose that recommendation is a good sign."

Took out the vinyl, cued it up, heard a quick bit of drumming, wound the vinyl back, waited for the previous song to end—the usual. If I was alone in the station I don't remember it but I was alone in the DJ booth at least, headphones on, already fairly long hair below my shoulders, doubtless wearing some sort of band T-shirt—my basic look for the rest of life already well established, to the chagrin of others perhaps, but I know what works for me.

I started the song, the little buried clatter of drumming began, and then the guitars and beats fully kicked in.

And time stopped.

What can I tell you about that gap in my experience, that rupture, not a rapture or not just a rapture, but a rupture, a schism, a division,

*something that changed the universe as I saw it because it was something
I had never seen or sensed before?*

*What can I tell you that can seem acceptable, credible perhaps, when
it was about something as mundane as an album, a song, a series of
notes in a vinyl groove?*

*Time, of course, has a way of dulling the view and vision of many
things, and of introducing other points of comparison, different memories. To have other moments of sublime, serene joy, amazement, is to have
a rich and good life, and on that front I have been generously blessed.*

*They include moments of emotional overload, the sensation of going
to bed for the first time with a person I loved dearly, the feeling of looking
out over an ocean to see snow-capped mountains rising up out of the sea,
the sense of accomplishment when a surprising gift was given, when
hard work led to great reward, when all the dreams seemed to come true.*

*The downsides and failures, oh I've experienced them, sure, but let's
talk about the joys now, the counterpoints to the negative. Those are moments I treasure, private or public, alone or with many friends, or even
one close one.*

*Did any, though, did any truly, totally, thoroughly leave me so com-
pletely and utterly in awe, like there was another universe revealed to me,
that all of a sudden I was aware of something new, something more,
something else, and it was within my grasp, within my hearing, it was
being given to me just like that? Only this moment did that.*

It stunned me.

And . . . time started.

When time started, I realized that, indeed, I had been standing
there literally agape, just . . . looking at the vinyl as it spun around.
I must have cued up something and played it next, but how and
what?

What *had* happened?

I was dimly aware I had been rooted to the ground since the song had fully begun, just standing there, slack-jawed, amazed—I felt a glow on my face, I wasn't horrified, I was smiling still, full of joy. A happiness from being bowled over completely, possessed . . . sent.

Like I was out of my body, but I wasn't somehow, I was there the whole time but I was not there at all. I was to the side, just by an atom's worth, no more, and yet a million miles, light-years away, immeasurable distances.

In struggling for the words, I frustrate myself, but still I must reach for them. In listening to and loving the song from that day to this one, I wonder what it was exactly, that feeling. Forget "shock of the new," I've had that happen, before and since, been taken with pleasant surprise by a hitherto-unheard song, or viscerally hating something else equally freshly experienced. This was more, and nothing before and nothing since has felt like it.

Take this away with you if nothing else—that was the uniquely profoundest moment of my life to date, and I have no shame in saying that, and I have no problem with ascribing it to something so 'simple' as a record. Because if everyone has had or will have something similar happen to them—whatever the context, whatever the source of creation—then we are all truly an amazingly fortunate species.

Time stopped and started and somewhere in between was a moment, an experience, a state of place and mind, which has never happened for me again.

After that, perhaps unsurprisingly, it was just a matter of finding the records. But also waiting, as I learned that the last full album actually had come out two years previously. I started to read the UK music press around that time to find out what further information I could. Before the Internet became commonplace, the idea of a weekly press that talked about cool things with rapid turnover was shockingly great, used as I was to the tedium of *Rolling Stone* and their conviction that the world needed yet another Jerry Garcia interview first and foremost.

By the time the *Tremolo* EP emerged in early 1991, I was primed and expectant, rewarded and gratified by the reactions that the music provided. I remember taking it home and playing it on the shared system that four of us in the apartment near campus rented. Xana looked up from where she was sewing, frowned a bit and said, "Are you sure there's not something wrong with the disc?"

"Oh no, it's meant to sound like that."

"Then are you sure there's not something wrong with the stereo?"

And so time went on—the contours of "Soon" were now long familiar to me but the seemingly bottomless series of mantras composing the song, circular and tightly wound, sprawling and slow but looping ever backwards, the rising and falling sighs beyond immediate comprehension, the endless beat, all kept me rapt. The unfamiliar universe suggested by the first play had become a well-known one, perhaps, but only in the musical sense—if that makes sense. I knew the approach and what was being reached for now as something concrete, but the glow from first impact lingered. What was shock was now aspiration, a reaching outward and upward, a drive to utter exultance.

I also started gathering a sense of community around that time, fellow radio station people similarly touched by MBV and by other bands clearly following in their slipstream. (All too clearly in some cases—while shoegaze has now almost reached common currency as a genre name of sorts, it was cooked up with an air of contempt in circles tired of what they saw as Yet Another Band in love with MBV not too wisely but too well.)

I remember one of my fellow MBV-loving cohorts then was freshman student Walt Disney. Looking extremely good for his age, not to mention his condition given his cremation after his death back in the '60s, Walt was named by parents who had to know exactly what they were doing. Personally I'm surprised he didn't strangle them when he grew old enough, but such is the nature of familial love. We mostly met at radio station meetings and compared notes on the news we had heard, found ourselves just waiting, waiting, as 1991 dragged on.

And then, somehow, there it was, picked up in that record store as mentioned, the promo copy now mine. I honestly don't remember much about the first playing of the album or anything, instead it was almost as if it just . . . had always been there? Hard to say, but unlike the volcanic encounter with "Soon," *Loveless* blended into my life effortlessly, the simplest of meldings.

So, of course, I played it and played it again. Quite an awful lot in fact. I still do to this day, though I admittedly did reach the point that was identified by Andrew Eldritch of the Sisters of Mercy in an interview once, talking about his own favorite records. As he put it, you reach a state where all you have to do is look at the sleeve of an album, or even its spine, and everything about that album comes rushing back to you. So the replayings in recent years have been spaced further apart, and newer obsessions end up getting heard more often—all very natural.

What mattered at the time, though, was getting used to it there and then. Such scope, such range—such were my thoughts, and while the roots may be clearer now, and the descendants might have cheapened part of the thrill through overuse in turn, it's still something monumental, something, quite simply, huge. *Loveless* is nothing if not aiming for a scale hard to easily measure, the work of a band that was never going to play stadiums wanting to create the most enveloping and overriding music possible.

Sipping at my desert island champagne and idly wondering what else the genie could conjure up, I could predict my reactions now to the songs readily enough; they're the ones I started evolving at the time. The album is of a piece, there's no flaw, nothing to remove—if something went now, I would feel it and miss it. That, I think, is vitally important—not only song for song, but note for note.

The creation of *Loveless*, as told since in interviews and books, is a story of trying to get something exactly right, of Kevin Shields searching for a way to get everything down to the last tone, driving his record company boss insane along the way. Comparison points are made to Brian Wilson and all that—not without reason, given the Beach Boys' mid-60s experiments with reverb and vocal textures. Still, the better and more obvious connection to be made is with the Bomb Squad, Public Enemy's production team. Shields was a PE fiend and similarly wanted every beat, every note, everything to count—to make nothing left to chance, to focus.

I think, in retrospect, it must have been his relentlessness, and that of his band, that contributed to the first impact of "Soon," whatever the attendant results afterwards. For all the talk of blur, queasy feelings, unsettled overdrive, vast soundscapes, swaths of echo, incomprehensibility, *Loveless* aims not only to be heard but to be inescapable, not merely majestic but commanding. Each song could be its own specific exercise in a form then transmogrified into either a monster or a ghost (and when the latter, like "Sometimes," like the kind of ghost that haunts a darkling plain rather than lurking around mere coffins).

So between sweep and pinpoint precision is where *Loveless* lies, sticking into your head like goo while amps explode or seem to. Regardless of the strength of that first experience with "Soon," *Loveless* still sends me somewhere else in a gentler fashion. It often seems like it's out to tear itself apart with the craziest smile on its face, leaping into the abyss for pleasure rather than pain. Parting with it would be impossible—and no matter that it's a canonical album in many quarters now, treasuring it above all others is, to me, an important blow *against* that canon, an eternal blast of pride against deadwood.

Why so? As I realized the truth of *Loveless*'s vast impact on my soul over time, I also found my own grounds for critical love of many things, on many levels. Relativism, in moral, theological, ethical terms, is hardly a new concept. Neither is reader-response theory, the idea that it's not so much the creator of a piece as the individual audience member that matters. Somewhere out of my squelching and arrogant manhandling of these and other ideas I approached as close to an aesthetic guideline as I'll ever have, the idea of 'radical subjectivity'—which isn't all that radical. But it is subjective, to a fault (and that's the point).

Simply put, the canon is denied. Instead there are as many canons as there are people, and all that matters about a song or a group or anything artistic is how you yourself react to it—if you like it, hate it, change your mind about it, really get into it, treat it lightly, become a scholar poring over every last thing about it. Everything is up for grabs; celebration and condemnation is yours to declare, not yours to accept. *Loveless* is the centerpiece of my canon. It is the album for me, it is flawless to me. I *know* this. My understanding of this destroys all other attempts to create canons elsewhere, destabilizes them—it creates freedom by allowing me to choose my own path.

There will be debate—in fact, there must be debate, for without debate and discussion and interaction these canons cannot connect, react, intertwine. But there are no rules—not necessarily for creation, but definitely *not* for reception. That someone dismisses something airily that someone else can quote chapter and verse about is not a sign of the former's inability to appreciate something but a sign of the power of the individual mind to make decisions as it chooses. I've heard *Loveless* trashed more times than I can count, scorned as dull, rhythmless, overdone. Yet I'm perfectly fine with all those descriptions.

This is because we have all made our choices about what to focus on and what to skip over, what to dissect with a mental scalpel and what to turn from with a shrug. What we hold dear to our heart we are sometimes lucky enough to be able to share with others, either on the shared ground of similar intensity of appreciation or perhaps with the hope of offering a new perspective, of changing a doubtful mind. But in that we hold to our own decisions sometimes with fierce, unswerving devotion, we hopefully recognize that in others, as the discussion continues.

Yet though there is no canon outside that which IS in our head, the power of that canon is immense. We may never order it, no lists need to be drawn up, maybe favorites as such are never consciously considered. There is no true need to prioritize the internal canon, flexible and ever-changeable as long as we wish it to be.

The power of that canon, though, is irrefutable. It is ours and ours alone, individual, unique, all-encompassing within the scope of a single soul. Our lodestones and our touchstones, our bêtes noires and things we love to hate, all are there. And in my canon—musical but not just musical—*Loveless* is supreme, untouchable.

Perhaps unsurprisingly, the album is also a direct link to my favorite concerts of all time.

MBV played twice in L.A. during 1992, on two separate tours. The first time through was originally supposed to be an opening set for Dinosaur Jr., but J Mascis had fallen asleep for ten months, so picking up an opener or two along the way (by the time they made it to L.A. it was Babes in Toyland) MBV soldiered on. Needless to say, I got my ticket within seconds flat of its going on sale. Plans were made, days counted down . . . all of us who were going wanted our riots in our head really badly, waiting on the moment.

The Roxy is a small place, crowded floor edged by seated areas. Of course, we were all on the crowded floor, and the feeling of the crowd matches the feeling of that album cover—bright, indistinct, overwhelming. When the show was underway, it was one long miasmic cascade backward and forward, a massive chaotic flow and sway. The band hit the monster-ass boogie groove of "Slow" and it was as if we flowed through the stifling air of the club like carp kites in a humid wind.

It was the rhythm section that was the enjoyable surprise that night. Colm O'Coisoig looked appropriately intense, frenetic at his quickest and loudest behind the drums, but Deb Googe . . . if I ever played bass, I would play it like her. Bouncing with seeming nervousness on one leg, then the other, she was finding the groove of each song even as she played, halfway between nervous restraint and participatory cool. She seemed only to look off sidelong at her bandmates, controlled but aware, just playing the hell out of that thing.

Bilinda Butcher and Mr. Shields himself had the guitars, the microphones, the slurred blend of singing. . . . I don't recall anyone saying "Hi," but everyone onstage seemed happy enough to be there in a low key way, while we were cheering our damned fool heads off. I'd say about half of *Loveless* ended up being played, but I don't remember all the details now, just snaps of memory: the strobe-paced flicker of the film projected for "Soon," the look in Bilinda's eyes as she sang (not staring or insane but something not quite normal either). Then there was "You Made Me Realize."

It's not on *Loveless*, having first emerged as an A-side back in 1988, and it's almost straightforward post–Hüsker Dü pop-punk with dreamier vocals, though it has one part in the song where everything drops out but an open D chord rapidly played again and again by all the guitars and bass before slamming back into the main arrangement. So when the time came the band, this time including O'Coisoig on frenetic drums, played said open D chord . . . for fifteen minutes.

I know this because at a certain point I started checking my watch and estimating backwards; the rumors had just started to go around that they did this type of thing at every show as their final song. A few years later when I had the chance to interview Shields—and he turned out to be one of the most chatty, talkative and polite fellers I've ever interviewed—he noted:

"When we did that song, it transformed the audience into a different thing altogether. All the people at the front could behave no differently from the people at the back. It put everyone into their own head, because they couldn't talk to each other either."

I remember all the swaying seeming to intensify a bit, all of us just crammed into that spot, the heat and the light and the feeling that we were all going to eventually faint at some point, though it never came to that. O'Coisoig's face looked like he was possessed, a manic grin as he blasted away on the drums, everyone else just bent over their instruments as if wanting to wear them all to bits through repetition. How they signaled to each other that it was going to end I don't know but all of a sudden they were back in the song, a final verse, and that was it. Crazy.

But of course wonderful. So when they toured again later that year, playing a larger venue this time, I wasn't going to say no. It was a different experience, though, less claustrophobic since there was more room, but also because this time around I stood back from the stage and just watched carefully, drifting instead of getting fully caught up, no bad thing, but a change of pace. The set list was the same, and I admit I had been hoping for more surprises, but what the hey.

Then "You Made Me Realize" started, and I thought to myself, "OK, I am going to take an exact measure of the time here as soon as they start the chord." They began, I noted my watch, and then waited to see what would happen.

They kept playing, of course. From my perspective it was quite fun, guessing who knew what was forthcoming and who had no idea. I could see the clumps at the foot of the stage, people all crammed in, but they were starting to fray a bit towards the edge as the chord kept hammering out. I just watched and nodded and let my mind drift.

They kept playing at fifteen minutes. I was exhausted already, sure, but not completely trashed, so I was happily into the feeling being generated, the combination of repetition and minisecond strum and maximum volume. (Shields again, from our interview: "The [show] in Los Angeles, it was a shame, because it wasn't loud. . . . Loud in a caustic way, but not in a low-frequency way, not in the stomach way. In the ears, yeah. I think we definitely tried to push that as far as we could ever push it. But I think in the future I want to make it a lot more physical, in a body way.")

They kept playing at twenty-five minutes. I swear I saw people literally staggering towards the exit, just having to leave, not being able to stand another second of it. But then I also saw people moving forward, almost as if they couldn't be controlled—moths to the flame.

They kept playing at thirty minutes. I really have no idea what I was thinking at that point, beyond wondering how or when it would end. Would it end at all? It seemed like they were aiming for something impossible—it would match with their music and with *Loveless* and the dream and vision and new reality I had encountered. In later years I described "Soon" as the sense of a fragment that had fallen out of the sky from somewhere, that the 'real' song was continuing to play out there endlessly, on all frequencies, in full measure. Here, now, with another song, they were aiming to recreate that, to actually create that in full—to see what would happen.

They kept playing at thirty-five minutes . . . and then, back to the final verse, a last slam through it, and it was over.

Completely—the band never played another show. Without planning on it, without knowing it, likely the band didn't know it then either, I had seen the end of the live incarnation of the musicians that had created the most stunning moment I'd experienced, matching that with something equally distinct, unique, bizarre.

And that is why I'd relax under a palm tree sipping Moët & Chandon and look at *Loveless* and think. Because it tells me about the time when I was taken out of this world, and returned to it changed.

4

VARIOUS ARTISTS
History of Our World
Part 1: Breakbeat
and Jungle Ultramix
by DJ DB
Profile, 1994

BY MICHAELANGELO MATOS

T'S EASY TO SEE THE WORLD THROUGH A DAY-GLO PRISM
WHEN YOU'RE SELLING HOLOGRAMS AT THE MALL OF
AMERICA. THAT'S WHAT I SPENT TWELFTH GRADE DOING,
for a husband-and-wife-run company called Hologram Land. Of
course, holograms aren't Day-Glo—a light hitting laser-cut foil at
a 45-degree angle gives you an untainted spectrum. But it gets at
the environment well enough. It certainly doesn't seem contradic-
tory with everything else that was opening my eyes at the time:
Keith Haring, Sonic the Hedgehog, and Bust-a-Move for Nintendo,
Daisy Age hip-hop, early-90s pop-house and stab-pattern rave, all
codified by a multicolored, playful pop-mindedness, bubblegum-
bright and cartoony.

And it looks a little silly written down, not least because what I
got from it can be summarized in one infamous acronym: PLUR.

This matters, at least to those of us who spent a few crucial years wearing ridiculous oversized outfits while driving from state to state to see DJs whose names we'd forget a week later, playing records we'd never remember, illegally in warehouses (or occasionally, if you were from the Midwest like I am, in barns) while high on drugs. Unless you were me—the only time I got high at a rave-not-club was in 2000, long after "the scene" and/or my participation in it had peaked. (E followed by acid—it *ruled*.) Peace-Love-Unity-Respect is pretty corny on paper, even if it's worth trying to live up to in real life, and it's utterly hopeless as a slogan if you expect to be taken seriously by the unconverted. You can say that of Satanism, too, but at least danger gets respect. Me, I'll take cheeseball color-bonkers reconstituted pop-cult signifiers over whatever iteration of pentagram, fang, and silhouetted tree you wanna top with a pointy, unintelligible font. Consider yourself warned.

Recently, a friend gave me a poster-sized black-and-white flyer from Minneapolis dance-music cognoscenti Disco Family Plan— the first of several—from 1991:

Get down. Get down. Get down.
THE TOTALLY STOKED MENTAL TRACK OF THE WEEK—
EPILEPSIA BY EPILEPSIA ON HIT HOUSE RECORDS
HOUSE TECHNO TRANCE
SMASH SEXISM
FIGHT RACISM
END QUEER BASHING
GET DOWN.

I had several of these (not the one just quoted) taped to the inside of my high school locker around the same time I was selling holograms while Knott's Camp Snoopy's indoor amusement park buzzed away around the corner from Hologram Land's second-floor perch. "Disco" was on its way to gaining the hipster-kitsch cachet it would hold secure by mid-decade, but in 1992 it still had a frisson of the forbidden. DFP's mating of disco's far-off hedonism with further-off *Better Homes & Gardens*–style happy-shiny design-for-living appealed to the cynic in me as much as the optimist.

Here's another, smaller print object, not to hand but burned in memory: RAVE KRISP-E'S. The first real rave flyer I saw up close—a Kellogg's Rice Krispies cereal box with colored "E"s scattered through the bowl. The card's primitive Photoshopping was, at the time, impossibly futuristic, nostalgia turned on its head right before subversion fell into kitsch.

Most important of all, the flyer implied a subculture—not the only one, but the one that drew me in—suburban in nature but without the studied casualness that typified indie rock, an indifference I couldn't have faked at that point if you'd force-fed me 'ludes and strapped me to a chair at a Warhol retrospective, or the equally cool attitude common in hip-hop. Mall-punk, particularly after Green Day, whose ignition was still some time away, was probably the closest thing the '90s had to rave—sloppy, resolutely uncool, energy energy energy, stuffed in its early stages with obvious thrills that make adults who've grown out of it wince. The difference is that the mall punks, bless 'em, were (are) discovering something that had existed for a while at least. Ravers were convinced we'd found the future. Even at seventeen I was already enough of a student of rock history and criticism to know better, but I was also young enough not to care—especially since I was doing it while surrounded by kitsch psychedelia in a giant entertainment-industrial complex that wasn't Day-Glo but might as well have been.

The reason I worked at the Mall of America was simple: My mother, two sisters, and I lived right across the street from it in Bloomington, Minnesota. (Most of my family still does.) We'd previously lived in a two-bedroom basement apartment in Richfield, a neighboring suburb, and while there and at my great-grandaunt's place in the city where I spent weekends, I'd begun devouring all the music I could get my hands on and all the books about it I could find at the library. One day at a used-clothing shop I saw a flyer for a Saturday midnight radio show called "Radio Depth Probe" that spun house and techno, which I was curious about from British magazines, and I began taping the two-hour show every week. It went off the air when its station switched formats in 1992, about a month before we moved to Bloomington.

While selling holograms, I became friends with a coworker named Allen, who liked much of the same music as I did, dressed better, had a girlfriend, and drove. In April, 1993, we went to a puppet theater in Uptown Minneapolis and danced alongside about seventy-five funny-dressed people while a man in a *Cat in the Hat* hat—known as DJ Cat in the Hat—played records through a crappy PA. He mismatched his beats at least three times. The house lights were low but being on diffused the dark party vibe. The smart drinks were powdery and overpriced. A month later, we arrived at a warehouse on the outskirts of St. Paul that wasn't yet ready. The thirty or so people already there were as nervous about protocol as we were, and as excited about stepping into a scene of their own. When the doors opened, the walls were covered with liquid-projection graphics and programmed colored lasers zapped in time to the music. The ceilings were thirty feet up; everything echoed. For the next four years, I went to every party like it I could find.

I have never been as right there and ready for an album as I was when I found a copy of *History of Our World Part 1: Breakbeat & Jungle Ultramix by DJ DB* at the Mall of America's third-floor Sam Goody in spring 1995. I'd stopped working at the mall a year and a half earlier, leaving holograms behind a few months after graduating high school. I had skipped college, gone to live in the city, gotten work as a restaurant cook, and was going to as many shows and raves and buying as many records as I could afford, often more. I visited my family all the time, either riding my bike from the city, which took between an hour and an hour and a half, or taking the bus to the mall, usually stopping in to buy CDs first.

History of Our World Part 1 had been compiled and mixed in 1994 by DJ DB, a Londoner-turned-New Yorker whose work I was already familiar with. In 1994, DB had collected and mixed *Acid Resistant*, whose twenty cuts of squirting, careening 303 fuckery emanated almost entirely from a couple of DJ/producers from Cologne, Germany, who would later form the nucleus of that city's Kompakt label. More importantly, DB compiled five CDs for Profile Records' *Best of Techno* series, in particular 1993's epochal *Volume Three*, which introduced me to stomping, heavily Germanic trance—back when the style was good and ruthless, before it became an arpeggiated synth-twinkle nightmare—and the breakbeat hardcore that was turning, more assuredly by the month, into jungle. DB had a fervid panoply of scenes to cherry-pick from, but he also had great ears, especially for stuff that was later overlooked or forgotten entirely. (Eden Transmission's throbbing-gridwork "I'm So High," from *Volume Three*, may be the greatest drug record ever made.) If DB's taste in trance ensured that I could never hate the genre entirely, no matter how hard it tried to make me, he was frighteningly on target when it came to jungle.

Then again, so was pretty much anybody who spun it back then. A year before buying *History*, I'd attended the first Furthur three-day outdoor-camp rave in Hixton, Wisconsin. My musical highlight was provided by Minneapolis's Drone, whose name signified trance (or even ambient) but who played what, at the time, we called "breaks." I walked in on him tearing up a barely populated tent with a succession of hard-charging variations on the basic formula: reconstituted drums from the Winstons' "Amen, My Brother," wobbling sub-bass, sound bites from action films, dancehall ragga, or hip-hop, and squeaky cartoon vocals. After awhile, I wandered off; when I returned an hour later, he was still at it. Back in the Twin Cities, I congratulated him on his set; he responded that the party had been so disorganized he'd played three hours instead of the one he was scheduled. He'd had to resort to B-sides he hadn't wanted to play, he lamented. The joke was that the second go-round I caught sounded every bit as good as the first.

History of Our World Part 1 is a history lesson and a mix tape, a growth chart and a party record, an essay and a freestyle chant, five years in twenty-five tracks from five labels in sixty-five minutes that misses dozens of equally great records but leaves nothing out. It celebrates its moment in real time before your ears, which

makes it easier to grasp, especially if you were living in that moment secondhand. Most of my jungle knowledge came from compilations and occasional mix tapes I picked up from Cynesthesia,
the boutique that served as Minneapolis's rave-ticket and map-
point headquarters for pretty much all of my rave-going days.
(The place was run by an older woman whose sister dated my
grandfather, though I wasn't aware of the connection for years.)

DJ mixes are often the most potent way of hearing post-rave
dance music, since it's usually designed to be mixed. That was true
of jungle as well, but most of the non-mixed compilations that
drew me into the music (Moonshine's *Speed Limit 140 BPM Plus* series foremost among them) worked better than most because
prime jungle had more ideas per track than most music of its ilk
did per album. As its practitioners began speeding up the breakbeats that maintained its bottom, nearly everything else—the samples, the melodic refrains, the vocal chants—sped up too, apart
from the basslines, which slowed down, giving the music its
unique fast/slow feel. As the sound-surfaces sped by, it began to
behoove the producers to include new elements more often;
quickly enough, as you can hear on *History*'s first third, the tracks
went from simple tracky space-age hip-hop ready-mades to structures that felt pop—verses, choruses, bridges—even when they
didn't resemble it any other way. This is how most of the individual tracks on *History* are shaped.

But it's not how *History* itself is shaped. The songs' hooks hang
out long enough to embed themselves as hooks, but not as
songs—indeed, DB left plenty of great moments from these
tracks out of the mix. But none of them are missed. There are
lots of DJ mixes as rich, that keep better momentum, that offer

more surprises. But even if he'd called the thing *A Bunch of Records I Picked Up Last Month at a Garage Sale* and scrambled the tracks' chronology, *History* would still have the most satisfying arc, would still feel like a complete, ordered statement, would still tell (or appear to tell) a story as thrilling as any in pop. True to his title, DJ DB programmed *History* more or less chronologically. But as he would demonstrate with the two follow-up albums (1996's *History Part Two* and 1999's *Shades of Technology*, both terrific), he was a DJ first, and his first commitment was to building a specific aural arc.

It begins with a spoken-word snippet from Touch's horrifying 1971 generation-gap cautionary single, "Once You Understand." "Mr. Kirk?" "Yes?" "Do you have a son, Robert Kirk, age seventeen?" "Y-yes?" "I'm sorry, Mr. Kirk. You'd better come down to the station house. Your son is dead." "Dead?! H-how?!" "He died of an overdose." On "Once You Understand," this comes at the end, before a sickly kiddie chorus repeats its chant: "Things get a little bit easier/Once you understand." Here, 4 Hero dust the sample in cold computer pixie dust with a high-pitched riff like a telephone malfunctioning and repeat the cop: "Come down to the station house; come down to the station house; come down to the station house. Your son is *dead*."

WHOOMP! A sampled kick drum stomps, giving way to a looped, sped-up breakbeat from the Isley Brothers' "Get Into Something," Ronald Isley's exhortation to "give the drummer some" turned into chipmunk talk that exposes the opening sample's pathos as a sick joke—on Mr. Kirk, on his foolish son, on the hopelessly square "Once You Understand," on the drug faddism and generation gaps that play out in more or less the same manner every few years, and on you the raver, who by hearing and ostensibly dancing to this new song is implicated as a potential overdose. This is grim stuff, but it's also weirdly inviting. If these guys can laugh at something that harrowing, maybe we can have some of what they're taking, or at least watch from a relatively safe distance while they skirt the edge. Another vocal sample duets with the turbo-Isley, chanting what sounds like "gener-*a-tion*"—another manifesto? Is that an accident? Before you have time to wonder, a thick keyboard bulldozes into the middle of the sound field with a butt-simple three-note figure, mostly there to wobble the speakers but in this context announcing another of the jungle's audio-brutalist elements. This is the reverse-negative underside of rave's holographic rainbow optimism. Like Carl Craig saying that Kraftwerk "were so stiff they were funky," or Talking Heads trading on being so straight they were weird, early rave's cartoonishness was so twee it was scary.

After a final "Your son is dead," DB cuts straight into the House Crew's sampled diva shouting, a cappella, "Gotta keep the fire burning," before a bank of synths play the fanfare-riff that forms the lingua franca of early jungle (and house, and techno) as much as the breakbeats or basslines did. On headphones, the riff jumps from right speaker to middle to left, but it feels more than just cute—the movement signals the onrush of the beat, or the genre, or the drug. After the theme is established, the song's primary beat emerges from some shakily programmed drum-machine fills, but the dodginess just adds to the massed excitement, and DB plays on the rushed/rushing cut-and-snip quality of the early tracks by quick-cutting between them rather than overlaying them (which he does a good deal of later on). On the segue from "Keep the Fire Burning" into DMS's "Vengeance," he overlays

some of the title samples for continuity but keeps the actual
tracks basically separate.

We started with a sick joke and a moody diva, so next, with
"Vengeance," we get ruffneck rap attitude, from a double-speed
Run-D.M.C. quote. "I'm the king of rock, there is none higher/I
won't stop rocking till I retire," twee-D.M.C. hectors, a Silly Putty
image of hip-hop being stretched to the breaking point, the music's repeat-the-good-part-for-eternity motivating principle carried
to an absurdist end. "I won't stop rockin'! I won't stop rockin'!"—
not just that, but it now sounds like it *can't* stop, because its nervous system is working faster than the rest of it can comprehend.
The beat underneath is sluggish compared to the sample, but the
sample has so much momentum it hardly matters.

Then the breakthrough: Open Skies' "Ozone Nights," misla-
beled on the CD as "Deep in Your Eyes," the twelve-inch's B-side.
D.M.C.'s final "Till I re-*tire*" is replaced with a simple, tinny break
before we're ambushed by mnemonic piano and a system-shock
diva vocal: "It would be OH! Soooo niiiiice. To be with *you*. To be
wiiith you." (As in, it would be "Ozone Nights," geddit?) It's shrill
and hysterical, right at the edge of panic, tremulous without being
particularly "soulful," a heart-in-mouth jump that breaks the mix
open, only to cut to spazzy synth-wows like a computer malfunctioning, or a balloon flying through a room as it lets out air. The
diva squeal completes the disc's initial movement from twitchy-
speedy nerve-wracking to full-on ecstatic; whatever its borrow-
ings, from here on the language this music speaks is its own.

That language stays frenzied a while longer: Kaotic Chemistry's
"Drum Trip II" builds off an epileptic repitition of a b-boy chant:
"Do it now, get ill," over clean breaks punctuated by a heavily

processed snare like a Pac-Man chomp. Plinking keyboard figures, horror-movie atmosphere, and a diva "yeah-yeah" as stratospheric as Open Skies'—only cheering from the sidelines rather than under the spotlight—gather and push the momentum. We're accustomed to the hyper motion; now we just want to see where it goes, and with a swift piano sweep we find out: "Total ecstasy-ee-ee," another diva tells us over a statelier-than-usual house-piano ostinato.

EQ's "Total Ecstasy (Remix)" is the first track on *History* to sound comfortable in its own skin and not bursting out of it. The endorphins are still firing, but they've settled enough to take things as they come. The breaks are crisp and smoothly repetitive; synth-strings even the tone almost subliminally; even the rave-blare bridge is less a breakout than a signpost—oh, that's where we are, the warehouse with the funny colors on the walls where everyone smells like Vicks Vapo-Rub. Sure, I'd love some water—thank you. I can tell you're a good person too, and your fuzzy hat feels amazing against my temple. I'd love to come to your after-party, and your friend is just as beautiful as you are. Does she want some gum?

There's some more female a capella madness before the next transition, and while the "aaaah!"s are certainly church-like, the spirit is different—more gothic (not Goth), fixing the eye on the steeple, not the pew or the pulpit, the queasiness of judgment lurking around the corner, if not fully present for a while yet. To prove it, "Peace Maker" fixates on ride-cymbal jangle and a light-saber synth pattern before robot voices gurgle up and the instruments are bathed in steel wool, mechanical processors giving them a cold gray glowing echo. The walls are turning metallic and

the details are blurring, though I seem to remember the basic setting from the collective sci-fi unconscious. It's cooler than I
thought, actually, but what's that lime green pinpoint doing in the
upper left-hand corner?

Knowing Omni Trio's "Mystic Stepper (Feel Better)" before
hearing it on *History* helped freeze me in place when I first regis-
tered its appearance during the final twenty-four seconds of
"Peace Maker," but that isn't mandatory. The intro is a repeated
fine-grained four-note pattern, with odd harmonics creeping in,
that could portend anything from ambient wisp to death march.
Shining its beam through Nebula II's accreting robo-murk is the
most important thing DB will do in the entire mix. His neat stacking and on-the-beat sound-bite encores will remain frequent tools,
but the lingering overlap is an announcement: We're not just
changing lanes, we're moving from the county road to the inter-
state, with "Peace Maker" as the exit lane.

Once you've made it over, the change in landscape is immediately noticeable. Till now, even the most deftly reconstructed beats
and depth-charge sub-bass had a kind of sonic two-dimensionality.
Where "Mystic Stepper" begins for real is its opening drumroll,
and it's the most *produced*-sounding part of the record: a kick like a
tympani, snares that crack distinctively even during the feverish
speed-rolls constantly punctuating the rhythm. That intro's ominous twinkle stays put while a sampled diva holds a long note.
They're the net; the drums are acrobats. Then a command: "Feel!
Feel good." Or is it a command? The diva here is an angel of
mercy, only like the soothing/uneasy rest of the track, she doesn't
sound too sure of herself.

After a minute, neither does anything else, because Rob Haigh, the producer behind Omni Trio, whips the tablecloth out from under his finely laid china: he reverses the drum track, sending everything flying, while a couple of church bells hammer coldly on the sides, the destabilizing becoming its own weird hook with its own rhythmic logic. If "Total Ecstasy" signaled rave's anthemic giddiness as a convention to be harnessed and brought out for a hook or for show, Haigh's weird bridge does the same thing with its runaway momentum and the odd, almost accidental timbres resulting from all those mangled samples.

I treasure "Mystic Stepper" the single, because Haigh keeps shifting around his motif without ever quite resolving it. DB treasures it because it establishes jungle in its fully mature form—that's how he uses it here, anyway. So when he pushes stop on the Technics that the record is playing on after a second refrain, he closes the book on the music's ascension. We've made it up the mountain. Now we get to admire the scenery: The skeleton-clatter pirouettes and piquant melodies of Omni Trio's "Renegade Snares" and Nookie's "Gonna Be Alright"; the bug-eyed acid riffs and drums, pitch-shifted till they tweak like divas, of 4 Hero's "Journey from the Light"; the hazy, not-quite-identifiable loop underpinning JMJ & Richie's "Case Closed" (not strings, but faded till they might as well be); the Jamaican-patois double-dutch of Phuture Assassins' "Roots 'n Future"; every unbridled second of the House Crew's unsurpassed "Euphoria (Nino's Dream)." At end, with a Ray Keith remix of Baby D's "Let Me Be Your Fantasy" and DJ-SS's "A New Breed of Ravers," the beats begin to sound half-speed even if their rate per minute hasn't budged. With a turn of the Technics power switch (and over a looped new-age lady intoning, "And feel that your whole being is revitalized"), DB sends the whole thing into a skid that takes some ground with it.

No one uses the phrase "information overload" anymore, mostly because it's a little too awestruck. It describes a condition we've long grown accustomed to, one that's only intensified in the past two decades; when something stops being alien, you stop noticing it completely.

Jungle was information-overload music, and for me it came along at a perfect information-overload time—rampant hormones, kiddie-fun rides at indoor shopping centers, map-point voice-mail hotlines to parties in barns, caves, and abandoned warehouses. All at once, jungle signified past (signposts from pop history, fairground-ready keyboard hooks, and helium-pitched vocals transmuted Saturday-morning cartoonishness into Saturday-night fever), present (constant mutation, connected to a scene happening *right now*), and future (aggressive technological savvy). It was familiar enough to grab onto and alien enough that I could learn its rules, then claim it as my own. It was, in short, everything I wanted music to be, not least because for a good while it felt like it was still growing, still changing, as yet not tied down to a definitive, diminishing-returns version of itself. It was so much more *alive* than anything else out there, even stuff I loved.

I'm using past tense deliberately. Jungle hasn't died, and neither have I. I still listen to a lot of music, much of it current, and there are good jungle records still being made. But *History*'s ascension is what I fixate on, and as uncomfortable as it is to admit, this has everything to do with nostalgia. Sure, the album is labeled *History* and enacts a version of it, but its sheer restlessness gives the concept too much motion to feel calcified. Yet that's where my relationship with the music stands. By the late '90s, when jungle seemed to have dried out sonically and creatively, I basically left it behind, and despite entreaties from smart people who've stuck with it and an occasional glimmer of genius when I tune in, I'm never fully able to dive back in. It's like an old lover you look up every so often just to see if they're doing all right, but with whom you wouldn't necessarily want to rekindle the flame.

My love for the music was intense and full of abandon, the way the relationships you have in your late teens and early twenties tend to be (and your late teens and early twenties themselves are): memorable and hyperreal and important. But I was also peripheral to its inside workings, both as an American in love with a largely British scene and as a raver who spent as much time trying to figure out what it all might mean as I did abandoning myself to the music. (Maybe it would have been different if I'd taken drugs, though I know myself well enough to have my doubts.) *History of Our World* is really a history of someone else's world. But at the same time, it's my history alone, of a world where I still get to dream in Day-Glo, where peace, love, unity, and respect cohabit snugly, where the light hits everything at a 45-degree angle and reveals a perfect spectrum.

5

DIVINE STYLER
*Spiral Walls Containing
Autumns of Light*
Giant, 1992

By Scott Seward

"Am I An Epigram For Life?"

HALTING. HESITANT. THE SOUND OF SOMEONE NOT
COMPLETELY SURE WHERE THEY ARE OR WHERE
THEY'RE GOING. OK, IT'S ALSO THE SOUND OF
someone not yet fully awake and possibly groping for their bong
in the darkness. What's he mumbling about? Why do the electronic squiggles above his words remind me of a halo of stars
around a cartoon cat's recently frying-panned head? His words become clearer. He's worried about crossing the river Styx. And who
wouldn't be? His voice has a definite note of fear. This isn't really
what you would call a "song," and anyone looking for a good example of how *not* to open your album (if you plan on selling any)
need look no further. This dude sounds like he's going on a trip
against his better judgment. A journey. It's a challenge of sorts. He

seems to be trying to say: "I don't even know if I wanna go! Are you sure you want to come with me?"

I did. And do. A thousand times over. For now and forever. Divine Styler's Spiral Walls Containing Autumns of Light (which appeared with little fanfare in 1992 on the mostly forgettable Reprise subsidiary Giant Records) was the very first album I thought of to answer the question of what to bring on a trip to nowheresville. There was no hesitation. I even live on an honest-to-God island only reachable by plane or boat, so I know a little about what one needs for maximum offshore comfort. Most of the ingredients required are 80 to 100 proof. I am not, however, island-born. Too much city living has corrupted my senses. There are times when I'd gladly trade in the soothing lap of the tide or a gorgeous sunset for some Indian food or a used record store to browse in. While what most people prize about the sand and surf life are the peace, quiet, and gentle rhythms, I find that I crave a fairly steady barrage of elements not easily found in Shangri-La. That's where the death metal comes in. Lots and lots of death metal. And Baltimore club music. Hell, anything. Marching bands, Stockhausen, Maynard Ferguson's piercing trumpet call, any and all sounds that can and will remind me that all of life is not defined by a sunset, and that I am not, in fact, dead yet. Simplicity and meditation can come later. I have too much on my mind. Choosing Divine's album as my hypothetical one and only source of aural plenty makes perfect sense. (Not to mention it's the only album I own five copies of. Just in case! Like extra batteries for the hurricane flashlight.) It is all of life and much of what I would want to remember of the world and its shadows. It is not a retreat from humanity, but one can retreat into it at will. It rocks majorly. Sadly, you've probably never heard it. It feels like a gift. It's sullen and desperate and peace on earth and good will toward men. With the exception of Gothic stonecutters.

TOUCH

The sound of a heartbeat. Then a slightly dazed and loping electro-shuffle. The sound of robots drunk on God. Divine is completely open and vulnerable. Or asleep. There are disorienting stops and starts until, eventually, everything stops completely. Divine is now rested and alert. A thumping one-man call and response. He is prostrate. This is a show of strength and a call to arms. We have reached the end of song two on this "rap" album and we are rhymeless. If anything, "Touch" is even more oblique and disjointed than the opener. It's a heck of a way to start a party! The lesson of "Touch" seems to be that it's not easy to give up the past or past weaknesses. Maybe.

There was a noose around my neck and tears in my eyes, but I was too drunk to be deadly and the rope was too close to the ground, which meant I had to kneel in order to get enough weight on my neck to do any damage, and this awkward (and slow) process gave me too much time to think. Despite being at my bleakest, this was not gonna be the moment when everything went black. I was, without a doubt, a big miserable oversensitive crybaby. We've all been there. So I did what many Americans do when life becomes too close for comfort: I moved. Back to my childhood home and out of the big city (in my case, the big city was Smelladelphia, Thugsylvania. Home of Scrapple, The Sun Ra Arkestra, Frank Rizzo's sainted corpse, leading jazz bagpiper Rufus Harley, and Randall "Tex" Cobb). It was time to recuperate and reevaluate. Time to learn how to stay alive. So much had happened since I had moved away from home in 1987 BC (Before Compton) and during those early '90s dog days AD (After Dre). I wouldn't be the only person trying to figure out my place in the universe. (It turns out I don't have much of one. I am here by the grace of arbitrariness and long-lived Yankee heredity.) The going would be rough. Divine Styler and case after case of baby peas would help to set me free.

IN A WORLD OF U

A love letter to Allah and the first show-stopper on the album. Not a moment too soon! We needed some sort of life-preserver to hang on to. The drums are live, tight, and funky. Everything is live, actually. This will be Divine's band for the album, The Autumns of Light: *Kendu Jenkins on drums, Tony Guarderas on bass, Jeff Phillips on guitar, and Divine on keyboard, guitar, and vocals. Such a smooth conversational croon here. Divine's voice is like a fine wine with hints of chocolate, butterscotch, cloves, tobacco, and hemp. He is in a contemplative mood as deep as well water. Everything is fresh and clean. The acid-inflected snake-charm guitars do their dance. Never wanting this song to end is the first step on the path to redemption.*

A crumbling infrastructure. No money. No jobs. People fleeing by the thousands. A genocidal war on drugs. Violence. Loss of hope. AIDS. A president who thought it was a good idea to throw the mentally ill out onto the street during the middle of a drug epidemic. American cities could be hell on earth in the '80s. It seemed like the rural and suburban citizens of the United States couldn't care less. (I try my best not to gloat—because it really isn't funny—when the scare stories come on television about drugs like meth and "hillbilly heroin" sweeping through the country. *And how it isn't just an urban problem anymore!* Ha! Like it ever was. How you like me now, you chickenshit, white-bread, redneck Opie

Taylor–looking motherfuckers! Sorry. I wish you all well.) They said that cities were a lost cause. Blow them up and start over. Dirty, rotting husks filled with crime and insanity, which was kind of true at the time. A trip of a few blocks to the store could mean running a gauntlet of illness, need, and menace. Nowadays you have people retiring to cities! Who woulda thunk it? I can't help but feel that this country went through some sort of brutal senseless war during that period and that nobody wants to talk about it. It's like it never happened. So many dead and lost and gone and locked up for life. Entire neighborhoods . . . poof! And, yes, you guessed it, despite the neglect and misery there was vibrancy and life and the radio was rocking with yet another generation of craftspeople fashioning art out of the bare minimum and creating hope out of hopelessness. And it had a beat and you could dance to it! There was hip-hop (the music that crack built!) and house music and techno and R&B and even rock in some quarters that felt like life and death and fresh air in increasingly airless rooms. People are resilient like that. Divine Styler was just one of millions making marks and signs on brick and concrete that future alien civilizations could look at and perhaps grasp that pettiness, greed, and fear were not the only things that this doomed human race held dear.

Love, Lies And Lifetime's Cries

Uh-oh. Divine's knocking on heaven's gate, but they won't let him in. This is the first real sign that things are not well in the Styler household. Divine rambles over horror-film synth—He has "taken himself to the farthest walls of hurt"—and he is beginning to realize that time is a sham. He is slowly breaking through, but he thinks he is stuck.

I used to sit for hours, in the pre-Dre universe (Dre being the African demigod of music known for his tempestuous spirit and restless creative energy as well as a force of nature that almost single-handedly changed the shape of rap music), listening to the a cappella version of Eric B & Rakim's "Follow The Leader," because I wanted to know everything that Rakim knew. I wanted to be Rakim. I bridled when he rapped: "In this journey, I'm the journal, you're the journalist. Am I eternal or an eternalist?" I didn't want to be the journalist. I wanted to be the journal. And eternal. I wanted the knowledge that Rakim effortlessly conveyed, even when I didn't understand it. Or when it had little to do with my own life in any way, shape, or form. This, of course, was silly. In some ways it was just another manifestation of the childhood OCD that had made me a herky-jerky mess as a youth. This idea that knowledge could be gained by osmosis, tactile confirmation, and repetitive voodoo, and that a sense of spirituality could be attained by becoming or swallowing whole the person responsible for my excitement is what made me sit on my bed as a child with a portable record player spinning "I Feel Love" over and over until I had Giorgio Moroder's synthesizer parts down to mimed perfection. I didn't want to learn how to play "I Feel Love" on the synthesizer and I didn't want to learn how to rap like Rakim. I wanted to be the spirit of their words and sounds as if I had created those words and sounds alongside them. This is all textbook stuff. I have no idea which textbook, but one of them. It wasn't until I was older that I came to realize that my only job as a listener was to embrace the beauty of life through sound and that I didn't need to take or steal anything from anybody in order to make myself stronger or feel less alone in the world. We are all as strong as we believe we are and we are always alone.

This epiphany is one of the reasons why you won't get any phony history out of me regarding Divine Styler. It would all be second- and third-hand, and quite frankly, none of my business. Just stuff that I read on the Web in interviews and reviews. I wish him well and all the love and happiness that the world has to offer, but I cannot speak for him as a person or about incidents in his life I know little about. I can only really speak about the sounds that come out of my speakers when I play the music he has made and make note of how the recorded persona of Divine reacts and interacts with the music surrounding him. I can give you this much information: Divine moved to California in the '80s and hooked up with Ice-T and Ice's Rhyme Syndicate (which included Afrika Islam; Divine's production partner; Bilal Bashir; future House of Pain member; Everlast; and a host of other DJs, rappers, and Ice-T confederates) and through him would record what would be Divine's 1989 debut, *Word Power*. Credited to Divine and The Scheme Team, it is a singularly funky, strange, chaotic, and bewildering album. Let loose in the studio on Ice's dime, Divine and Bilal and their pals made a hallucinogenic feast for beat lovers, linguistics professors, and Muslim conspiracy theorists. And people like me who just marveled at the weirdness of seeing scrappy headz like Divine on MTV when that channel was more suited to the Bell Biv Devoes of the world (I ain't hating on BBD, I'm just saying. . . .). Chock-full of ideas both half-assed and strong, out of print for years, and featuring two of Divine's funkiest and most powerful cuts—"Ain't Sayin' Nothin" and "Tongue

Of Labyrinth"—*Word Power* is as fucked up as the day is long and serves as some freaky yardstick for any iconoclastic outcat of the future to measure their own drip-painting output with.

LIVERY

The interstellar performance of "Love, Lies and Lifetime's Cries" culmi-nates in a drumroll that lands at the feet of jeep beat nirvana in the guise of "Livery." A verbal exhortation that rides the push and pull of one-man-band basement synth, echo-rich drums, and funky chicken gui-tar scratching the henhouse floor. "Come to the jungle of boogie to the livery" Divine cries. It's mumbo gumbo that swings hard in the name of enlightenment.

When I moved home from the city in the early '90s for my rest cure, I ended up living in a rental house that smelled like dog urine with my brother Daniel Saxton Bunnybrain and ex–Violent Children guitarist turned ninety-pound bearded biker Warren Kennedy. I got a job at the supermarket on the third shift (eleven p.m. to seven a.m.), and I worked there forty to fifty hours a week for the next two and a half years. I lived on cigarettes, bad coffee, candy bars, and monotonous classic rock radio. Grunge was start-ing to hit in a big way, all the Top 40 stations were already starting to play choice Nirvana and Pearl Jam tracks, but the big-wattage rock institution that got piped through the store at night didn't trust it and refused to acknowledge those upstarts from Seattle. They went to great lengths to avoid it too! They had to play *some* new tunes in between "Baba O'Reilly" and "Rocky Mountain Way," so they gave a momentary boost to people like Sass Jordan,

Brother Cane, Jackyl, Mr. Big, and Big Head Todd & The Monsters. I was no grunge nut, but it was kind of excruciating after awhile to watch them opt for James Taylor's newest over anything in flannel. Some sort of weird misplaced sense of pride. Joe Walsh wore flannel! Grunge was as American as apple friggin' pie. Well, eventually they caved. They had to. And when they did, it was Alice in Chains and Pearl Jam *all night long*. To this day, when I see a picture of Eddie Vedder I smell the bleach that the floor crew used on the bathrooms.

The supermarket is where I learned the Zen of pea stacking. Alone, all night, slicing open box after box, I really got a chance to think about my life. Where I went wrong. What not to do next time. During break I would read fashion magazines or one of my many Jiddu Krishnamurti books or just stare off into space in a topsy-turvy day-is-night/night-is-day delirium. My favorite task was "blocking" the store. When everything was up on the shelves, we would go through the aisles one by one stacking cans and jars and boxes until every shelf was a solid wall of products. I don't think I have ever enjoyed doing something work-related more in my life. It was like I was born to do it! On some nights, when we had extra-large loads of product to unload, price, and stock, we wouldn't have time to block the whole store. It was such a horrible, deflating feeling when that happened. I would walk out to my car in the morning in defeat. I learned so much during my time there. About life, myself, other people, and the long-term effects of oily coffee, diner food, and candy bars on the human stomach, but most importantly how to be alone and still and observant while still engaging with the world around me.

GREY MATTER

Divine's genius and serpentine linguistic stylistics in full flight. The one-two punch of "Livery" into "Grey Matter" is hard to beat. "Grey Matter" was the only single off of the album (said single is almost thirty-five minutes of mixes that stretch and elongate the original song with forgettable "jazzy" embellishments that add nothing to the original's swift disregard for just about every pop chart that exists). If anything, they just render Divine's metaphysical scatting more bizarre by isolating his voice on top while sub-Boz Scaggs "Lowdown" bass roots around in the cellar like a pig looking for truffles. Mostly it sounds like Divine didn't have a whole hell of a lot to do with the single. And it's telling that there is a radio edit for one of the mixes, but not for the album track! And, the album track is the last song on a very long single filled with superfluous mixes! I love it when label bosses get scared. Fuck it, he got an album out of them, and briefly got to be label mates with Morbid Angel, Pudgee Tha Phat Bastard, and Oingo Boingo). The expertly deployed use of synth and live funky drumming creates a shuffling groove that is pure contact high. Starting the album with this near-perfect slice of astral rap would have made way too much sense. You gotta eat your beans before you get any pie.

The Wu-Tangification of the universe has made hard-to-decipher lyrical code par for the course on even the most major of major-label rap offering these days, but when Divine released *Word Power* in 1989 there weren't that many fearless cosmic warriors creating their own language out of Islamic mysticism and surrealist poetic imagery. Word strings falling like liquid silver onto the heads of like-minded seekers of caves and mountaintops were hard to come by even in a genre so filled with exemplary wordsmiths.

Maybe if you had combined the Poor Righteous Teachers and Kool Keith you would have had an approximation of where Divine was coming from at the time. Years ago, I had a conversation with a coworker that went a little something like this:

> Me: So, do you like the Jungle Brothers?
> Her: Nuh uh, they dirty!
> Me: You mean their lyrics?
> Her: No!!! I mean they nasty, their clothes are always dirty and they *look* nasty!
> Me: Oh. I kinda like the way they look!

And I did. I loved the Jungle Brothers. There was a time when I would have killed for them. Them and EPMD and Schoolly D and a whole lot of other people. Killed for them like I would have killed for my friends and my two six-packs of Meister-Brau a night and my Muriel Spark first editions. They meant the world to me. That sample of the guitar riff from Junior's "Mama Used To Say" on the JBs' *Done By The Forces Of Nature* was worth more to me than all the tea in Chinatown. Divine and his pals were dirty back then too. Like me. Like my friends. The highlight of Everlast's "I Got The Knack" video—the only single that went anywhere for him from his debut, thanks to a deft and obvious "My Sharona" sample—was the sight of the Scheme Team slam dancing crazily, the dust literally flying off of them. They were my dirty hippie rap gods. Public Enemy and N.W.A. might have made me want to burn the world down and start from scratch, but the JBs and Divine made me believe that a new world could be built on top of the old using the goodness that was still left as spare parts.

HEAVEN DON'T WANT ME AND
HELL'S AFRAID I'LL TAKE OVER

A sluggish dreamscape, but no mere "interlude" or ha-ha "skit." Divine's lost soul vocal gymnastics fight a sleepy drum machine in order to be heard by God. Allah be praised and Allah be a little confused perhaps by this young man's vigorous testimony, but if I know Allah, and I do, he's digging that Garry Shyder-esque fuzz guitar set for mosquito as much as anyone.

My brother, Dan Bunny, was the one who gave me my first copy of Divine's *Spiral Walls* LP. He had two double-vinyl promo copies for some reason. As a kid, I had hated my brother with a passion, even though we were both miserable drug-swallowing dirtbags who shared a lot of the same interests. But when we were teens, despite our animosity, we couldn't help but hip one another to various cool sounds that had slipped over our transom. He clued me in to acts like Kurtis Blow, Syd Barrett, Budgie, Tonio K, and Motörhead. I gave him the lowdown on bands like Crass, Rudimentary Peni, Scratch Acid, and Die Kreuzen. And as much as we both loved hard rock, we also immediately embraced rap as soon as we knew of its existence. We had grown up in a suburban Connecticut home that was always filled with the sounds of R&B, jazz, and funk. We were ready for rap. Thanks, Dad! My brother had also been the one who had first played Chubby Checker's *New Revelation* album for me. (An album that haunts me to this day. The only album I thought of besides Divine's to take to a desert oasis.) *Spiral Walls* was released when I was still in Philly, but I was too dispirited at the time to care about anything. But now, safe in the woods and slowly wiping the cobwebs from my eyes, my life was beginning to matter to me again and the album never left my turntable (just as Slayer's *South Of Heaven* never left the tape deck in my '89 Cavalier). I could definitely relate to Divine's search for understanding. We were both trapped in a world we had never made.

MYSTIC SHEEP DRINK ELECTRIC TEA

The lysergic funk turns deadly on "Mystic Sheep." The abrasive electro-industrial multitracked vocals will wake you from your reverie in a hurry. In fact, this song manages to stop the entire album dead in its tracks. Its bracing bottomless-pit techno beats combined with concrete overshoes make for D.I.Y. gabber-rap of a high order.

In 1992, RCA Records released a curious album by a group calling themselves Me Phi Me. Me Phi Me's album was a strange mix of PM Dawn–inspired rap, moldy funk samples, Eastern philosophy and religion, African American Greek fraternity sloganeering, and twelve-string classical guitar. It even featured an out-of-left-field guest cameo by that super-smooth king of the white-boy samba, Michael Franks. (As it happens, I am finishing up a critical survey of Michael Franks' career entitled *A Fatal Case Of Popsicle Toes: One Man's Misguided Obsession With The Somnambulant World Of Michael Franks*; it will be published in the near future.) Hardly anyone remembers Me Phi Me's debut. Some of the members of Me Phi Me might not even remember it. And I bring their album up to point out that they only made what is possibly the *second* strangest rap album of 1992, with Divine's being the first. The contender for 1991 might be the frenetic and captivating Bomb Squad–helmed Son of Bazerk album. In 1993—The Year of the

Chronic—the noisiest rap album award would have to go to the Jungle Brothers and their experiment in hermetically sealed, cannabis-grown avant-gardism, *J. Beez Wit The Remedy*. The freak-of-the-week award for 1997 would have to go to Prince Paul and his claustrophobic epic of beat-queasiness, *Psychoanalysis (What Is It?!)*. All of these albums were put out by big-time record labels. They were all exploratory by nature (even Me Phi Me's hard-to-digest effort). And the same could be said for PM Dawn's '90s discography, and they raised their freak flags pretty damned high. Hardly anybody bought them. (Prince Paul's album was actually reissued by Tommy Boy Records after its initial release on an indie label in 1996. Tommy Boy was apparently trying to find an album that would sell even fewer copies than their candidate for 1996's least-remembered rap oddity: the dark, sluggish, and depressed *Truth Crushed To Earth Shall Rise Again* by Everlast's formerly hit-making House of Pain. How commercially dubious could this album have been? Well, Divine Styler is an unofficial fourth member on it, and he is featured prominently throughout. *That's* how commercially dubious.) I would call these albums ahead of their time if I believed in such a thing. But I don't. They were very much of their specific time. I definitely see a line of continuity that runs from the Jungle Brothers (and A Tribe Called Quest and De la Soul) to Divine to groups like New Kingdom and then on to present-day space-cowboys Dälek and Clouddead. The thrill of discovery binds them together (well, that and certain sweet fumes, maybe). Not that you can't discover amazing details and sounds in Nas, Jay-Z, and a hundred other rap superstars. You can. And almost any R. Kelly album is as strange and transfixing, in its way, as anything that Divine Styler has produced. But Divine and the freaks and geeks of the current indie-rap world that I admire all have a three-dimensional capability to envision rap as being and sounding like whatever they want it to be and sound like. An open-ended universe of sound that doesn't play by the rules that say that Nas and Jay-Z are "technically" two of the best rappers alive. To paraphrase Rakim, I never sweat the technique. I want to fly high above the treetops on mystic wings of song. Technique is the last thing I'm worried about.

WIDTH IN MY DEPTH

As delicate as "Mystic Sheep" is cacophonous, "Width In My Depth" finds Divine asking the hard questions—"God, what am I?" "Why should I deserve me?"—and being rewarded with a peace of mind that heretofore had been denied to him. Ahhhhhhhh. Like the man says: "No one ever said patience was a deadly quasar." Damn straight.

If love is a flame with no smoke, then *Spiral Walls*, as an experience, is not an album for those who worship the smoke.

THE NEXT

"The Next" is a tour de force of bubbling burbling brown-sugar organ ("My space is my machine") and one of Divine's finest vocal performances ("Did I curse my love with dead hexes?"). He coos, scats, flutters, raps, and exhorts Sunday-preacher style along over under and above the beat in inimitable fashion. I used to make way too much out of the line: "My mentor says I've dropped too much acid/Mommy thinks I'm a psycho-spastic." That was my "Aha!" moment when I first heard that. As if it explained some-

thing. It doesn't. It couldn't. It never will. Art stands alone and free
of the breath that expels it. All music and words belong to the universe once released from our mortal grasp. Many people who hear
that line don't even speak English. To them it is simply a disembodied voice's assertion of existence.

After less than three years back in the bosom of my family, after
one ill-fated love affair, after time and reflection and daylight sleeping, after ruthless self-examination and psychic toughening and
many, many hours of experience with a box-cutter, I was ready to
head back to the city for round two. I had made Divine's album a
mirror (don't think I don't realize that) and used the image I saw in
it to craft a happy ending onto this last phase of my life. I wanted a
new beginning and I made myself believe that he did too. Which
is all bullshit, but, hey, whatever works. And it did work at the
time.

EUPHORIC RANGERS

*A tribal rumble and a cry from beyond the grave of birth. Divine is naked
and unashamed. There is nothing ever to be ashamed of. There is nothing
that he can't say. He sees the light. We, all of us, see the light. And it's
beautiful.*

"Why not Savoy Brown, Angela Bofill, The Strapping Field-
hands, The Sun City Girls, The Hi-Lo's, Bohannon, The Ravens,
Heavy the World, Beckett, Mandrake Memorial, Severed Heads,
October Tide, Eyehategod, Faze-O, Joe Tex, Thin Lizzy, Jack Blan-
chard & Misty Morgan, Dog Faced Hermans, DJ Technics, Babe
Ruth, The Bizarros, Mott the Hoople, Ultramagnetic MC's, Half
Man Half Biscuit, Junior Wells, Magic Sam, Rosalie Sorrels,

Bloomsbury People, Spread Eagle, Wide Boy Awake, Charles Mingus, The Monochrome Set, Felt, Denim, Go-Kart Mozart, The Bonzo Dog Band, The Damnation of Adam Blessing, Captain Beyond, Hampton Hawes, SSD, The Necros, Lil Son Jackson, Amon Düül II, Fun Boy Three, Bubble Puppy, Funkadelic, Weldon Irvine, Magna Carta, The Unspoken Word, Katatonia, or Ulver? Or Mozart, Bach, Brahms, Ellington, Mahler, or Ives for fuck's sake!"

"Those are all fine choices. Perfect choices. But I'm sticking with Divine. I think the world of him. And it's not out of some desire I have to be clever or perverse. Anyone with an open heart and mind will find just as much richness in this album as I do."

"Do you even know anything about Islam or that kind of thing?"

"Nah, I never really paid much attention in school. And I never did go to college, much to my regret. But I do know that we are all one and that my love for the world is infinite and that there is no ending or beginning. There is only a constant flow of energy made of the heavens. And that's a start."

"If you say so. If I were stuck on an island I'd want some fuckin' bass, you know what I mean? Get me some Maggotron and knock the coconuts right off the fuckin' trees, you know?"

"Yeah, I hear that. You'd go all Maggozulu on that island's ass."

WALK OF EXODUS

With the crack of a snare drum an epic of mystery and grace is born. I could shed a tear just thinking about this song. It is the well-deserved rest after a long journey. And yet it has a heightened atmosphere, a drama built into it that is riveting to me. It sums up a life's experience, but after this brief respite, perhaps first a hot meal and something cool to drink, there is more to see and do. The journey is never over. Oh, and again, I beg of you, beware of Gothic stonecutters.

In 1998, Divine released his third and last, as of 2006, full-length album, *Wordpower 2: Directrix*. It was a stunning ultra-futuristic album filled with shiny cyborg beats and Divine's undiminished ability to captivate with unlikely spitfire rhymes both mythical and sublime. Nobody can write a cryptic millenarian song about the hidden role that vowels play like Divine. Songs like "Satan Dynasty Killer" and "Microphenia" knock my block off to this day. *Wordpower: 2* was also the first album I ever wrote about in public for cash money. This was yet another new chapter in my life that was Divine-related. By 1999, I had lived in Philly again for years and suffered my share of setbacks, but I no longer feared life or change or the passing of time. I might not have been ready to take on an entire Satanic *Dynasty*, but maybe a minion or two. It is now 2006, and I'm even further away from that young man who needed to learn balance from rap records and the shelving of peas. I look out the kitchen window and I can see the lagoon that leads to the ever-present indifference of the ocean. I can hear the love of my life and our two small boys playing in the back bedroom. I can hear the crows as they shred my last nerve with their incessant cawing. Jesus, I'm bored. Islands are for the birds. Literally. Don't ask me how we ended up here. It's a long story.

AURA

Ha! There are no happy endings! Divine saved this glitch in the system for last. Oh sure, he could have ended his album with the perfectly appropri-

ate and mesmerizing "Walk Of Exodus," but that would have been too perfect. He had to screw with time and space one more time via this slab of tricked-out Allah-loving woozery. It's just his way of saying: Have you been paying attention? Life doesn't end on an upbeat note. It never ends. We all go on playing our part unto infinity. I'll just take this time to add a big "fuck you" to future hysterical historians looking for hipster ghosts to devour. I'm not your pet griot trickster monkey god, motherfucker! Put down the pen, Jeeves, and stop looking for an excuse to use the word diaspora. I'm out of here.

6

JOHN MARTYN
Solid Air
Island, 1973

By Simon Reynolds

Picking my favorite record of all time, identifying the album that means the most to me, singling out the one I could least bear to never, ever hear again—such a task would surely make my head explode. But the desert island scenario (and I'm curious: who came up with this conceit first, historically?) actually makes narrowing things down much easier. Something with a very particular bundle of attributes would be required, a tricky-to-find combination of consoling familiarity and resilient strangeness. You'd need a record that could retain the capacity to surprise and stimulate, to keep on revealing new details and depths despite endless repetition. But it couldn't be too out-there, too much of an avant-challenge, because solace would after all be its primary purpose. Which in turn would mean that the selection would have to feature the human voice, as a source of comfort and surrogate company—a criterion that sifts out many all-time favorites that happen to be all-instrumental (Aphex Twin's two *Selected Ambient Works* albums, Eno records like *On Land* and his collaboration with Harold Budd *The Plateaux of Mirror*). But, equally, songs alone couldn't sustain me on the island—I'd need some element of the soundscape, the synesthetically textured . . . food for the mind's eye . . . something to take me out and away.

Four albums sprang to mind based around a framework of songs-plus-space (or songs-in-space, or maybe even songs *versus* space). (Actually, there's a fifth album in this vicinity, but Lester Bangs bagged it last time around: *Astral Weeks.*) All are from roughly the same period in rock history—the early '70s—and all can be characterized as post-psychedelic music in some sense. Tim Buckley's *Starsailor* is just too wild, too derangingly strange; its restlessness would stir me to rage against the limits of confinement, rather than adopt a sensible stoicism, and its eroticism would be no help at all. Robert Wyatt's *Rock Bottom* is rich and lovely, but the album's emotionally harrowing arc (it was made shortly after the fall that left him paralyzed from the waist down) might be too wearing for someone in such dire straits; even its ecstasy is on the shattering side. *Stormcock* is brilliant and beautiful, but Roy Harper's diatribes wouldn't warm my lonely soul, and besides, it only consists of four long tracks, all pretty much chipped from the same block of sound.

So my choice is John Martyn's *Solid Air*. There's something about this album that suggests "island music." And I don't just mean that it came out on Island—probably the most highly regarded record label on Earth at that point, a haven for the visionary, the esoteric, the not-obviously-commercial. The other day I was searching through my stuff for a review I wrote a long time ago of the reissue of another John Martyn record (1977's *One World*, which is hard on the heels of *Solid Air* as much-loved album/potential D.I.D.), only to be pleasantly ambushed by the opening line.

> John Martyn was a castaway on the same hazy archi-
> pelago of jazzy-folky-funky-blues as other burned-out
> hippie visionaries of the '70s (V. Morrison, J. Mitchell,
> etc.).

Ha! That list should have included T. Buckley, R. Wyatt, N. Drake (a close friend of Martyn's and the inspiration/addressee of *Solid Air*'s title track), and probably quite a few others too. "Archipelago" still seems like the right metaphor. These artists didn't belong to a genre; each of them had their own distinct sound, but there's enough proximity in terms of their sources, approaches, and vibe, to warrant thinking of them as separate-but-adjacent, a necklace of maverick visionaries sharing a common climate.

The cover of *Solid Air* invites aqueous reverie. A hand passing through sea green water leaving an after-trail of iridescent turquoise ripples, the effect is idyllic on first glance. But then you notice that the image is a circle of color on a black background, introducing the possibility that we're inside a submarine looking through a porthole, and the hand's owner is outside, drowning. *Solid Air*'s title track, we'll see, is about someone who's figuratively drowning, unable to resist the downward currents of terminal depression. One of the best songs is called "Dreams By The Sea," which might resonate for a homesick castaway, except these are "bad dreams by the sea."

Water flows through the entire John Martyn songbook, from "The Ocean" to his delightful cover of "Singin' in the Rain," while two of his post–*Solid Air* album covers feature images of the sea. *Sunday's Child*, from 1975, shows the bearded bard standing in front of crashing surf, while *One World*'s cover is a painting of a mermaid diving up out of the waves and curving back into the ocean, her arched body trailing a glittering arc of sea-spray and flying fish. In that review, I dubbed the album "a *Let's Get It On* for the Great Barrier Reef," a comparison inspired mainly by the reverb-rippling aquafunk of "Big Muff" and "Dealer," two songs that mingle the language of sex and drugs such that you're not sure what brand of addiction they're really about. *One World*'s final track, the nearly nine minutes of almost-ambient entitled "Small Hours," was recorded outdoors beside a lake.

Solid Air, though, has just one song that actively *sounds* aquatic, "I'd Rather Be The Devil," a cover of Skip James's "Devil Got My Woman." After almost fifteen years of loving Martyn's version, I finally heard the original "Devil" in the movie *Ghost World*, where this out-of-time specter of a song harrows the teenage soul of heroine Enid. Most songwriters would have flinched from attempting such an *unheimlich* tune, but Martyn's cover is so drastic it fleshes this skeletal blues into virtually a brand-new composition: imagine the clavinet-driven funk of Stevie Wonder's "Superstition," if it actually *sounded* superstitious, witless, and twitchy with dread. "I'd Rather Be The Devil" starts as a sickening plunge, a dive into seductive but treacherous waters. Roiling with congas and clavinet, the glutinously thick groove rivals anything contemporaneous by Sly Stone or Parliament-Funkadelic, and Martyn moves through the music like a shark. Lyric shards come in and out of focus: "my mind starts a-rambling like a wild geese from the west," "stole her from my best friend . . . know he'll get lucky, steal her back." But mostly Martyn's murky rasp fills your head like a black gas of amorphous malevolence. The song part of "Devil" gives way to a descent-into-the-maelstrom churn, a deadly undertow of bitches-brew turbulence. Then that too abruptly dissipates, as though we've made it through the ocean's killing floor and reached a coral-cocooned haven. Danny Thompson's alternately bowed and plucked double bass injects pure intravenous calm; John Bundrick's keys flicker and undulate like anemones and starfish; Martyn's needlepoint fingerpicking, refracted through a delay device, spirals around your head in repeat-echoed loops of rising rapture. This oceanic arcadia is something music had touched previously only on Jimi Hendrix's *Electric Ladyland* with the proto-ambient sound-painting of "1983 . . . (A Merman I Should Turn To Be)/Moon, Turn The Tides . . . Gently Gently Away."

Listening to this split-personality song—glowering storm-sky of dark blue(s) funk/shimmering aquamarine utopia—it's hard to believe that only a few years earlier John Martyn had been a beardless naïf with an acoustic guitar, plucking out Donovan-esque ditties like "Fairytale Lullaby" and "Sing a Song of Summer." What the hell—more precisely, what *kind* of hell—happened in between?

Arriving in London from his native Scotland in the mid-60s, John Martyn hung out in the city's folk cellars, learning guitar technique by sitting near the front and closely watching the fingers of Davy Graham and Bert Jansch. Soon he was performing at spaces like Les Cousins and Bunjie's himself. He signed to Island (one of the first non-Jamaicans on the label) and in October, 1967, at age nineteen, released his debut album, *London Conversation*—fetching but jejune Brit-folk. Like many of his contemporaries, he

gradually fell under the spell of jazz, especially John Coltrane and
Pharoah Sanders. He later described Impulse as the only truly
pure label in the world. *The Tumbler*, from 1968, featured the
flautist and saxophonist Harold McNair, while *The Road To Ruin*,
his second collaboration with wife, Beverley, involved jazz players
Ray Warleigh, Lyn Dobson, and Dudu Pukwana. But neither of
these records really transcended an additive, this-plus-that approach; they fell short of a true amalgam of folk and jazz.

It's not known if Martyn learned and drew encouragement
from, or even heard at all, the voyages of Tim Buckley, who was
on a very similar trajectory from pure-toned folk troubadour to
zero-gravity vocal acrobat deploying the voice-as-instrument. But
Martyn did talk in interviews about digging Weather Report (particularly the chromatic electronic keyboards of band leader Joe
Zawinul) and Alice Coltrane (he called her "my desert island disc"
but didn't specify which particular disc of hers he had in mind!). A
less-likely influence was The Band's *Music From Big Pink*, especially
the Hammond organ sound, which he mistook for electric guitar,
and described as "the first time I heard electric music using very
soft textures, panels of sound, pastel sounds." He and Beverley
Martyn recorded one album, *Stormbringer*, in Woodstock, with
some members of The Band playing. But that was something of
an aberration in the general drift of his music towards a jazzed flu-
idity. The ideal of a "one-world" music possessed the imagination
of many at this time—Can and Traffic, Miles Davis and Don
Cherry—and throughout this period, at the cusp between the '60s
and the '70s, Martyn was also listening to Indian classical, high-life,
and Celtic music. (He would later record an electric version of the
Gaelic air "Eibhli Ghail Chiun Chearbhail.") This all-gates-open

receptivity was part of Martyn's refusal, or more likely *inability*, to tolerate divisions, his compulsive attraction to thresholds and in-between states. And it would culminate in the untaggable and in-divisible alloy of folk and jazz, acoustic and electric, live and studio, song-form and space, achieved on *Solid Air*. "I think that what's going to happen is that there are going to be basically songs with a lot of looseness behind them," he told *Melody Maker* at the end of 1971, less than a year before recording the album.

As jazz entered Martyn's musical bloodstream, it affected not just his songwriting and approach to instrumentation, but his singing too. The clear diction of folk gave way to slurring that turned his voice into a fog bank of sensuality tinged with menace. Folk privileged words because of the importance it placed on mes-sages and storytelling, but Martyn had come to believe that "there's a place between words and music, and my voice lives right there." One characteristic Martyn mannerism—intense sibilance—can be heard emerging in his cover of "Singin' In the Rain" (on 1971's *Bless the Weather*, the immediate precursor to *Solid Air*), where "clouds" comes out as "cloudzzzzzzz," a drunken bumblebee bumping against your ear hole.

If Martyn's music grew woozy "under the influence" of jazz, during this period he was equally intoxicated by . . . well, intoxi-cants. The ever more smeared haziness of his voice and sound owed as much to the drugs and drink entering his biological bloodstream; dissolution and the dissolving of song-form went hand in hand. Martyn had always felt the bohemian impulse (he'd gone to art school in Glasgow looking for that lifestyle, only to leave after a few months, disappointed) and on his debut album he sang the traditional folk tune "Cocain." But with its jaunty lyrics about "Cocaine Lill and Morphine," the song sounds like it was recorded under the effect of nothing more potent than tea. *Bless the Weather*, again, is the moment at which the music first really seems to come from *inside* the drug experience. "Go Easy" depicts Martyn's lifestyle—"raving all night, sleeping away the day . . . spending my time, making it shine . . . look at the ways to vent and amaze my mind"—but it's "Glistening Glyndebourne" that hurls you into the psychedelic tumult of sense impressions. The title sounds like it's about a river, and the music scintillates with dashes and dots of dancing light just like one, but it's actually inspired, bizarrely, by an opera festival in a stately home near where Martyn then lived; the suited formality of the upper-class crowds provoked him to reimagine the scene.

"Glistening Glyndebourne" was also the track that first captured what had become the signature of Martyn's live performances, his guitar playing through an Echoplex. It seems likely that he was, unconsciously or not, looking for a method of recreating sonically the sense of the dilated "now" granted by drugs. Martyn initially turned to the machine thinking it could provide sustain (a quest that had previously and briefly led him to attempt to learn to play a jazz horn). He quickly realized that the Echoplex wasn't particularly suited to that task, but that he could apply it to even more impressive and fertile ends. Set to variable degrees of repeat-echo, the machine fed the guitar signal onto a tape loop that recorded sound-on-sound; the resulting wake of sonic afterimages enabled Martyn to play with and against a cascading recession of ghosts-of-himself, chopping cross-rhythms in and out of the rippling flow. The Echoplex appeared in discreet, barely discernable form on *Stormbringer*'s "Would You Believe Me," but

"Glistening Glyndebourne" was something else altogether. Its juddering rush of tumbling drums and Echoplexed rhythm guitar was the dry run for "I'd Rather Be The Devil."

Solid Air starts with "Solid Air," twinkles of electric piano and vibes winding around Martyn's close-miked acoustic guitar and bleary fug of voice. For most of my years of loving this album I never knew the song was about, and for, Nick Drake, and I almost wish I could unlearn that fact (especially as I've always secretly felt that Martyn deserved the mega-cult following that his friend and Island label mate has, as opposed to his own loyal but medium-sized cult). But the phrase "solid air" still retains its mystery. Listening to it just now it suddenly flashed on me that "solid air" sounds like "solitaire," raising the possibility that it's a punning image of the lonely planet inhabited by the melancholy Drake, cut off from human fellowship as surely as any desert island castaway. More likely, though, is that lines like "moving through solid air" attempt to evoke what depression feels like, suggesting both the character in Talking Heads' "Air" who's so sensitive he can't even handle contact with the atmosphere, and someone trying to make their way through a world that seems to have turned viscous. The song, written over a year before Drake committed suicide, is at once an offer of help, an entreaty, and a benediction: "I know you, I love you . . . I could follow you—anywhere/Even through solid air." Sung with a sublime mixture of maudlin heaviness and honeyed grace, it's a huge bear-hug to someone in terrible pain. But, with the advantage of hindsight, it also feels like a lullaby—rest in peace, friend.

There's a symmetry to the way *Solid Air* is constructed. Side two starts like the first side, with a soft, slow whisper of a tune gently propelled by a languid but huge-sounding double-bass pulse. In texture, tone, and tempo, "Go Down Easy" is very much a sister-song to "Solid Air," but this time the air is thick not with melancholy but with a humid sexuality that's oddly narcotic and ever so slightly oppressive. It's a kind of erotic lullaby: the title/chorus seems logical enough, the kind of thing lovers might say, until you actually contemplate it, and then it sounds more appropriate to an agitated animal being quelled or a child being calmed down at bedtime. "You curl around me like a fern in the spring/Lie down here and let me sing the things that you bring," croons Martyn, drawing out the chorus "go down easy" into a kind of yawn of yearning, as he draws his lover into a space where breath becomes tactile and intimacy almost asphyxiating.

On *Solid Air*, John Martyn is a hippie with a heart of darkness, equally prone to brawling and balladeering, his voice constantly hovering between sweet croon and belligerent growl. In an interview, he talked about wanting to be "a scholar-gentleman . . . I'm interested in spiritual grace," and this side of Martyn—the idealist, albeit one whose ideals his all-too-human self tended to fail— comes through in songs like "May You Never" and "Don't Want to Know." The former (his most well-known song, widely covered, mostly famously by Eric Clapton) is a goodwill message or blessing to a friend; that empty social formality ("best wishes") fleshed out with specifics, bad things to be warded off ("may you never lay your head down without a hand to hold," "may you never lose your woman overnight"). An anti-hex, if you will. Lines like "you're just like a great big sister to me" and "you're just like a great big brother to me" show that this song's domain is *agape* as opposed to the *eros* of "Go Down Easy." Eros, in Martyn's world, is the danger emotion, the destabilizer, source of addiction and division (stealing your best friend's woman in "I'd Rather Be The Devil").

If Martyn had only ever recorded delicately pretty, heartfelt songs like "May You Never" and "Don't Want To Know," he might have been as big as, oh, Cat Stevens or James Taylor (although his thumpingly physical and rhythmic acoustic guitar playing always put him several cuts above the singer-songwriter norm). "Don't Want to Know" is an even more desperate attempt to ward off malevolent forces with a willed withdrawal into blissful ignorance: Martyn says he doesn't "want to know one thing about evil / I only want to know about love." It's a kind of shout-down-Babylon song (even though his voice is at its softest), with a strange apocalyptic verse about how he's waiting for planes to fall out of the sky and cities to crumble, and lines about how the glimmer of gold has got us all "hypnotized." Martyn often talked about wanting to leave "the paper chase" behind, move out to the country, live a purer lifestyle. But if this song envisages corruption as an external contaminant that you can escape by putting distance between yourself and it, "I'd Rather Be the Devil" and its own sister-song "Dreams by the Sea" treat evil as an intimate. In "Devil," it's inside his lover, his best friend, and most of all himself ("so much evil," moans Martyn midway through the song), while in "Dreams," a song fetid with sexual paranoia, he goes from imagining there's "a killer in your eyes" to a "killer in *my* eyes." The track is tight, strutting funk, Martyn's *Shaft*-like wah-wah coiling like a rattlesnake. At the end, it's like the fever of jealousy and doubt ("Nah no nah no / It can't be true . . . Nah no nah no / It's not the way you are") breaks, and the track unwinds into a

lovely, forgiving coda of calm and reconciliation, laced with trick-
ling raindrops of electric piano.

There's one more pair of songs on *Solid Air*, and in these Martyn figures as incorrigible rogue rather than outright monster.
"Over The Hill" is deceptively spring-heeled and joyous, its flut-
tery prettiness (mandolin solo courtesy Richard Thompson) dis-
guising the fact that Martyn here appears as a prodigal rolling
stone returning in disgrace. "Got nothing in my favor," he blithely
admits, while flashing back to "Cocaine Lil" with a line that con-
fesses "can't get enough of sweet cocaine." Babylon's own powder, coke is a drug that stimulates desire for all the other vices,
from sex to booze. "The Man In The Station," on the opposite side
of the album, catches the roving minstrel once again wending his
way back to the family hearth, but this time he seems less cock-
sure and more foot-sore, ready to catch "the next train home."
These two coming-home songs would sound especially right on
the island, where I'd need music that both acknowledged the fact
of isolation while offering consolation for it. The album ends with
"The Easy Blues," really two songs in one: "Jellyroll Baker," a Martyn concert favorite whose blackface bawling is the only bit of
Solid Air I could happily dispense with, and then the light cantering "My Gentle Blues," which almost instantly flips into a sweetly
aching slow fade, draped with a poignant if dated synth solo
played by Martyn himself.

I've sometimes argued in the past that rock's true essence is juvenile, a teenage rampage or energy flash of the spirit that burns
brightest in seemingly artless sounds like '60s garage punk or '90s
rave. *Solid Air*, though, is definitely *adult* music. Crucially, it's
made by an adult who hasn't settled down, who's still figuring

stuff out; his music shows that growing pains never stop. This aspect of *Solid Air* also owes a lot to its historical moment: Martyn as open-hearted hippie emerging from the '60s adventure to confront the costs of freedom (the problem of being in a couple but remaining fancy-free; drugs as life-quickening versus drugs as "false energy" or numbing tranquilizer). *Solid Air* is post-psychedelic also in the sense I mentioned earlier. These are songs, like the self that sings them, blurring at the edges and melting into something larger. This expanse was designated "space" by the cosmic rock bands of the era, but Martyn's utopian image of healing boundlessness was "the ocean." In "Don't Want To Know," the vengeful verse about cities a-crumbling ends with the wistful line "waiting till the sea a-grow."

The oceanic "only connect" impulses of '60s rock were political and musical at the same time. In the '70s, these twin dreams collided with political reality and with a music industry that was becoming more segmented by market, and less of an anything-goes possibility space. By the end of the '70s, Island's Chris Blackwell would inform Martyn that his meandering muse had driven him into a niche marked "jazz," a pigeonhole that every tiny piece of the singer's artistic being revolted against. Only a few years earlier, in happier times, Blackwell produced Martyn's number-two masterpiece, *One World*, its title track a disillusioned hippie's plea as plaintively poignant and ardently apolitical (because seeking to abolish politics?) as Lennon's "Imagine" or "One Love" by Martyn's label mate Bob Marley. But the track's sentiment is also a musical ideal, the call for a "one-world" music being made by many at the time. Martyn had already reached it on *Solid Air*: a body music that feeds the head, a sound woven from the becoming-jazz of folk, the becoming-electric of jazz, the becoming-acoustic of funk (not that Martyn, an earthy fellow, would ever use such Deleuzian jargon). The schizo-song of "I'd Rather Be The Devil" is where it all comes together, while coming apart. Sonically traversing the distance from the Mississippi levee work camps in which the young Skip James toiled to Miles Davis's *In a Silent Way*, "Devil" captures the ambivalence of "blue": the color of orphan-in-this-world desolation, but also of back-to-the-womb bliss. The two halves of "Devil," like the play of light and shadow across the whole of *Solid Air*, correspond to a battle in John Martyn's soul— between monster and water baby, danger and grace.

7

ALICE COLTRANE

Journey in Satchidananda

Impulse!, 1970

By Geeta Dayal

LASHBACK TO AGE NINE. OUR YEARLY FAMILY VACA-
TION WAS A ROUGHLY FOUR-HUNDRED-MILE DRIVE UP
TO NEW HAMPSHIRE, WHERE WE'D SPEND A WEEK
every summer in a cottage on a lake. My dad would usually drive;
the vehicle was an Oldsmobile Cutlass Ciera station wagon that
featured faux wood paneling on the exterior, and an enormous
springy backseat that was a very close approximation of a sofa. I
spent many an impatient hour in that car, my only solace the cassette deck in the front. I never got to sit in the front seat, but being
an impudent nine-year-old, I attempted to dictate the music anyway. My mother would usually put in a tape of Hindu religious
chants, but I wouldn't stand for it. All that mantric repetition irri-
tated me (funny, how my favorite music these days is techno). I already had a favorite band by age nine—the Beatles—and I wanted
to listen to my *White Album* cassette tape. I thought of it as little

kids' music—"Bungalow Bill" and "Rocky Raccoon" are great sing-along kids' songs, after all—but there were some things I couldn't understand. I would sing along to "Happiness Is A Warm Gun," too, which disturbed my mother enough, but what bothered her even more was "Sexy Sadie" and the ensuing "Mom, what does 'sexy' mean?" conversation. My dad didn't know who the Beatles were. The year was 1988.

I already had a favorite Beatle—George Harrison. I thought George was cool because he seemed to appreciate India and its culture. I figured we could be friends. From what I could tell, he spent a lot of time chanting and meditating, eating vegetarian food, growing his hair long, hanging out with Hare Krishna devotees, the whole bit. The other Beatles dabbled in that sort of thing too, but George seemed quieter—more modest, less bombastic. I couldn't really understand, though, why I liked George Harrison but I didn't like my mother's religious chant tapes, which just irked me. I think I liked George's wonky adoption of Indian culture better than my forced assimilation into it.

I became fascinated with people who got into Indian culture voluntarily, but weren't born into it like I was. I never thought of them as hippies; then again, I never understood what a hippie was anyway. Grow up Indian-American and you grow up thinking that incense sticks and flowery silk dashikis are normal.

I thought being vegetarian was normal, and that all the other kids, who were meat-eaters, were weird; it was just the way I was raised. My dad, a kooky science professor who moonlighted as a tabla player, would reel off phrases in Sanskrit and wax philosophical about the power of mantras and sonic vibrations. I attended numerous fire sacrifices (before you ask, nothing gets sacrificed except some melted butter and handfuls of dirt). I had to go to the Hindu temple on weekends. I received a sitar as a present from a swami once. I would peruse ancient Vedic scriptures like the *Srimad-Bhagavatam*, not just because they were lying around the house, but because I was curious. I learned about other galaxies, other planets, astral planes, theories of reincarnation, and legions of demigods and goddesses. The walls of my house were adorned with giant paintings of multicolored gods with multiple arms. If you have six arms, it's all the people with only two arms that are strange.

I was secretly proud of my upbringing, as much as my increasingly rebellious teenage self despised it. Because as colorful and offbeat as Indian culture was, it was conservative in other ways. I didn't want to be the demure Indian girl my parents wanted me to be. I didn't want to get married. I wasn't into the rich silk saris, the blinding gold jewelry, and the sickly sweet sweets. I didn't want to be a doctor just like my brother; I didn't want to be a scientist unless I could be a *mad* scientist. I harbored fantasies of being an outlaw journalist like Hunter S. Thompson, or an abstract expressionist, or something else that my parents would wildly disapprove of. At Indian parties, I was the kid standing in the back, the loner, the one wearing the black Joy Division shirt while everyone else swirled to Bollywood hits.

It wasn't until many years later that I would come to appreciate Alice Coltrane.

Journey in Satchidananda, released in 1970 on the jazz label Impulse!, features Pharoah Sanders on soprano sax and percussion, and Rashied Ali on drums. There are two bass players—Charlie Haden and Cecil McBee—along with an oud player, a tamboura player, and a tambourine player. There are bells. And, of course, there's Alice on harp and on piano.

Alice looks resplendent on the album cover, in her giant Afro and long dangly earrings. She's robed in what looks like a long, loose Indian *kameez*, striking a cool, pale blue pose against a burnt orange background.

Alice's husband, saxophonist John Coltrane, had died three years prior, in 1967. The following year, Alice, overwhelmed with grief, released the record *A Monastic Trio*. She was clearly coming to terms with him through her music: compositions like "Lord, Help Me to Be" and "I Want to See You" speak to her grief. In 1969, she put out the vastly underrated record *Huntington Ashram Monastery*, which underlined her retreat into Hindu spirituality. Her mourning here is more muted, with the exception of the haunting piano ode "IHS." The title is an acronym for "I Have Suffered."

Alice had recently met Swami Satchidananda, the Indian yogi who was becoming a favorite with countercultural figures like Allen Ginsberg; it was Satchidananda who gave the opening address at Woodstock in 1969. He became Alice's spiritual counselor. Infused with new strength from her guru, the knots of raw pain that were palpable on Alice's two previous records uncoiled into something smoother and silkier on *Journey in Satchidananda*. The strange title of the record was apt. Satchidananda wasn't just a person; to Alice, he personified a destination, an oasis on a desolate desert island. As Alice herself writes in the liner notes: "Anyone listening to this selection should try to envision himself floating on an ocean of Satchidanandaji's love . . . Satchidananda means knowledge, existence, bliss."

Few albums are as blissful and sedate as this one. The title track announces itself with a deep, deliciously thick bassline and the insistent drone of a tamboura. Alice's harp materializes in a kaleidoscopic swirl of tone color. Pharoah Sanders' saxophone begins its slow, passionate swell, fades out, and the harp effortlessly rolls back in to take its place. The dreamy trajectory continues in the second track, "Shiva-Loka," a reference to the heavenly planet inhabited by the Hindu god Shiva. "Stopover Bombay" is a more upbeat number, foreshadowing Alice's marathon journey to India that year. "Something about John Coltrane" is meditative, but not downcast; it's clear that Alice has moved to a new place in her life.

It's hard to pin down Alice's spirituality. Her detractors scorn her as an eccentric hippie with amorphous views and music to match, or a scattershot Yoko Ono of jazz, benefiting from her late husband's glory. Though Alice delved deep into Hinduism, her ideas were open and all-encompassing, folding in inspiration from the ancient Egyptians and from gospel music, among other things. *Journey in Satchidananda* was released the same year as another album by Alice, titled *Ptah, the El Daoud*—a reference to Ptah, the primordial deity in Egyptian mythology. A year later, her strikingly schizophrenic masterwork *Universal Consciousness*—equal parts noisy chaos and seraphic calm—spoke to her pantheist mindset, with references to Allah, Krishna, and Amen-Ra.

But Alice's ties to Hinduism seemed to grow stronger as the years progressed. She often appropriated various ancient *bhajans*, Hindu devotional songs, shaping them into celestial instrumental jams that bore little literal resemblance to the traditional sung melodies while somehow retaining all of their feeling. On her 1972 album *Lord of Lords*, she juxtaposed a Hindu name for God,

Sri Rama, with the name "Ohnedaruth," her spiritual name for John Coltrane. In 1976, Alice did a relatively obscure record based entirely on *bhajans* titled *Radha-Krishna Nama-Sankirtana.*

Alice Coltrane, born Alice McLeod, went by the name Swamini Turiyasangitananda until her death. She was a female swami, and her spiritual name incorporated my own. My name is Geeta, but it should be spelled "Gita"; it means "song." Gita and Swamini Turiyasangitananda. Her music possesses the unique ability to make me calmer, more open-minded, and more introspective, but we have a connection deeper than any conventional marker could indicate. Her music has the ability to summon my childhood past, scrubbed of all the culture clashes and teen angst and impatient expectations. In her hands, it's calm and colorful, even beautiful. In a rare interview with The Wire *in 2002, she looks effulgent in a bright orange silk* salwar kameez. *In those clothes, she looks a lot like my mother.*

You play music with your thoughts, Turiyasangitananda often said, more than you do with your fingers. The deep trance states her meditative music provokes permit me to travel backward and forward in time, to distant worlds and galaxies, to ancient civilizations and heavenly planets. She reminds me of a less recent past—a past going back far into the beginning of time. "Many of the Celestial instruments can be played without the use of hands or without any physical contact whatsoever," Turiyasangitananda once wrote. "Your mind, your heart is the only approach to them." My heart, Alice's heart, on a desert island.

8

MILES DAVIS
Bitches Brew
Columbia, 1969

By Greg Tate

THE FUNNY THING ABOUT *BITCHES BREW* IS I DON'T KNOW THAT IT WOULD EVEN MAKE MY TOP 10. IT'S NOT EVEN MY FAVE AMONG ELECTRIC MILES ALBUMS a position held by Dark Magus. It is, however, my favorite album of all time. I came to this conclusion after discovering the Brit music mag *MOJO*. Every month they pop that question to musicians and celebrities. (Both Ike Turner and Bootsy Collins chose Fleetwood Mac's *Rumours* by the way, go funkin' figure). Letting my subconscious answer first provoked *Bitches Brew* to rise up from the murky depths as the prime, unmediated answer. I had to go figure out why after the fact. The music itself, I came to realize, was secondary to the vast conceptual dimension of that particular and quite groundbreakingly peculiar Miles project.

Miles once said that the only way to achieve anything new in music was to take the best musicians around and get them to play beyond what they know. What makes *Bitches Brew* so captivating is that you hear Shorter, Maupin, Corea, McLaughlin, DeJohnette, and Zawinul stabbing in the dark all the way through it, having to invent a language they'd never spoken before and render it flesh, blood, sinew. *Bitches Brew* is jazz's great Frankenstein's monster, its Bride of Funkenstein even. It rewrote the rules for concocting jazz in the studio, too. Miles apparently would stop and start the band, parceling out newly conceived parts between takes like one of those filmmakers who don't let cats see the script until the day of the shoot. The album also boldly answered the question of what harmonic jazz had to say to itself and for itself in the wake of Coltrane, Coleman, Sun Ra, rock and soul, hippie and Black Power—all the hot mess that had jes' grew around and to some extent out of jazz in the '60s. (Dexter Gordon once told me he considered the bebop generation in all their antiauthoritarianism and unimpeachable Black Genius to be the forerunners of the civil rights movement, making me realize no bebop, no Beats; no Beats, no Bob Dylan, no Beatles, no counterculture.) *Bitches Brew* has outlasted its historical moment of production and influence, though, because it's so gorgeously messy, glacial and, full of black-hole undertow. Chalk that up to the wise decision to combine the acoustic bass of Dave Holland and the electric bass of Harvey Brooks, a move that gives the project the acoustic's nimble rumble and the electric's liquid locomotion in tandem. Why more bands haven't explored this sound since is a stone-cold mystery to me, but it's one of the reasons why my own band, Burnt Sugar, even exists.

Bitches Brew remains the undiscovered country today because you can still hear it anew every time, the same as you must see anew any canvas by Jean-Michel Basquiat, because likewise it is an album of ciphers and gestures, signs and runes, hints and

haints, mysteries and prophecies. It's a record that possesses cult
knowledge about the creative process made musically manifest in
ways that don't so much insist as swell, swim, smash the shore, retreat to the horizon, suck in like a tsunami, blow hard like a typhoon, pretend to come in like a lion, always go out like a lamb.
An album, then, of feasts and feints, Falstaffian gorgings, Ma-
hatma Gandhi–worthy fastings, electronically muffled screams
and even more ghastly silences, suspenses, noises in the attic
courtesy Bennie Maupin's Beetlejuicin' bass clarinet and Wayne
Shorter's suspension-bridge-building solos, as if the whole damn
Calatrava oeuvre simply demanded to be redrawn on soprano
saxophone. And Miles' horn scheme—the loving way he pushes
the rhythm forward with phrasing that singes the skin and gooses
the neck in ways that suggest all the things the world could be
now if Charlie Parker had been a drummer in the James Brown
band. No other trumpeter has ever sounded so comfortable teas-
ing, seducing, and pimp strolling the funk from so lofty a height
and so far behind the beat.

Of course the other reason I'm so partial to *Bitches Brew* is because without it I would have never embarked on my true love,
Burnt Sugar, a band whose genesis lay in simply wanting to pursue
the *Bitches Brew* bold approach, that of dragging in as many badass
contemporary acoustic, electric, and electronic and digital improvisers as one could imagine to play way beyond what they know;
to call and respond in novel, just-devised vernaculars; to go beyond the pale, beyond the event horizon, turn supernovas into sin-
gularities and Curtis Mayfield licks into symphonies.

For these reasons, for the life-altering memories, the unfadeable
glistening gems contained within, *Bitches Brew* would get my

wiggy-jiggy black ass through the slow drag nights and days of
isolation, loneliness, desperation, danger, depression, and madness
that forced exile on a desert-isle outback could surely drive a citi-
fied furthermucker like yours truly to.

9

SCORPIONS
Virgin Killer
Mercury, 1976

BY DAVE QUEEN

V*IRGIN KILLER* IS FOURTH ALBUM BY SCORPIONS ROCK
BAND FROM HANOVER, GERMANY. THEY WERE RARITY
AS HEAVY METAL BAND WITH GOOD GUITAR PLAYING.
The album was released in 1977 and produced by Dieter Dierks,
formerly of Ash Ra Tempel. Best song is title track, which is like
"Giant Steps," with drummer Rudy Lenners playing befuddled
Tommy Flanagan role (Lenners was gone by the next album, but
the band never did as extreme a track again), although he does
good job on "Hell Cat," which is like *Check Your Head*-era Beastie
Boys. Least good is "Backstage Queen" (no relation), listless remake of Led Zeppelin's "Celebration Day." Two of nine songs
are sung by lead guitarist and Hendrix devotee Ulrich 'Uli' Roth,
who sounds like excellent guitarist singing in second language,
after having drunk as much as possible to consume without
choking on own vomit. Ambiguous album title (referring either
to killer of virgins or killer who is a virgin) pioneered use of
meaningless but dangerous-sounding two-word album titles in

music (see Hellhammer's *Apocalyptic Raids,* Sodom's *Persecution Mania,* Manic Street Preachers' *Generation Terrorists*). 1977 was important year in music, as Andreas Baader, Gudrun Ensslin, and Hans-Martin Schleyer all died violently, latter found in trunk of car with pine needles in mouth. (In reality, *VK* released in 1976, but who remembers 1976 for anything except Andrea True Connection?)

German rock scene began with 'space-rock' bands, reflecting new worldwide consciousness made possible by Werner von Braun's rockets. However, Germany has produced artists of many other styles as well, from Hamburger School to Silver Convention to Milli Vanilli. Latter responsible for inexplicable controversy in Amerika where consumers demand right to judge on artist on looks. (UK like that too, except they never grow out of it, although they aren't as bothered with honesty in presentation.) In post-occupation (France, Germany) or post-colonial (Australia, Canada) societies, opposite is true—glamorous appearance taken as indicating lack of serious artistic purpose. Making Avril Lavigne most revolutionary artist in world music history. (Canada is country similar to East Germany—country only existing as function of more powerful ones, whose ruling establishment indoctrinates population with propaganda extolling society's superiority to those of closest neighbors. Also both places famous for frightening Amazonian women—Olympic shot-putters in Germany, academics and singer/songwriters in Canada.)

First Scorpions album *Lonesome Crow,* title of which may make sense as an allusion to Jim Morrison or Ian Astbury. ("Secretary of State Marshall smiles, he is glad the defeated nations of Europe are fooled.") Album features guitar prodigy Michael Schenker, who recorded his parts while still in utero. Schenker later joined

English space-rock band called UFO, whose most successful album was *Force It*. Cover depicts couple—rumored to be Genesis P. Orridge and Cosey Fanni Tutti of Throbbing Gristle of "Zyklon B Zombie" fame—'forcing it' while surrounded by faucets. This was around the time Farrah Fawcett, woman who married cyborg, displayed perky nipples on every teenage bedroom wall in America. Original cover art was dark painting of human hand encircling scorpion, later editions displayed orange medieval (extraterrestrial?) city encircled by outsized pediparps. Neither were successful in making album sound like later Scorpions records. Michael Schenker became Sly Stone of guitar gods, in terms of professionalism and comprehensible career decisions.

Second album, 1974's *Fly to the Rainbow*, recorded at Munich's Musicland Studios (explaining titular proximity to "Fly Robin Fly," used in Wild Man Fischer biopic *Derailroaded*, in scene where Mark Mothersbaugh is explaining how disco had "a beautiful body but no brain"), and while album introduced Schenker's replacement (amazingly wunderbar Uli Roth, who later moved in with Jimi Hendrix's girlfriend), image had clearly not been sorted out— *Fly* has baffling pastel cover featuring gloved figure in purple with propellers for feet, back cover is even worse, with figure bent over and band credits printed on ass. There's one cowbell-metal song about messianic rock star (not David Bowie, but he's mentioned in lyrics), sci-fi sound effects, and excellent drummer (Jurgen Rosenthal) who unfortunately got drafted. This wasn't great time to have to serve state apparatus in fresh-meat capacity, as 1974 was when Red Army Faction's surviving and non-incarcerated members attempted, mainly unsuccessfully, to forge links with Sozialistiches Patientenkollektiv (SPK), group of Heidelberg psychiatric patients who believed capitalism caused illnesses and coined chicory-tipped catchphrase "Kill Kill Kill for Inner Peace and Mental Health", and French writer Jean-Paul Sartre interviewed Andreas Baader, whose preserved brain was recently stolen from Tübingen University's Neurological Research Institute.

With third Scorpions album, 1976's *In Trance*, visual focus is finally in place. This is first time the band's computer-print logo appears (strangely appropriate for animal-named band, as exoskeletal arachnoids have probably most machine-like construction in nature), and technological theme develops through songs like "Robot Man" and album's cover, photo of woman looking transported by desire while squatting over large end of guitar—a Strat with brazenly protruding whammy bar. Viewer is unable to communicate with her, so completely does cold, sharp technology of guitar hold her in mesmerizing grip—all that's visible in composition is glimpse of knee, hands on guitar, and woman's face in St. Theresa-like profile. But then, on desert island, one would have enough time to develop one's imagination to the point of developing connection strictly out of mental necessity—a figure on cardboard or paper assumes humanity, not necessarily blank slate for one's own projection but complex and dynamic living being, as German band Can suggested in their score for film *Deep End*, in which lovelorn pool attendant has session of underwater love with lifesize cardboard cutout.

Also, it's sure thing that woman on cover is European, and as anybody who ever watched films or purchased or stolen magazines from dusty second-hand shop where nobody seems to work (it's not really 'stealing,' it's just getting tired of waiting around for somebody to show up at the till, and there usually isn't one of those either, just a cashbox of the type you'd find at a rural school hot dog day), European hippie girls' display of underarm hair is 'code' for a willingness to fuck anyone, anywhere, at any time, although obviously in the back of VW van is best. Despite enthusiastic promiscuity, these women not 'slutty' in least, just European and liberated and believe that bodies and sex are beautiful things, especially with innocent travelers carrying backpacks and phrasebooks. [Then again, I regularly find myself living in squalid flophouses with up to 16 illegal immigrant barmaids (due to homelessness stemming from my absolute aversion to work of any kind) and I never get any of this action, which I assume is because I don't wiggle a whammy bar quite as good as Uli Roth. But then, nobody ever has, before or since, although the Dutch/Indonesian guitarist Eddie Van Halen's baroque-bricolage has an outsider-art theme-park charm, and Ritchie Blackmore's attempt to throw his career down the toilet since the day he started almost justified his having a career, up until *Machine Head* at least, and half Negro/half Amerikan Slash doesn't use whammy bar at all.] Roxy Music's *Country Life* cover also appeared around this time, featuring frauleins Eveline Grunwald and Constanze Karoli, sister of third great German guitarist of the time, but while Roxy presents archetypal tableau, *In Trance* altogether more revealing, perhaps even invasive, of far more primal intimacy. (Big Black's *Songs About Fucking* cover being the [proudly] dumb Amerikan variation.) This was the first Scorpions album to be produced by Dieter Dierks, of Catholic/Jewish heritage.

1979's *Lovedrive* fits robot/automaton fixation marking ('euro'd,' now) German music of the time. Kraftwerk known for their studied, precise demeanour and songs of objectification/non-sentience

like "Showroom Dummies" and "The Model," Devo's first album
recorded in Conrad Plank's studio. The cover model's unblinking
presence may also have influenced Starship's "Nothing's Gonna
Stop Us Now" and the Kids From Fame's "Mannequin" (I think
that was from the episode where the standup comedian got strung
out on amphetamines). Limousine setting (later parodied on the
Fatima Mansions' *Lost in the Former West* cover) nails Eurotrash
rich with far less deference than Roxy Music, works as rueful,
ironic comment on band's world-encircling status—as did songs
like Tokyo-set "Another Piece of Meat," reggae "Is There Anybody
There," and pregnantly-titled instrumental "Coast to Coast."
("Meat" features solo by briefly-returning Michael Schenker,
pilled-up Merseybeat riff, and lyrically concerns women who became delirious, "screaming for more blood", at kickboxing
match—clearly, they're meeting more interesting people than the
"Backstage Queen"s of even three years previous, perhaps key to
their continuing success.)

Following album, *Animal Magnetism*, features various women in
various trances. One of them is alluded to by "The Zoo", album's
closing track and introduction of new style Scorpions use to great
effect in later albums ("China White", "Rhythm of Love"), martial, mid-tempo plod. Title seems inspired by film *Christiane F.*,
teen comedy about Berlin party animals. Another is on cover as
part of tableau later pastiched by Bruce Springsteen (*Born in the
USA*) and Loverboy (*Get Lucky*). Springsteen album is extrapola-
tion of Lynyrd Skynyrd's folk-music-of-the-oppressor, while post-
colonial collective Loverboy ("Hot Girls in Love") shows at least as
sharp command of English language as Scorpions. As on
Lovedrive, picture is of couple, not unaccompanied model (David

Bowie's "Helden" plays key role on *Christiane F.* soundtrack), but setting is very different—stylized opulence is here replaced by pastoral neo-realism (dog and beer can present), although location and era is disconcertingly vague—perhaps '60s Kansas transplanted to '70s California. This cover is more focused in thematic attack, as there's unavoidably explicit suggestion as to what the model might do next, unlike on *Lovedrive* where anything could happen and even the backstory is difficult to figure out.

Perhaps this lack of subtlety explains why *Animal Magnetism* (like Led Zeppelin's similarly nuanced *Presence*) is the runt, if not the redheaded stepchild, of the catalogue, rarely mentioned in Scorps' fans best-of lists. That was probably just due to anti-Amerikanism, but band squashed the issue anyway by subsequently going massive in that country with a European cover sensibility triumphantly restored. *Love at First Sting* embodied the title, in which the cover stars are clearly entranced by *each other*— this was the Scorpions album popular with the lucky high-school elite who got actual wet spots on their car seats.

The cover of 1982's *Blackout* was provocatively anomalous in the Scorpions gallery, in a *Having Fun with Elvis on Stage* sort of way—an airbrushed rendering of Rudolf Schenker, head wrapped in lobotomy bandages, his eyes being torn out by forks. The album was their biggest seller to date by a wide margin. The title track is about the dangers of picking up groupies while blind drunk, and having to look at them the next morning. The first guitar solo from "Arizona"—played by Matthias Jabs—is from George Harrison's "My Sweet Lord", making this mystic krautrock in the *Popul Vuh* mold. Klaus Meine's voice takes on a noticeably steelier, harsher tone afterward. Although not in the "oh, what a night" part, but maybe he didn't think the mic was switched on. The Nico homage "China White" is the link between "Kashmir" and "Billy's Got a Gun." The album's success was helped greatly by a song gleefully extolling the natural disasters that vex the Amerikan continent.

I don't know much about their career post-*World Wide Live.* That a band which had such previously acute visual sense produced an album cover like *WWL's* was a sad and surprising occurrence. Especially compared to the Mick Ronson-in-*Last House on the Left* contortions on the *Tokyo Tapes* (1978 live double) cover. That album (just ask the Axis, as Uli might say) included versions of "Hound Dog" and "Long Tall Sally," sped up to hardcore velocity, along with a pyrotechnic version of "We'll Burn the Sky," a fatalistic progenitor of Metallica's "Fade to Black" except without that Amerikan sense of melodrama that considers everything that happens in an ordinary adolescence as the most important fucking thing that ever happened in world history. But then, that sense of inflation is what made rock 'n' roll what it was. Foreign rock bands provide a good indication of how American culture is seen in the rest of the world, as if Amerikans were capable of giving a fuck about that. *Tokyo Tapes* includes "Kojo No Tsuki," a Japanese folk song ("Just ask the Axis," as Uli Roth might've said) that foreshadows later, more contemplative moments in the Scorpions catalogue ("Maybe I Maybe You" from 2004's *Unbreakable,* "Wind of Change" from 1987's *Crazy World*), and which also features some feedback buzzing straight from the Darmstadt school of electronic musique concrete. *Tokyo Tapes* kind of pisses me off because the CD reissue omits the live version of "Polar Nights," a standout ("Highway Star" as imagined by ZZ Top) *Virgin Killer* track, 'because of the limited lengths of this CD [this is a British EMI pressing]' and is now to be found as bonus track on the [didn't think there was going to be a 'the'] re-issued Scorpions album *Taken By Force*.

Which, sad to report, needed it, because *Taken by Force* is their worst album, recorded when the band was in a state of factional conflict. Roth left immediately afterward, leaving Rudolf Schenker and singer Klaus Meine in control. Chosen to replace Roth was Matthias Jabs, a student/acolyte of Keith Richards-like devotion. Not even Einstürzende Neubaten or Faust would end an album with a 7:20 composition called "Born to Touch Your Feelings," but at least there were four interesting tracks. "We'll Burn the Sky" is sung by Meine, as is "He's a Woman—She's a Man," which was re-recorded on 2000's *Moment of Glory* with the Berlin Symphony Orchestra. The song is more confrontational than later Dierks project Accept's similar "Love Child" ("Don't know who I am, a woman or a man/ I'm going insane"), perhaps even hostile, but subsequent revelations possibly render the song as a comment on Heidi Krieger, the East German Olympic athlete whose intake of government-administered steroids caused her to need an emergency sex-change operation. Then again it could be a dystopia about possible fashion trends among Canadian college-age women, which came to pass at *exactly* the time I was old enough to go to a school big enough to have a women's studies department. Then again, it would've been a 'desert island' even if it hadn't been a 'desert island,' but maybe not if I had gone someplace where women wore Scorpions T-shirts, and even then I would've been too repressed to do anything about it. Of course, now that I'm really old, they're everywhere.

Ulrich Roth didn't have any vocals on the album, for reasons
that probably made perfect sense, but two tracks were indelibly infused with his style, however divergent they were. "Your Light" is a
"Wait Until Tomorrow" / "May This Be Love"–type mellow track
that guitar-magazine readers grimly sit through doing their Hen-
drix-album duty, and "Sails of Charon" is a disco/metal/southern
boogie/classical stomp (without the 'classical' bit it would be like
Black Sabbath's "Voodoo," or U2's "Sunday Bloody Sunday") written in ancient Greek modes, at a belligerent Allman Brothers am-
bling tempo, which unfortunately sounds recorded very early on a
morning after a "big city night" and more unfortunately ends with
an acoustic coda. Perhaps the German/southerner shared love of
fast driving and shared experience of occupation by a foreign
army sparked Roth's idea for the song, but these were throwaways, compared to what had come before. In particular, the solo
on *Virgin Killer*'s title track, which takes the *Christiane F.* idea ahead
of that film's central artistic figure—"Boys Keep Swinging" with
bite, "Fashion" with chops, "The Great Curve" with teeth. ("Catch
Your Train" is "Don't Worry About the Government," with something in German.)

Like *Virgin Killer* (whose American cover, featuring five belligerent Germans menacingly advancing toward the viewer, was inappropriate for the European market), *Taken by Force* also had two
covers. For some reason, wherever I'm at, they only have a really
terrible one with the same layout on each side—individual pictures of all five bandmembers, the words 'Scorpions' and 'RCA' in
each picture, along with their individual names. (Accompanying
Schenker, Roth, and Meine are drummer Herman Rarebell, who
later had a solo single and video with his version of the Surfaris'

"Wipe Out," performed as "Herman ze German," and bass player Francis Buchholz, who resembles a young Ian Brown of the English band Stone Roses.) The other cover, which I've never seen in a record store, is a picture of a cemetery, with white headstones in rows extending infinitely into the distance. Like Metallica's later *Master of Puppets*, except it's a photograph, and instead of being a still life, there are two people who are killing each other.

NOTES

1. When Germany was defeated in 1945, the Allied powers split the country into four zones of occupation—the Amerikan, British, French, and Soviet sectors. Perhaps bands from the British zone were influenced mainly by the Beatles, as Scorpions certainly were, whereas artists from other areas (e.g. Kraftwerk) were more tuned into the Beach Boys. One singer whose solo albums had that L.A. sound was Christa Pffafgen, who later changed her name to Nico and joined a band called the Velvet Underground. Nico's 1974 album *The End* (produced by John Cale, the VU's Michael Schenker, who obviously had a boner for Nico as he produced a bunch of her albums over two decades and even made one himself [*Music for a New Society*] that sounded exactly like a Nico album, except with his own Elton John-type voice) includes a cover of the Doors song also of that title. The line "The West is the best" is pronounced with a 'v' sound for the 'w' in 'west,' a stylistic flourish indulged in by

many German vocalists. Eastern Europeans prefer the
opposite effect, using 'w's instead of 'v's. ("There's a
wideo on the telewision"). After "mother, I want
to . . ." Nico does a long unaccompanied death rattle
that sounds like Mom is midway through the "maggot
stage" of the average necrophiliac's Decomposition
Stage of Attraction. Then there's some stage-musical
jazz-funk with a psychedelic guitar solo from Phil
Manzanera of Roxy Music.

2. Roxy Music was an English equivalent to Steely Dan,
   in that both bands progressively refined their sound
   into evanescence (without necessarily getting Xtian
   about it, "Psalm" and "Turn That Heartbeat Over
   Again" notwithstanding), and weren't really rock but
   came from such rarefied places that rock people were
   afraid to criticize them. *Katy Lied* was SD's *Virgin
   Killer*—the sound of a band finally realizing itself,
   which in the Dan's case meant becoming a full-fledged
   studio-only auteurist canvas for session scrawlers. *Katy*
   starts with an offputting frivolity, with three Jimmy
   Buffett sound-alikes, then the next two songs ("Daddy
   Don't Live in That New York City No More," "Doctor
   Wu") start dropping hints of fathomless bitterness and
   regret. On the second half, virginities are lining up to
   be killed—"Everyone's Gone to the Movies" escorts
   the innocent traveller across the boundary from trust
   to knowledge, the Zapruder-echoing "Chain Lightning" has Amerika being deflowered for the fifth or
   sixth time, and the end of the joyfully nihilistic "Any

World That I'm Welcome To" has the enervated protagonist in the "park" (same one as in *VK*'s "In Your
Park"?), "watching children playing." Using tact, poise
and reason, gently squeeze them.

3. 'K' is for Kraftwerk and Krafft-Ebing.

10

STEREOLAB
Transient Random-Noise Bursts with Announcements
Elektra, 1993

By Douglas Wolk

"What are your influences?"

There is an LP by the German synth-pop band Propaganda on whose sleeve this text appears:

"There is a poem of Goethe in which these lines occur:

> *'Und umzuschaffen das Gesschaffene*
> *Dass sich's nicht zum Starren waffne*
> *Wikt ewiges lebindiges Thun.'*

which can be roughly translated:

> *'and refashioning the fashioned*
> *lest it stiffen into iron*
> *is work of endless vital activity.'"*

The poem, it turns out, is called "Eins und Alles," and the album sleeve misspells a few words, but the point is taken.

The refashioned is comforting and familiar—you can say "bourgeois" if you like, especially if you're suspicious of comfort. Refashioning the fashioned provides the illusion of newness, the truth of change, and the pleasures of narrative continuity: something has come before, there is a foundation upon which something is being built. The young person's first question to artists is almost always about influences; we get our first approximation of what a band is up to by a quick comparison to other bands.

Friends of mine who saw My Bloody Valentine play have said that the extended blast of noise near the end of "You Made Me Realise" was the greatest sound-moment they've ever experienced. I'm very fond of MBV's later records, and I was there, standing toward the back, when they played New York in 1992 (with Pavement and Superchunk opening). "You Made Me Realise" just sounded like a big ball of noise to me, and not a good one. The friends who loved it most were toward the front. It was a matter of optimal speaker placement, I suppose.

Six or seven years later, I was at Irving Plaza, another club in New York, waiting for some band or other to get their fancy equipment set up, and whoever was DJing that night put on Stereolab's

"Jenny Ondioline," the album version from *Transient Random-Noise Bursts with Announcements*. It came out of those huge speakers at immense volume, like a liquid rainbow. Rainbows are symbols of corniness, but it is impossible to scoff when you're looking at a real one. "Jenny Ondioline" turned up so loud I could feel it in my cells wasn't *orgasmic*, the way people have described the My Bloody Valentine tone-burst—it wasn't sexual at all. It had the feeling, like a rainbow, of something whose natural order is being revealed, in glory.

I stood there, pointing my head straight into it, barely moving, breathing only when I remembered to, for eighteen minutes. That was the greatest sound-moment I've ever experienced.

(A study I once read claims that the best music ever is the music you heard when you were twenty-two-and-a-half years old. *TRNBWA* came out when I was twenty-three-and-a-half years old.)

I'd heard Neu!'s name mentioned in connection with Stereolab, but didn't understand the connection until one day I went into a coworker's office, and she was playing something that sounded very familiar. Wow, I said, is this like a remix of "Jenny Ondioline"? No, it was Neu!'s "Für Immer." (Neu!, you ask? German band, early '70s, first two albums have an unmistakable central riff/rhythm called "motorik": a steady pulse, a single chord with swirling ornamentation. This isn't the place to get into it.)

As little as they like to discuss them, Stereolab is bluntly forthright about their influences, and in 1993 those were Neu!, Faust, the Velvet Underground—the usual suspects. On *Transient*

Random-Noise Bursts with Announcements (oh, God, let's just call it
TRNBWA most of the time), they don't exactly hide their music's
origins. There's a possibly apocryphal story about a Stereolab set
list somebody swiped from the stage that included none of the
song titles from their records; instead, it simply listed the artists
who had inspired each song.

Even so, they're not terribly interested in recapitulating their favorite bands' *songs*; what they take off from is *sound*. They adore
the I-IV riff from the Velvets' "Sister Ray" and the Modern Lovers'
"Road Runner" and so on—their first few albums dress it up in
everything they've got in their wardrobe—but they treat it as a
way to concentrate on timbre in rock without letting too many
chords get in the way.

By *TRNBWA*—their second, third, or fourth album, depending
on how you're counting—Stereolab had figured out that there's
one thing even less intrusive than a two-chord riff, and that's a
one-chord riff. Hence the Neu! homage of "Jenny Ondioline," and
even when they're playing songs as (relatively) harmonically complicated as "Pack Yr Romantic Mind," they spend the whole album
following Neu!'s conceptual ideal of orbiting a specific sound. It's
the sound that's the core of "Jenny Ondioline" in particular, in
which a steady beat propels a single chord: a focused yearning upward. A leaning-into sound.

That sound is also not the sound of a live band: it's the sound of a
recording. Stereo doesn't mean you perceive a sound source differently with each ear—that always happens. Stereo sound *comes*

from two sound sources. It's an artificial creation, assembled in some kind of studio or laboratory. There's an ideal for what it sounds like—of reproduction, of speaker placement and physical positioning—but unless you are motionless and in exactly the right place and have perfectly calibrated equipment, you'll never hear it. It changes as the body moves; in the real, less-than-ideal world, it dances with you.

Transient Random-Noise Bursts with Announcements keeps reminding its listeners that it is an artifact of this bizarre mediation—that, in fact, the mediated product is what matters, rather than the performance it has transformed. The front cover is a reproduction of a hi-fi test record from the '60s: a glorious needle touching down on a glorious turntable. The recordings are punctuated with fragments of historical recordings about their own recording-ness; "Golden Ball" begins with a string of intentional recording "glitches," flattening Laetitia Sadier's voice into a distorted smear, and ends with a needle scratching across a record, getting stuck somewhere, being dragged off.

"Hi-fi." As a friend of mine says, "fidelity to what?"

One way of thinking about the difference between vinyl and CDs is that CDs don't exactly provide "perfect sound forever," as the original slogan went: they provide sound of a consistent and very high standard, with an upper limit of the 44.1 kHz sampling rate. They can never be more perfect, or more continuous, than that. Vinyl sound is much more fallible—there's so much that can go wrong between the microphone and your speakers, and it usually does. But, because analog recording is continuous, it's *potentially* more perfectible. That's what high fidelity is about: a very tiny kind of *tikkun olam*, working toward closing a gap between perfect sound and one's ears that can't entirely be closed but can come infinitely near to being closed.

Stereolab, it doesn't take a genius to notice, are vinyl fiends. They started out releasing vinyl on their own label in 1991, and have continued to release vinyl seven-inch singles long after it has become simply a gesture of their ideology. I've only ever heard *TRNBWA* on CD, but it's clear to me that its native format is the vinyl double LP. ("Jenny Ondioline" is side three. The last song is "Lock-Groove Lullaby.") More specifically, its native format is the limited-edition gold vinyl double LP (a two-dimensional golden ball) that the band's own label, Duophonic, pressed and then destroyed most copies because it didn't sound good enough.

Back in early 1993, I occasionally talked with a woman who worked at Elektra Records, which had just signed Stereolab and was getting ready to release *TRNBWA*. One evening, she called me, exasperated. There had been a marketing meeting that day; to promote the album, they were going to release a vinyl seven-inch single with "Jenny Ondioline" and a different version of "Golden Ball." Look, she'd said, it's cool and everything, but I just don't see what vinyl singles have to do with a band like Stereolab! I am happy to note that she didn't last much longer at Elektra Records.

I've picked up an awful lot of experimental and avant-garde records and CDs over the years, and I treasure them, as Stereolab treasures theirs. But both "experimental" and "avant-garde" have literal meanings that it's easy to forget. Art is only experimental if its practitioners don't know what the result of their experiment is going to be. Avant-garde art is the vanguard of something that comes after it, or is meant to come after it.

TRNBWA is not an experimental record; it's not an avant-garde record. It's a pop album, with ten pop songs. (Popular? No, not really—one single scraped up to number seventy-five on the British charts, and it wasn't even actually on the album—we'll get to that. But still, you know, pop songs.) But Stereolab integrate one formerly experimental, formerly avant-garde idea and practice after another into their recording. You can call it theory turned into praxis, or raw materials turned into a finished product, or more accurately a precision tool kit developed over decades' worth of trial and error and here put to work.

(The album's title, it should be noted, is a reference to something not at all experimental, and certainly not avant-garde—it's recycled from a turntable-testing record that was not even meant to give pleasure, but to facilitate it. Arguably, experimental and avant-garde records aren't meant to give pleasure either. Or, if they do, it's a happy coincidence.)

There is a whiff of Whig history to thinking about Stereolab like this. It's the culmination of all that stuff those bright but misguided experimentalists managed to develop, but weren't enlightened enough to use for pop! Krautrock and electronic experimental music were just waiting for Stereolab to come along and fulfill their potential! Well, I know—and I admire the inspiration and labor of the people who performed the experiments, and who strove in the unrewarded vanguard. But do I personally privilege pop over

exp./avt.-gd.? Hell yes. I keep my Tony Conrad and Hans Reichel
and Conet Project albums around for mostly symbolic I'm-so-
glad-this-exists reasons, but when I want to reexperience that
yearning-upward leaning-into feeling, it's time for Stereolab at
whatever volume I dare.

The sound, and its volume, is the key. The record collector craves
novelty, but also craves feeling a certain way *again*—the way some
record made him or her feel once. Songs are secular incantations;
playing them again and again after they're familiar can be a version
of an athlete's irrational pregame habits, ritually enacting something that you once did before the desired result happened, in the
hope of making it happen again. And songs wear out, some faster
than others. The point of the desert-island exercise is finding a
record that doesn't wear out quickly. So it's Stereolab for me, because my significant experience wasn't discovering *TRNBWA*, but
hearing it loud enough to feel it. Playing it loud enough (again) to
feel it doesn't *remind* me of earlier, happier experiences; it gives me
the physical sensation I loved then and love now. It's reliable.

The record collector is, no denying it, a fetishist. Which is just another way of saying that there are things that consistently give her
pleasure. (Admirable, really.) Every record, in a collector's hands,
becomes the reification of some kind of glory, a manifestation of an
ideal. There's a pirated squib of text on the back cover of *TRNBWA*:
"for people who desire the finest in sound . . . always demand:
STEREOLAB ULTRA-HIGH FREQUENCY DISKS." It's a joke,
and not a joke. The demander's fetishes are the creator's fetish too.

Stereolab are, of course, fetishists: they're ideologues and sensualists, and that's a fine combination for knowing what gives you pleasure. But they aren't utopians, and one of the things they fetishize here is human imperfection and unreliability.

TRNBWA opens with a mistake: Andy Ramsay's snare flourish at the beginning of "Tone Burst" is not quite right, its first two cracks just slightly too close together. A few seconds later, whoever's playing the organ fumbles a beat, wanders into dissonance, plays an erroneous chord a few times to make it sound intentional. Then, about a minute and a half into the song, something really messed-up happens as Laetitia Sadier's lead vocal starts. She's singing quietly and tenderly, in French, to a lover, or rather to someone she addresses as being *like* a lover: "Tels deux amants de longue date/Nous nous retrouverions une aprés-midi. . . . " The rest of the song, startled, fades down a few notches, then a few more.

This isn't supposed to happen. Common wisdom has it that the performance is where the music happens; after that's done, you've got all the time in the world to get the postproduction right. The awkward mix of "Tone Burst" just underscores the fact that *TRNBWA* is a *recording* as much as it is a performance.

When she finishes her lyric, the band fades back up again, even louder than it was at first, and eventually somebody—probably co-songwriter Tim Gane—starts playing a guitar solo. The solo doesn't have much to do with the song, though—it's more of a paraphrase of Lou Reed's guitar spasm from the Velvet Underground's "I Heard Her Call My Name." Eventually whoever's playing the organ just starts hammering the keys with his or her fists until the rest of the band stops playing.

I may be misremembering this, but I think Jim O'Rourke, who later produced a few Stereolab records, once noted in an interview that he tries not to record pop bands playing "correctly." It's not that practicing parts robs them of spontaneity—if you're playing a composition, it's really not especially spontaneous. It's that overpracticing can lead musicians to play their parts *right*—with objectively near-perfect timing and intonation—and it's a lot more interesting to hear musicians playing *like themselves*. That's one of the things I love best about *TRNBWA*: I can't really tell who's playing the keyboard or guitar parts, but they all sound like they're being played by a specific confident but not-wholly-accurate person, and if you substituted someone else, they'd sound significantly different.

Just as Stereolab's recordings are not exactly their performances, they're not the same thing as their compositions, either. At least in the early days, their demos were skeletal and quiet and almost nothing like the finished product. Only a few have ever been commercially released, mostly as ridiculously scarce flexi-discs. There supposedly exists a single with a demo of "Tone Burst," but it's rare enough (twenty-eight copies, assuming it's not a hoax) that it's effectively hypothetical. I've never heard it. A "country" version of "Tone Burst" made it onto one of Stereolab's singles-and-rarities compilations, though. It shares its lyrics and melody with the song on *TRNBWA*, and still seems more like a different entity than an alternate version.

The closest thing to a Stereolab demo on *TRNBWA* is its most mysterious song, "Pause," which is blanketed in recording-studio gestures. Its slippery little plastic-film melody—two voices, an organ, a barely stroked guitar, a barely touched string on another guitar, and finally the hiss and tap of a primitive drum machine—bobs above and below the surface of a "numbers transmission" (a tape of a shortwave radio station broadcasting an espionage code). At the end, there's a minute of feedback-waltz murk frosted with vocalese. If all double albums were called upon to trace their relationship to the "White Album," this would be "Revolution 9" and "Julia" as the same song.

The core of *TRNBWA*, and Stereolab's career, and maybe my lifetime of listening to music, is "Jenny Ondioline," named after an early synthesizer and not a woman. It opens with a very simple sound that would've been inconceivable without its avant-garde ancestors: a six-note motif played twice by a flotilla of guitars, like something out of Glenn Branca or Rhys Chatham's guitar-orchestra pieces. After the fanfare, we move on to the six-minute section that's the main body of the song, or at least the part that was trimmed down into several configurations' worth of singles. It's a sustained F-sharp-major drone (F-sharp is the last note of the introduction), with occasional C-sharp and B chords thrown in there to relieve the tension, and a *motorik* beat. It is sublime; cf. my giant-Irving-Plaza-speakers epiphany above. It blurs and dissolves everything around it, including language.

"Life on Earth is a bloody hazard, it's a fact," the first line appears to go, although it's open to debate, since Laetitia Sadier sings it in a very heavy French accent, and the lyric has nothing to do with the melody line except for the syllable count. The two "a"s are both accented. The rest of the lyrics are even less clear. I wouldn't have guessed that a line in the chorus is "I don't care if democracy's being fucked" if some fan hadn't transcribed it that way on the Internet. Neither, it appears, would anybody who played it on college radio in the summer of 1993.

The words, in any case, aren't the part anyone remembers; the vocal hook is an "ooh" that Sadier and Mary Hansen share. Late in the second section of the song, the band drives and drives their F-sharp-major chord along a magnificent plateau—every time they seem about to drop down to the "ooh," they don't. And then they do, when you're not expecting them to. I've been listening to that song for almost thirteen years as of this writing, and it surprises me every time.

Finally, the recording jump cuts back to the introduction—whose first two notes now echo the "ooh." That would be a fine way to end the song, but Stereolab aren't even halfway done. They fade into another six-minute section that's basically identical to "Exploding Head Movie," one side of their first collaborative single with Steven Stapleton's long-running experimental project, Nurse with Wound. (NWW are even bigger record fetishists than Stereolab: their first album included a comprehensive list of Stapleton's favorite obscuro experimental records that's still used by collectors as a guide.) The new section is even closer to "Für Immer" than the "life on earth" section (this time the drone is in E, the same key as Neu!'s record), which means that it's even closer to the Massive Chord That Goes On Forever And Lives In Their Dreams. After a few minutes, Sadier and Hansen start singing

something that's more a mantra than a song—the words they repeat are "lift, hope and struggle."

That section ends with a tiny flourish, and bleeds right into a
stereo test record's reminder that this is a recording: "The following sequence is recorded equally on both channels, but is out of
phase. . . . " If there's an end to that sentence, we don't get to
hear it, because now Stereolab are playing the E chord again, at
punk rock speed and density, leaning with their forearms on some
keyboards. Punk rock is where they came from, historically
speaking (and by "history" here I mean economic history, the
punk-into-indie-into-alt sequence of movements that valorized
starting an unfancy band and putting out records on your own fan-
cifully named label): it's a kind of music that's usually thought of as
more about performance than a recording. But this is—forgotten
already?—a recording, and over the next two minutes there's
enough *musique concréte* tape mischief that this section of the song
would be irreproducible in performance.

That cross-fades into a final two-minute section: the E chord,
slowed back down to a brisk, wobbling pulse, surrounded by cobwebs of synthesizer that sound like overtones. Play the earlier sections of "Jenny Ondioline" loudly enough, and you'll think you
hear those overtones; here, the thickly bunched roar of guitars
and organs has been stripped away, and only the halation that used
to hover around them is left to ride the *motorik* pulse for the song's
final stretch before it rounds the horizon of the fader.

(At last, the CD track counter flips from seven to eight, and
"Analogue Rock" begins. It might be another section of "Jenny
Ondioline," my ears always say at first. It's at exactly the same
tempo, and it's another mantra: "All good things to come / Will

come/Wellcome" [*sic*]. But it's structurally different from the ubiquitous eternal now of "Jenny O," and slowly the spell fades.)

Non-guitarists who are reading this may be asking: why is the E chord important to "Jenny Ondioline"? The simple answer is that it's more or less the home chord of a guitar in standard tuning. The low and high strings of the guitar are both tuned to E, two octaves apart; when you play the simplest form of the E chord, you don't finger either of those strings, and they ring out as no other guitar chord's root tone does. As with the way Neu! used it, building a song around an E drone means "we're thinking about resonance"—literal, rather than cultural.

The other peak of *TRNBWA*, "Crest," is six minutes long. It feels epic, expansive, complicated. It has two guitar chords and a two-line lyric, which I never realized until I focused closely on it. Its length is arbitrary—they could play it for two minutes or twenty. But it's not a drone song; it's a rock song, thanks to Duncan Brown's Sisyphean bass part, which ascends and plummets, ascends by another route and plummets again. (The only non-amateur cover I've heard of any of *TRNBWA*'s songs is a "Crest" that Sebadoh recorded for a session on John Peel's BBC Radio show in the mid-90s. Their version is 3:42, and seems exactly as long as Stereolab's.)

Mary Hansen and Laetitia Sadier sing, "If there's been a way to build it there'll be a way to destroy it/Things are not all that out of control," four times for each verse—toward the end they sing "la la la" a few times too. The first half is a slogan; the second half is a reassurance, and a weird one: either things are out of control or they aren't. . . .

"Jenny Ondioline" wasn't a hit, and "Crest" wasn't a single. The almost-a-hit from TRNBWA wasn't even on the album—it was "French Disco," an extra track appended to the "Jenny Ondioline" single. The story goes that the band was away on tour when they found out that "French Disco" was catching on, and didn't get to respond quickly enough to push it higher than number seventy-five on the British chart—although they did eventually release a remixed version as a single, retitled "French Disko." It's a more immediate song than anything on *TRNBWA*, with a huge guitar riff in its heroic chorus ("La resistance!"). This may be more Whig history, but that's also why it doesn't quite belong on the album— it would have stuck out too much. (Perhaps Stereolab's own resistance was to repeating themselves: the riff is very close to the one Gane came up with for "The Seeming and the Meaning," from 1992's *Peng!*) My old band the Media used to open our practices with a medley of "French Disco" and the Ramones' "Now I Wanna Sniff Some Glue," with which it's surprisingly compatible.

Before the release of *TRNBWA*, Stereolab opened a handful of shows with "Jenny Ondioline," in a twelve-minute version (the "lift, hope and struggle" section was there, the final sections weren't). Later in 1993, they occasionally played "Our Trinitone Blast," "Crest," "Golden Ball," "Tone Burst," "Lock-Groove Lullaby," and "I'm Going Out of My Way." By the end of the 1993 tour, "Jenny Ondioline," "Crest" and "Golden Ball" were the only *TRNBWA* songs that appeared regularly in their set, unless you count "French Disco." "Pack Yr Romantic Mind" didn't get played live until 2006.

I said that Stereolab are sensualists and ideologues, but they're also realists: again, they live with and love imperfection. Sadier's lyrics are about not pleasure but the *possibility* of pleasure, and the world that makes it possible or impossible. That first song, "Tone Burst," is truer to its title and their ideology than it seems. Hearts burst, metaphorically, and there are sunbursts; a tone burst? She ends her lyric "La son profond de ta voix / Tel un rayon vivant ouvrira mon coeur." Her lover's (or like-a-lover's) voice, she says, is a vibrating ray that will open her heart. The sound is the key; she can feel its resonance. She doesn't say anything about words.

No song on *TRNBWA* includes its title. "Golden Ball" mentions a ball, and the sun; that's as close as we get.

A detourned *Calvin & Hobbes* comic strip my friend Craig did around the time *TRNBWA* was released: Susie is interviewing Calvin, and asks him what his influences are. He turns away, exasperated, saying "forget it—I'm not doing this interview until you can think of some better questions."

It's actually a fair question about Stereolab, though. Their influences and their ideology of sound really are significant if you want to understand the band, and it's possible to swim and crawl deep; their refashioning of the fashioned is as vital as Goethe suggested it could be. But in fact the Stereolab of 1993 are *better* than any of the bands and avant-gardists who prefigured them and are perhaps stiffening into iron by now (and yes, that's Whig history yet again, and yes, I'm saying they're better than the Velvet Underground, not more *important* or more *groundbreaking*, I'm saying they're *better*). What makes them better is that their library, all their thought and study, is refracted through their sensualism. Their passion for the amorphous, imperfect, not-yet-fully-realized body is right on the surface of *TRNBWA*, from the joyful error at the beginning to the winsome dissonance at the end. It endures, as a matter of form. It may fade for me someday, but it hasn't yet.

October 24, 1996: Stereolab, touring behind *Emperor Tomato Ketchup*, are playing at the Loeb Student Center at NYU in New York. It's sucking. The sound mix is terrible; the band's visibly not into it. After about half an hour, Tim Gane leads the band offstage and announces that they'll be back when they get some things sorted out. They come back ten or fifteen minutes later and tear into most of *TRNBWA*, which sounds just fine. This, they can do.

In 1999, I interviewed Tim Gane, and brought up the subject of *Transient Random-Noise Bursts With Announcements*. He winced: it had come out nothing like he'd wanted it to. "Making that record was pure hell," he said. "In the end, I hated it, and I've pretty much hated it ever since."

11

SPIRITUALIZED

*Ladies and Gentlemen
We Are Floating in Space*
Dedicated/Arista, 1997

BY DAPHNE CARR

L ADIES AND GENTLEMEN WE ARE FLOATING IN SPACE
HAS BEEN CALLED THE BEST BREAKUP ALBUM OF ALL
TIME. IT WAS HAILED IN ITS DAY FOR LAYING BARE THE
story of Spiritualized's guitarist, singer, and songwriter Jason
Pierce's very public dumping by longtime keyboardist and girlfriend Kate Radley. Though she left Pierce for the Verve's Richard
Ashcroft, in the midst of the great Britpop moment, Pierce vehe-
mently denied that the album was in any way about her. If there
was any love object in the album, it was "the spoon," his equally
public passion for heroin. The "love letter to heroin" interpretation comes from the fact that while the whole album radiates sadness, longing, and desire, there is only one single female pronoun
sung throughout. The only other women mentioned in the whole
album are the formal addressees of the album's first word.

"Ladies and gentlemen, we are floating in space" are the words
spoken to open the album, and they're uttered by Radley, whose

voice never appears solo again in the whole seventy minutes. The words stand outside the music: they frame it. The same gimmick ends Spiritualized's first album, *Lazer-Guided Melodies*. In "200 Bars," Kate begins counting while Pierce sings about finding love in that measure of time. The song ends when Radley announces "two hundred," and you realize she's been there all the time, holding Pierce steady.

My friend Anna's dad was a military pilot, and he told her that all the emergency instructions in the airplane cockpit are made in female voices. It keeps people calm. Perhaps this is why Kate, then-girlfriend of the spaceman flying this craft, whispers these lines, which are lifted from a children's story. *Ladies and gentlemen . . .* I hate to be a bother, but I would like to point out that we are not tethered to the ground. Don't be afraid, but we are drifting and may even be lost. Would you care for some tea?

Science fiction fans are familiar with drifting: craft lost in space, crew left awaiting rescue but growing eerily aware that there may be no salvation. Then there are the prim lunar outposts, colonies established by imperialist Earth-types that devolve into civil war. When the homeland connection is cut, it's up to them to make up new rules. It is all too fitting, then, that I follow the impulse and ask that my rhetorical exile take place in space, that Spiritualized's *Ladies and Gentlemen We Are Floating In Space* come along as magna carta to a territory whose map I will never expand, only endlessly detail. That's some heavy shit, but what else is eternal banishment for? I'll raise a cup for memory, bliss, and basslines as that blue planet Earth comes into view.

To get to the part about the album, I have to bring you two chapters into the story. The first chapter involves falling in love and feeling like it will last forever. That chapter ends at a pay phone in Chillicothe, Ohio.

For graduation, some girls got cars, some girls got money, but I wanted to go to audio engineering camp. So there I was in Appalachia the summer before college, spending fourteen hours a day cleaning tape heads, setting up mics, and learning signal processing. I was one of four girls in the program, so we got to live in a little white house at the foot of the hill near the studio. The seventy-five or so guys in the program lived in cabins up the hill, and every night they'd build a bonfire and sit around playing acoustic guitars. It felt not unlike life during the gold rush, except that I came and left a lady. After all, I was in love with a college boy back East.

This was 1997 and I'd had e-mail for two years, but no one at the camp had a cell phone, so there was always a long queue for the pay phone. I'd been there a week without talking to my boyfriend, and was anxious to tell him about my adventures and to see how he liked the zines I'd sent him. The night before I left home, I had a going-away party for myself that doubled as a launch for the last issue of my zine *Array*, cleverly titled "disarray." The issue featured a dozen little essays (OK, rants) about leaving home, and one story I'd written mostly while on acid—my first foray into published fiction. The story was about a cartoon character invented by an artist who hated his girlfriend and his job and who wanted to have a nice little anime-style fantasy fling with another woman. And wouldn't you know it, the boy fell into the frame and the cartoon ended up much more than a character, rebelling against him and coming to self-consciousness of her own creation. I think it ended with her tears causing the ink of her own

figure to smudge and wash away as shadows moved across a bedroom wall. Now you know why I'm not in fiction. Anyway, it was
my big girl statement, a sort of "She's Leaving Home" note but
without the wretched string section. I would need that soon
enough.

At the pay phone, I dropped the quarter in, got through, and
my beau hung up on me. Confused, I called back, and the same. It
happened about ten times before he would actually talk to me, but
then only to break up. What had changed? In one week. The story,
did he see the parallel? I was cut free with no explanation. I hung
up the pay phone in the dark, with the bonfire crackling in the distance and the San Diego speed-metal guy happy to get his turn at
the phone. I was numb, then I was floating, and sooner or later I
would become conscious that I had a broken heart. I was nineteen
and alone for the first time in my life. Too much, just too much.
Oh god, OK Daphne. Push play and just lie down.

The opening mantra, "All I want in life's a little bit of love to
take the pain away," falls over starry synths already familiar to fans
of Spiritualized's two prior albums, *Lazer-Guided Melodies* and *Pure
Phase*. It was Pierce's sonic signature by the time of his first significant breakup, with his musical partner Pete Kember in the legendary '80s British lo-fi psych band Spacemen 3. Tympani outline
each phrase. A second Pierce enters with his reedy angel voice distorted, telephone-style. Swells of guitars and strings confirm the
structure: a canon. It's Pachelbel's Canon actually, a warhorse perhaps more comfortable as mid-sequence in a wedding compilation
than as opening gesture for an art-rock masterpiece. It's an odd beginning, a canon. No narrative arc, no moment of triumph, no
end. It's a cyclical structure and, as such, music theorists call it
feminine, so Pierce renders his opening endless and his senti-

ments emasculated. And what exactly is he saying over and over, endlessly? He originally sang that "Wise men say/Only fools rush in," but the album was delayed so that the lyrics could be rerecorded, changed to, "I've been told/Only fools rush in/But I don't believe/I could still fall in love with you." It turns out that even though Elvis told Pierce some wise things, the king didn't want his truths repeated. So no father figures either.

"Ladies and Gentlemen" is strung with bleeps that sound like hospital machines monitoring heart rates. The final bleep sounds as the synth haze burns off and the album changes directions dramatically. The second track, "Come Together," is likely the only song from the album you'll still hear played in public today. It's a surface-heavy blues-rock tune, flanging and wailing away with the London Community Gospel Choir in "come together" tow. On his "Come Together," John Lennon was rumored to be so blitzed he had to lie down to record the vocals. Pierce's song is more like a speedball: the sound of every synapse firing, the brain repeating come together stay together come together stay together. The tough psychedelic bluesman routine, to which Pierce would later retreat, is in critique and reference here. He can't say no, and he can't stop, and he knows it's destroying him. On "Come Together" he is warm in the middle of a lovin' spoonful. But sugar, we're going down.

"Cool, 'cause I'm wired and I'm out of my mind," sings a choir of Pierce's on "Think I'm In Love." The air up here is more rarefied, with musical gestures stretched out over long expanses of time. The dope is running down his spine, he says. Clouds turn to droplets and beneath us it is raining. The drums phase in and out, and become the most important sound the way someone who is on the edge of paranoia and possibly high can hear a faucet drip three rooms away.

From nowhere comes a list, similar to something out of a middle school self-esteem-building class, when a writing exercise might have read, "I think I am . . . /But I know I am . . ." The contrasting elements give students room to dream and a sense that their reality wasn't so bad either. Pierce's list enumerates anxiousness about friends, career success, and love, but it's hard to tell which side of the binary Pierce believes is true. Is he a bloated egomaniac or a misanthropic nihilist? "I think that you're my dream girl/Probably just dreaming/I think I'm the best babe/Probably like all the rest." He's one of many people, myself included, who believe themselves to be very important while knowing that they are very insignificant in the greater scheme of things. How to reconcile this space between is the trick, and it is a trick Pierce hasn't learned yet. So he makes music (and I write).

His dissatisfaction descends into obsession and anguish, to a moment of acutely felt sadness, in "Broken Heart," that by album's end is still unresolved. Of course, the nature of melancholy is that it doesn't seek resolution. It exists as a space of endless rumination on the subject of loss. Freud called melancholy the "unconscious loss of a love-object," suggesting that all melancholic moods reflect back to this original loss. Unlike sadness, melancholy looks upon the past with pleasure, sweetening the bitterness of unfulfillment in the present. Historically, melancholy types have sought out expanses like the sea or the night sky, places that trigger pensiveness. I think this is why most people actually sort of fear vacation, and why I didn't pick something a little more uptempo for my island. *Ladies and Gentlemen* may have been the product of one man's melancholy, but the true gift of it is that it renders a melancholic aura portable and instantly obtainable to its fans.

By the song "Think I'm In Love," Pierce's melancholy has clouded out the present. Here he's swearing off his dream girl and himself in the same stanza, allowing his dark predictions to become more resonant truths. And really, she never had a chance. He's longing for the ideal, lamenting inner loss, the failure of adulthood, his lack of innocence, and the incomplete. "Think I'm In Love" is really about being in love with his own sadness and listing all the ways in which he's failed to live up to his own standards. He's not flying; he's falling. He's not rocking 'n' rolling; he's twisting. All the emotions he wants to believe are true are false. They're underwhelming shams exposed through the clichés of pop's lyrical conventions. He knows that's bad art, but anyone who has suffered loss knows that before you can say anything new about the experience, you experience many feelings through tired metaphors overused long before the Brill Building. And Pierce is not unfamiliar with moons and spoons.

"All of My Thoughts" short-circuits emotion as the high wears off and addiction starts creeping. "I just don't know what to do with myself/cause all of my thoughts are of you," he sings. The track then falls into a melee of piano, guitar, and harmonica so ludicrously psychedelic it should have a vibrating op art warning label. Only the bassline rides clear. Each time it dies down, Pierce repeats, "Don't know what to do by myself." Clearly the answer for him is heroin. For me this is the point in the album, not just in Chillicothe, but also after every breakup, that I have to at least sit down. That first summer it was on a badly upholstered couch in the living room of my little white house, my crappy stereo further distorting the already-too-hot bass while I let the sound wash over me, waiting for something from the din to grab me directly. Ever since, every sitting has been not just for itself but for all the previous listening sessions. That's the nature of melancholy and, conveniently enough, it's also the nature of music. It only works when connecting the past to the present.

What happens next is Lynchian. High and descending into obsessive-compulsive nostalgia, our hero has a vision of times past. "Stay With Me" is all Spacemen 3 synths and early Spiritualized simplicity. The song unfolds like a surreal underwater fantasy, one I imagine made by some smackhead art-department prom planners. There are cardboard air-bubbles for basslines, pipe-cleaner seaweed strands of gently bent guitar, scalloped metallic green tambourine fish, undulating blue foil synths, and store-bought plastic sea horses arranged as arpeggio melodies that glitter in the light of a 1950s slow-dance mirror ball whose light casts weird, seasick shadows into darker regions of the underworld. Of course, Pierce is our junkie Neptune driving wild horses through this two-bit spectacle, attempting to look epic. It's a grotesque low-budget daydream layered so thick with hope that it descends into a static unreality that doesn't end, but only gives way to "Electricity," a speedfreaking rave-up in clear homage to Hendrix.

It's not formal homage, though; it's like a prayer. Pierce worships in the electric church as a '60s rock completist known for melodic and lyrical quotation of the psych canon and whose first single as leader of Spiritualized was a cover of garage rock icons the Troggs' chamber pop track "Any Way That You Want Me." Like Hendrix, Pierce has overdosed on the tragic bluesman persona, crossing copious intake with obsessive studio craft and coming out with something akin to religion. It's pompous to think this formula could still work in 1997, but it did, if packaged less like a wild ride on a mind-melting hippie caravan than a prescription for the "heart and soul" to be used as directed. The album's packaging is very safe.

The speed gained from "Electricity" pushes to the last hill, the "Home of the Brave." The fingers curl, the body braces for the beginning of the freefall. "I don't even feel it but lord how I need it/When I'm not with her, I'm not all myself," Pierce sings as a piano swirls in an increasingly murky space below. "I'm sure when it wears off, I'll be hurting," he sings, and it's clear that this is a body numb to pain, so numb that dangerous things can happen. Radley echoes "off a mirror, off a mirror," to report where he takes his breakfast. And I'm sure when she was in the studio, she didn't even know how he'd use her voice. Ah, the studio magic, the junkie justice. I guess he and I are similar in that way, though: beware the artwork of your ex.

Amid some free jazz chaos, the song plunges unannounced into the skronking and bass rumbles of "The Individual." This is a common sound in the Spacemen 3/Spiritualized milieu, and psych rock in general: the moment of the sick soul in limbo. Whole labels, like Kranky and Darla, trade in the genre of transcendental blissout wallpaper like this. Coming before the heart-wrenching realization and workaday honesty of "Broken Heart," "The Individual" is the moment before dawn when it seems possible that our hero might not make it. But in the silence, it comes.

"Broken Heart." A naked, honest prayer, uttered in pain. Moving through the whole cycle of naïveté, rejection, disbelief, frustration, misery, and melancholy, this is the moment of static sadness that is absolutely banal unless the song and the listener's mood are aligned. "Though I have a broken heart/I'm too busy to be heartbroken/There's a lot of things that need to be done/Lord I have a broken heart." I can make it until the jump to the fifth, "and I'm crying all the time," and then, as if it were a good country song, it forces me to join in. I might even wail. The worst part about this song is that the texture is so thin, there's no place to hide within it as I cry.

The strings are actually gross. The French horn's like some overly maudlin John Williams interlude whose only redeeming quality is that when I become aware of it, I know my own worst is over. This is the time when I decide whether to keep crying or to get up and do something, like look at myself in the mirror. I was once in love with a boy who said people never looked uglier than when they were crying, which should have been a clear indication for a melancholic that the relationship could only end in the loneliest of tears. I don't know what I look like when I'm crying, but I do think I never look calmer than right after, with a red nose and giant pupils framed by pink-red eyelids, my skin tight with salty tear-tracks.

Lately the thing that has rung most true to me about "Broken Heart" is the horrible reality of being too busy to be heartbroken. What does it mean to be someone who can't pause for even that? I'm too busy to be heartbroken: a terrible, adult realization. I think about not just lost lovers, but of my dead grandparents, great-aunt and -uncle, and friends who have suffered similar losses and who continue to go to work, take out the garbage, feed the cat. Now sometimes I have to schedule time to be heartbroken. I give myself seventy minutes. *OK. Push play and lie down.*

"No God Only Religion" starts and ends with church bells, but they're not for Pierce. The descending horn line, caterwaul of guitars, cymbal crashes, and furious drumming attest to the fact that the melancholic spell is broken and amid the ruin Pierce is asking, how did this happen? The song title suggests that the union made by any vow outside the electric church is lawful but unholy. That's a bitter hex. But his heart begins to mend in "Cool Waves," a gesture of acceptance late in Pierce's twelve-song program. He gives his reluctant consent, whispering, "if you've got to leave, you've got to leave" while the choir strongly reminds the "babe" who's leaving that "I love you, love you." Pierce sings like he's fading away. The obsession and drugs maddened him, but they also gave him something to do. What will he become without them? This is the question an addict fears most: what do I do with my time when I'm sober? "Cool Waves" ends with a distant fanfare not unlike the one the Beatles lifted from Bach for "All You Need Is Love." "All You Need . . ." is also the song played in the last episode of *The Prisoner,* a one-season British television show from 1967 about the unsuccessful attempts by a former spy to escape an island on which he's been placed for eternity because he knows too much. The difference between the prisoner and me is that I get to take an album along to my exile. And I don't know too much.

Which brings us to the last story. It's about Sam Stone, a soldier wounded in Vietnam who returns with a morphine addiction that destroys him. John Prine wrote "The Ballad of Sam Stone" in 1971, and Pierce cribbed the first two lines of its chorus as the opening for his seventeen minute and thirteen second final track. In Prine's story, Stone survived war just to come home and die alone of an overdose. No salvation. "Cop Shoot Cop" is a recapitulation of *Ladies and Gentlemen*'s addiction theme, with Pierce surrounding himself with lessons about cop/shoot/copping himself into a similar fate. Since the twelfth step of ending addiction is to use newfound spiritual awakening to help other addicts, then it is only fitting that legendary swamp pianist and now-three-decades-clean former addict Dr. John appears offering support and maybe a little *gris-gris* to the cause with patient legato chords. Pierce professes to believe he's "been reborn," that he "doesn't have the time no more," but as this is the last song, it is nothing but a junkie's promise. As in the beginning, the form doesn't suggest closure, but continual return. In this case, it comes as a winding down, a last note in the bass, a resonance dying to silence.

It wasn't until I started writing this that I ever listened to the last note though. I guess I always assumed I'd hear it when I needed to. That time hasn't really come yet, and I don't look forward to it. I look back.

12

DIONNE WARWICK
Legends
Arista, 1994

By John Darnielle

For Sam Deese

"I think my mom bought that single."
—Lalitree Darnielle, my wife, referring to
"That's What Friends Are For"

WHEN THE MOMENT OF TRUTH COMES, I REMEMBER ITS GENESIS. MEMORY IS FUNNY LIKE THAT. THIS IS THE SCENE THAT PRECEDES THE MOMENT; these are the brought-to-you-by details: I am standing in my living room, bleeding from my left temple, staring at the CD shelf on the east wall. A gun muzzle is poking me in the small of my back. It's really uncomfortable, which is an obvious point, but one that's got a real *oomph* to it when accompanied by an immediate physical reality. And then it's happening: I'm doing the totally ridiculous thing I've been ordered to do. I'm taking a CD down from a shelf. It's the only album I'm going to be allowed to take with me to some uncharted island off the coast of North Carolina, where I will surely die within the next ten days, if not sooner. Who's anybody kidding about this "rest of your life" business? I grew up in Claremont, I can't survive in the wild. So I'm reaching toward the albums, pausing at my more-complete-than-yours Smog discography for a minute before hesitating pregnantly over the St. Matthew's Passion, and then suddenly—instinctively, you'd almost say if you didn't know better or imagine that it mattered—I drop to a crouch, and I find the "W" section. I grab the triple-disc set *Legends*, whose fifty-two tracks draw on Dionne Warwick's tenure at Arista Records between 1979 and 1993. There are many roads to the grave, and this one is mine. Thank you, God, for Dionne Warwick. And just then, as my fingers touch the card stock of the outer casing—in the drawn-out split second before a rifle butt to the back of my skull knocks me cold—I remember a scene from my childhood, the memory of which, even now, guides my hand.

It is 1977. I am in a small room upstairs at my grandmother's house. We live here now. We moved here not long after my mother, in terror, herded my sister and me out to the car to escape my stepfather's increasingly violent rages. A year or so from now, he'll be back, and we'll move into a three-bedroom place across town, together, but for now we're here: in a two-story, four-bedroom, two-bathroom house in one of Claremont's older neighborhoods. We have moved four times over the last four years. I've learned how to entertain myself, because I am often the new kid in school, which is a solitary position to occupy. Mostly I read books and try to endear myself to children's librarians or teachers, whose company I generally prefer to that of my peer group; but, like any other kid, I also watch a fair amount of television. I have always loved music, and I watch awards shows when they're on, because I like to see the musical guests singing live. I get very excited when these shows come on; half the time I haven't heard the songs or seen the movies that're being pitted against each other, but I pick sides anyway, using whatever flimsy information I have—a film clip, a stray chorus, maybe a full performance during the presentation—on which to base my momentary partisan stance.

This year, Dionne Warwick is hosting the American Music Awards. That's all I remember; I don't know whether this was the first time I heard her sing or not. I just remember seeing her, feeling both confused by and attracted to her languor, her sense of self-assurance, her easy manner. Something in her approach suggested to me that there was a separate reality somewhere, one in which emotions were much subtler and less raw than they were in my reality. In this past-present moment, nine years old, watching her sing from down in the hidden heart of this diffferent emotional world, I am a little put off.

Two years later we've settled into that very modest house across town. I am older, and years make a difference in these times. I'm secluded in my bedroom; I spend my evenings in here. Most nights I am either pressing my ear up against a small transistor radio or watching a black-and-white television set. On a new show called Solid Gold, which I watch semireligiously, albeit with inchoate indie contempt, Dionne Warwick is lip-synching her new single, "Heartbreaker." I am again put off: I don't understand the song. The melody sticks in my brain like a popcorn hull between molars. I hate the now-omnipresent Brothers Gibb harmonies, hate them, *hate* them. The emotional weight of the song is beyond me, calling to me through a veil I can't breach. I want to press my face up against that veil to get whatever glimpse I might steal of life on the other side of it, and at the same time I want to keep well clear of it. I have this sense that once you've gone over to that side of things, you can't come back. Still, the attraction of the veil itself, and the allure of the unknown that it represents, is practically narcotic in its draw. "Heartbreaker" represents a ne plus ultra rather more sophisticated than your garden-variety point of no return: it's a quiet, nagging inevitability. I can't shake it. As the playback fades, Dionne is still lip-synching, gamely fostering the illusion that a fade-out is something an orchestra and a vocalist agree upon beforehand and then pull off in real time. This illusion, for reasons still obscure even now, is very important to me. Then the applause comes up, drowning out the horizon point between fade-out and silence, and Dionne smiles broadly.

Twenty-six years later, it's this wisp of a memory that will guide my hand toward a Dionne Warwick boxed set just as I'm losing consciousness in my North Carolina living room. The connection between moments: all we can really ask of pop music.

There's a book by Johnny Rogan called *Morrissey and Marr: The Severed Alliance*. It's a melodramatic title—you suspect that the author's got rather more invested in his subject than is fitting for a biographer—but it does its job. It sets a narrative in play. All that remains for the book, really, is to fill in the spaces its name has made available. "Alliance" as though there were a program for the pair to follow through upon, and as though the partnership bore some great cultural weight (which, to be fair, it did); "severed" as though outside forces somehow divided the two, driving asunder that which nature or history or love had once brought together. Clever.

I think of this book when I listen to any of the three discs that make up Dionne Warwick's *Legends*. Warwick made her name by establishing herself as Burt Bacharach's perfect foil. Possessed of a remarkable gift for investing airy phrases with both transparency and depth, she seems to have been offered first pick of the Bacharach-David bounty throughout the '60s. The records they made together are iconic in their near-invisibility; rather than re-membering or reliving them, one practically carries them around on one's body like a series of birthmarks. "Don't Make Me Over," "Anyone Who Had A Heart," "Walk On By," "Do You Know the Way to San Jose," "I Say A Little Prayer": in all, Warwick and the Bacharach/David songwriting team had twenty Top 40 hits over a ten-year span. In 1972, though, Bacharach and David scored a mu-sical adaptation of the 1937 film *Lost Horizon* that bombed rather spectacularly. It would be thirteen years till *Howard the Duck* would best *Lost Horizon* for sheer commercial and critical failure.

Information is spotty about what happened to the Bacharach-David-Warwick partnership in the wake of *Lost Horizon*; biogra-phies usually summarize things rather cryptically: "Warwick was forced to sue Bacharach and David," say, or "the union dissolved amidst numerous lawsuits." There are references, though they are few and far between, to recording sessions booked and rebooked for Warwick, and finally cancelled for lack of forthcoming mate-rial from the songwriters. The nine-year-old in me likes to imagine Warwick in the vocal booth, perhaps leafing through a magazine while seated on a stool, a gathering of musicians on the other side

of the glass in the tracking room, all of them waiting for something to sing and play. In my child's dream of how records are
made or not made, the musicians begin to leave one by one as outside commitments beckon: dinner's waiting for them at home, or
they have an AA meeting they can't miss. Eventually it's just
Dionne, angry and frustrated, shutting out the lights as she leaves.

The truth is doubtless more prosaic, involving legally binding
contracts that prevented Warwick from recording new material.
Nothing's worse for a singer's career than absence from the public
eye; the public heart doesn't grow fonder, it just moves on. So
Warwick sued Bacharach, and Bacharach sued David, and David
sued Bacharach right back, and the team that'd made emotional
ambiguity an abiding aesthetic concern for the pop charts, elevat-
ing it to occasionally sublime heights, dismantled itself somewhat
nastily, its principals going their separate ways. Warwick made a
remarkable album of light Philadelphia soul—1975's *Then Came
You*, produced by Thom Bell and featuring the Spinners on the
title track—but she was in unfamiliar waters now.

Four years later is when *Legends* begins.

I am in a burlap bag in a Beech V35B Bonanza, high above the
water. The airplane's engine roars like hell's own powerhouse. My
head hurts; my body hurts; my eyes hurt. I am humming to myself to keep from going insane. I am humming "That's What
Friends Are For" by Dionne Warwick and Friends.

The thing about "That's What Friends Are For," the weird
thing about it, is that it's actually quite good. When this particular
version of the song first came out, back in 1985, its release was
one of pop music's first responses to the growing AIDS epidemic.
In those days, people who knew they'd shortly die from AIDS-

related complications would often direct their associates to list the
cause of death as "cancer" or "terminal illness." The stigma attached to AIDS was no joke, and "That's What Friends Are For"
was somewhat brave in trying to reframe the discourse. But the
song itself came off like a string of Hallmark sentiments: stay
strong, remember the good times, believe in love. Back then these
struck me as two-dimensional slogans, Ace bandages applied to
broken bones. I was young, and I asked of music that it provide
me with vicissitudes. It was imperative for me that pain sound like
pain. Now I know for sure that I'm going to die, though, and I'm
listening to my memory of the song on a loop inside of my head,
and it sounds rather different to me.

In fact, it sounds profound, and somewhat wise. It's got the sort
of melody you can hum without having to think too hard about it,
which is a priority for me in my present circumstances, since if I
think too hard, I'll black out. In 1985, few A-listers wanted to think
much about AIDS, much less lend their names to a record about it.
The cast is therefore modestly star-studded and quite small in
scale: Elton John and Stevie Wonder the big names on the mar-
quee, Gladys Knight gamely chiming in, and Dionne Warwick,
whose project this seems to be—again, the single's credited to
"Dionne Warwick and Friends"—above and around and throughout the proceedings. It's a Bacharach/Sager affair, originally
recorded by Rod Stewart in 1982; the assembled cast for the
Dionne version brings its considerable talents to bear upon the
song before them. The '80s empty-opera-house-on-the-moon production tries to keep a safe distance between the song's soft,
wounded heart and the listener, but unless you've never seen a
man die—or unless you believe you're immortal—you can't miss

the considered, quiet ache in Warwick's voice when she gets to the second verse:

> And if I should ever go away,
> well, just close your eyes and try
> to feel the way we feel today
> and then if you can remember

The subsequent chorus, whatever its strengths or weaknesses, is rather an afterthought in the wake of "and then if you can remember," which is frankly brutal. "If you can" could be taken several ways, and some of them are horrible to contemplate. The last note of the phrase—the "er"—lands low in Dionne's register, which has always been where she was most effective anyway, and she lets it vibrate for a second or two before heading on. That line, and Dionne's willingness to stress its uglier possibilities, practically obliterates the good feeling that the chorus itself will try to engender; and even buried within the familiar Hallmark moment writ large ("keep smiling, keep shining"), there's an ocean of great sadness, a nod toward the despair that made the chorus possible in the first place. There's a helplessness to it, a terrifying fragility. There are dead people animating this only-somewhat-hopeful chorus. This, then, is the endless mercy of pop music, which makes my own selfish concerns seem small: the hidden histories, the silenced voices recalled in the near-silence of forgetfulness, all in a small pop production pieced together long ago when once it seemed necessary to do something, during a moment that began receding into the past even as it was coming into being, almost completely lost now, though not quite.

I turn inside my bag. Someone kicks me in the stomach.

It's in the very nature of pop music to pose as though it were weightless. Critics, or history, can describe or invest such weight as they see or see fit: but the dialectic is between an eager surgeon and a reluctant patient. Pop music revels in its own inconsequentiality; it seems to say that it doesn't mean much, if indeed it does mean anything at all: how *could* it bear much meaning, when all it does is repeat the same themes over and over again, year in and year out, using the exact same melodic and verbal phrases and constructions? Let a pop song run through its life cycle all the way to the end, though, and let the modes of production that governed its birth run their historical course—let them, I mean, be entirely replaced by newer technologies—and if a body still remains to be exhumed, see whether it hasn't taken on weight and substance.

For example, "I'll Never Love This Way Again," a song by Richard Kerr and Will Jennings, who also wrote "No Night So Long." It leads off the second disc of the *Legends* collection. Seen in its native habitat—1979—it barely even registers: it quietly places fifth on the year-end *Billboard* chart, which is no mean trick, but Blondie's "Heart of Glass" and Sister Sledge's "We Are Family" are in the number-one and number-two slots, respectively, while Donna Summer's "Heaven Knows" is at number four, with Kenny Rogers's "Coward of the County" speaking for an entirely different demographic at number three. "I'll Never Love This Way Again" is the nice girl of this quintet: good for slow dances, workable as background music, ready at a moment's notice to vanish from view.

It stands out prominently enough now, though, coming as it does from the misty depths of non-history, out there in the ether of occasional memory. It manages to gather power like an imploding star despite having some really questionable production choices against it: all the listener's straying attentions are herded toward the one great big hook at the center of the chorus, while the verses (which aren't bad) are given the bum's rush. A younger Dionne Warwick wouldn't have aimed quite so squarely for the cheap seats on a song like this, and a better arranger would have tried to inject a little variation into the repeated ramp-up-to-the-chorus moments. Besides all that, there's the song itself, which is not great; it gives itself away on first listening. There is nothing, really, to be gained from listening to it a second time. But therein, for me, lies its simple and effective pathos. Here is what Dionne Warwick, who once had the best of Bacharach for right of first refusal, has on her plate as of 1979:

> *You looked inside my fantasies*
> *and made each one come true;*
> *something no one else had ever*
> *found a way to do.*
> *I've kept the memories one by one*
> *since you took me in.*
> *I know I'll never love this way again.*

Warwick occasionally deploys some uncharacteristically bluesy chops here—check the delivery of "way to do"—as though hoping to infuse the song with a subtlety it would prefer to resist. But the song, unlike "Do You Know the Way to San Jose?" or "Alfie," each of which luxuriated in an exciting, ever-changing present day, has its eye on the future, a future that is the embodied antonym of subtlety. Poised on the cusp of a decade that will focus much of its energy on overkilling a few inconvenient, incipient countercultural paradigms that were never really going to take root anyway, "I'll Never Love This Way Again" reads the listener's palm and finds the rot at the root. It's sentimentalism at its worst—the "this" in the chorus is a cheap, mean trick—and its power, consequently, is deathless. Its ability to draw tears from dry eyes will not only never die: it will grow yearly, like calcium deposits on an unwashed faucet. In a way, it's as immune to time as "Twinkle, Twinkle, Little Star." It is a nearly blank slate.

And because it has so little to offer, its shallows become depths if you look at them for too long. The effect of this makes me dizzy. What must it feel like for the narrator of this song, knowing that she will shortly begin descending from heights she can never hope to see again in her life? The song won't say, or can't; the singer knows what the song is driving at, and has the talent to make the song stand on its own two legs. But it has no legs, or the legs it has are boneless. These two dimensions cannot become three. That is their tragedy. And so they take on the sorrows of the listener as a sponge absorbing water. But the sponge is as big as the universe, and the song will never stop giving of itself.

On the beach, alone at last, I lick my wounds and stare at my boom box. How long can its batteries last? Not long at all, I'd guess. But what do you say we pretend the situation's not hopeless, while we still have our sanity? Is everybody here up for a little of the young-Judy-Garland-style stiff upper lip? Is it cool if we just think out loud for a while? Is there any point in *not* talking to myself now? If I were Robinson Crusoe, I might forage for food, or craft a compass, or build a hut. If I were religious, I might pray.

Instead, I do what any reasonable person in my position would do. I listen to "I Know I'll Never Love This Way Again" for three consecutive hours, and I cry like a child.

"Arista Records," I whisper to the translucent-bodied vermin who've taken up residence in the hair on my legs. I say it twice, and I pronounce it two different ways: "AIR-iss-tuh," which is correct, and then "Uh-RISS-tuh," which is wrong, but which was how I pronounced it the first time I bought a record on the Arista label (the Bay City Rollers, "Saturday Night" b/w "Marlena," at the Zody's on Holt Boulevard, circa 1977) and contemplated the powder-blue-and-white color scheme with its vaguely chakra-like "A" logo. The design in general seemed an occult reference to the California skies beneath which I was then growing up.

Like you and me and everyone else we know, Arista is now a wholly owned subsidiary of Sony BMG. When it was launched in 1974, however, it was the music division of Columbia Pictures, which is to say that its central function was to ensure that a major player in the movie business wouldn't go hungry at the music-biz trough. Clive Davis, its founding president, was a Harvard law grad, and had until recently been president of CBS Records; he'd been fired amidst allegations of financial impropriety and the looming threat of federal investigation. Davis did not cop specifically to any of the charges leveled against him by the company, but he did admit to tax evasion; he then, in the wondrous way of show business, set about getting revenge.

He was no dummy. He signed Barry Manilow; he signed the Grateful Dead; hedging bets against the future, he signed Patti Smith. Later on, he would sign Whitney Houston and Sarah

McLachlan, and Kenny G besides; later still, long past the age when most record execs would have been put out to pasture, he partnered with an up-and-coming producer named Sean "Puffy" Combs, and the two sold twelve million albums in their first three years together. The world also has Clive Davis and Arista Records to thank for the commercial revitalization of Carlos Santana.

Dionne Warwick signed with Arista in 1979. "I Know I'll Never Love This Way Again" was her first single for her new label, and she won a Grammy for it. Icing the cake, she took home another Grammy that same year, in a different category, for "Déjà Vu," an Isaac Hayes–penned tune from the same album. *Res mirabilis*: she had dodged the guillotine, survived several eras of popular music, and come out swinging. I envision Dionne in '79 as a barbarian warrior rising from the dust of the battlefield, gore hanging from her fingernails, steely resolve in her eyes. The music business requires youth, vitality, newness; it eats its children when they reach the age of reckoning; it takes no prisoners. So, at any rate, runs the popular understanding of the established order.

By succeeding so riotously in the waning years of one decade and the waxing years of the next, Arista Records and Dionne Warwick make a statement that is practically all nuance. The former entity can be seen as a tenacious workhorse's raised middle finger to the business that would have had him take the fall for what, in truth, were industry-wide problems; Dionne, at this point in time, is an eccentric '60s American chanteuse hanging on with both hands to her hard-won position in the cultural pantheon. Neither party can reasonably be thought of as passionately engaged with the other. Arista looses its proven hit makers on Dionne; Dionne steps doggedly up to the plate. Together, they make money for one another, and they belly up to the buffet in what are generally fat times for the industry.

It is unromantic to think of music in these terms. Music, after all, is the stuff of dreams! The most abstract of the arts, the most primal form of organized expression, the least mediated type of formal communication—all that lovely rot! But for me, these hideous business details—of time and circumstance; of people eager to keep their heads above water even if it means pushing a few other heads under; of human pettiness and idiosyncrasy—are marginalia that infuse their central texts (the songs, I mean) with blood and breath. If songs are human stories, then how much more human are they when we feel that we've glimpsed the real human beings—petty or vain or desperate or high as kites—who stand behind them, holding them up like shields or masks? They comfort us precisely because they're not interested in spilling their guts, est-style, but in soldiering forward, undaunted by pain. Dionne Warwick's artistry has always been explicitly about this apparent paradox—between the pull toward believable emotional experience and the even deeper need for comfortable, buffering artifice—and her work at Arista, historically located at comfortable remove from her '60s high-water marks (now unfortunately romanticized almost beyond hope of rescue), splits that difference with gymnastic grace. Warwick's Arista years shuffle hope and resignation both internally (in the tunes, and their delivery, and their production) and superficially (in merely existing at all). If approached desperately enough, they blur the distinction between these two designations with what almost appears to be malice aforethought.

But I say "almost" again, and I mean it, because just before the batteries of my boom box expire, I hear "Déjà Vu." Perhaps it is just how hungry I am, or how near death, but it sounds almost intolerably emotional to my ears. It hits me like first love, all unknown quantities, something like those of "Heartbreaker" long ago, only now rolling down a much steeper grade. Perhaps all the stories of partnerships and contracts and alliances are red herrings strewn in our path by a merciful God who knows we can't stomach the bare facts as they are. Maybe our first visions were true.

Here's what happens: a mid-tempo riff is carried entirely by the keyboard, traversing an octave up a flatted fourth from its tonic and then down a full octave from there, lending a woozy feel to things. Where are we to rest and feel comfortable here? Where is our center? Is there no shore? But remember that this is an Isaac Hayes number, and that at his serpentine best, Hayes can elude the very center that his song exists to posit. It's clear from the outset that "Déjà Vu" has a specific aim in mind, but it's also a little hesitant about its object, like a person afraid to stare directly into the sun for fear of going blind. The thrust, the whole point really, is to impose a slight degree of discomfort, of mild tension. There are strings that are here precisely because they contribute quietly to this effect. The drums laze. I must have water. The FM radio–friendly popping funk bass rides down very, very low, and calls to mind both bourgeois scenes in overpriced restaurants overlooking the sea and tricked-out Oldsmobiles crawling the streets on summer evenings, all purple lights and hydraulics. I am going to die. I don't want to die. I am going to die. I don't want to die. Warwick's ad libs over the breaks are high and double-tracked with a mirroring whispered vocal, and are so loaded with implication that one scarcely knows where to begin, since there is no place to begin. There's only the center, the present, the middle of the road. In the present case, the sexuality that's often submerged in that middle rises a little closer to the surface, but by that time we are nearing the fade-out. She recorded this to save herself from the brink. She sang it because there was nothing else to sing. He wrote it to keep from slipping over the edge. It was there for me when I needed it. It crystallizes itself in time and its creators can only stare in wonder as it makes and unmakes lives like an infant God bored with his surroundings. I reach up to hit the repeat button. Please God. I just want to hear the first line again:

This is insane
All I did was say hello

13

ELTON JOHN
*Goodbye Yellow
Brick Road*
Rocket/Island, 1973

By Matt Ashare

LTON JOHN CAN REST ASSURED THAT ONE OF THESE YEARS HE'LL BE INDICTED, OR, UH, INDUCTED INTO THE HALLOWED IF TERMINALLY BORING ROCK AND Roll Hall of Fame. Hell, he's already a knight or something back home in the UK. So what if his only noteworthy activities over the past decade have included a silly, money-grubbing "piano men" tour with the god-awful Billy Joel and a tasteless (if lucrative), ham-fisted reworking of one of the best tunes he wrote at the peak of his partnership with lyricist Bernie Taupin over thirty years ago, the heartfelt ode to Marilyn Monroe "Candle In the Wind." And that's just one of four bona fide classics the dynamic duo nailed on their landmark 1973 double album *Goodbye Yellow Brick Road.*

Now, four hits in seventeen at-bats may not be all that bad in baseball, a game of averages over a long haul of a season. And *Goodbye Yellow Brick Road* did manage to keep Elton in the commercial game for a good two years on both sides of the Atlantic. But, on a purely artistic level, it's certainly no match for four-sided classics like *Exile On Main St.*, *London Calling*, or even *Zen Arcade*. As for Elton himself . . . well, let's just say that even a fawning Jon Tobler, in his uniquely uninformative liner notes for the thirtieth-anniversary deluxe edition of *Goodbye Yellow Brick Road* (a double CD with four bonus cuts), mainly praises the subject of his essay for *not* dying young, an astounding feat accomplished by millions of people every single day.

"Longevity as a rock star is the Holy Grail which extremely few have managed, but one artist who has been able to maintain his popularity over more than three decades is Sir Elton John." In other words, we're dealing here with someone who's got the staying power of a Bob Seger. Rock and roll never really does forget, now does it?

So, no, I won't be making any claims for the absolute superiority of *Goodbye Yellow Brick Road*. I won't even begin to suggest that it shook the musical world to its very core, or that nothing would ever be the same again once *Goodbye Yellow Brick Road* had left its indelible mark on the charts and legends of '70s pop culture. It's not worth anyone's time to argue for the universal relevance of an album that was perhaps just important enough to establish Elton John as a career artist, but that probably doesn't belong on any respectable list of Top 10, 20, or even 40 recordings of all time. Hell, it might not even make the Top 100. Not that I'm a big fan of lists or anything.

Besides, all talk of numbers was entirely and completely and irrevocably irrelevant to one ten-year-old who'd finally gotten the courage to ask his mom for a little cash to spend in the record store next to the supermarket in Cincinnati, Ohio, she'd brought me to for her weekly double-cartful of food for the family. Someone—that would be me—would have to help carry all those groceries from the back of a Ford station wagon to the kitchen. So someone—me again—was feeling emboldened enough to spend his mom's money plucking from that mysterious tree of forbidden fruit they kept tucked away in the record store. And, since "Saturday Night's Alright For Fighting" had definitely superceded Chicago's "25 Or 6 To 4" as my air-guitar song of choice, Goodbye Yellow Brick Road was all I had on my shopping list that day. That I'd also be getting "Bennie And The Jets"—my first-ever air-piano song—and a very familiar title track that was Beatles-esque before I even knew what the "White Album" really was (or, for that matter, that you could put "esque" on the end of just about any proper noun), sealed the deal. And the cartoon cover image of Elton stepping out onto a yellow brick road (à la L. Frank Baum's Wizard of Oz) was going to make this a relatively easy sell for my protective parents, in spite of the trademark platforms Elton's pictured wearing. This was a rock album that could, in the days before those nasty parental warning stickers, pass for a kid's album as long as dad didn't happen to notice a song called "Jamaica Jerk Off" (hey, it's a song about chicken, right?) or "Dirty Little Girl." It would be years before I'd realize that it made absolute no sense for Elton to be stepping out on to a road of yellow bricks when the album's title seemed to suggest that he was waving adieu to that mystical symbol of innocence. But I was a late bloomer who'd yet to fully develop a sense of bitter irony.

So no, I'm not prepared to propose that any album that provides a ten-year-old with that perfect balance of solace, stimulation, and pure escapist joy, all set to a strong backbeat, an infectious melody, and an overwhelming sense of magical realism is absolutely destined to leave a permanent mark on the world or even that person as he or she makes his or her way through life. (We are currently experimenting on rats and, while we have isolated the *Goodbye Yellow Brick Road* gene, we've yet to determine how the gene is triggered.) All I can say for sure is that it can happen—a ten-year-old kid *can* have his life turned upside down and inside out by something as simple as a double album of songs. Indeed, it does happen. And, every now and again, if simply by the law of averages, that album is bound to be *Goodbye Yellow Brick Road*.

I had no way of knowing or even imagining that ten years later I'd be teaching myself those tricky ninth chords that form the backbone of "Bennie and the Jets" or that a punkish, rowdy yet earnest cover of the tune would be one of the more popular encores for a band that I played in. Or that I'd rediscover a certain comfort as well as a new kind of inspiration in *Goodbye Yellow Brick Road* over and over again at various intervals of my adult life. But, before any of that could happen, I'd have to teach myself to hate the album—to write it off as silly kids' stuff or, more stridently, as just another symptom of the bloated, indulgent cocaine culture of the '70s that would force my heroes to rise up under the banner of punk and hardcore and convince me and my friends that anything that happened prior to '77 sucked (unless it was the Stooges, the Velvet Underground, and, well, the list would continue to grow as the exceptions began to outnumber the rule).

But enough about me. *Goodbye Yellow Brick Road* is such an epic, overstuffed, and oddly ambitious piece of work that I've yet to exhaust all of its supernatural resources. Nowhere else can you find everything from prog-rock excess to tender "Strawberry Fields" balladry to punkish, Stonesy guitar rock to blue-eyed reggae, all wrapped up in a package as neatly accessible as Elton and Bernie's masterwork. And that doesn't even take into account the underrated prowess of the Elton John Band—those long-haired guys pictured opposite Elton and Bernie on the inside sleeve of the disc. Guitarist Davey Johnstone, bassist Dee Murray, and my personal fave drummer Nigel Olsson were to hit a new peak on *Goodbye Yellow Brick Road*. It was no longer just the Elton John show, my friends. This was a rock band. And, while they would go on to rule the '70s with hit after hit after hit, it was on *Goodbye Yellow Brick Road* that their mettle was tested. And I'm still pretty sure they passed with flying, uh, colors.

What is it about *Goodbye Yellow Brick Road* that stokes my inner fire? For starters, it was the soundtrack to my formative years— Cheryl Tiegs and Farah Fawcett posters, unrequited crushes and crowded carpools, neighborhood kickball and schoolyard soccer games. And, just as you can't pick your family, it's impossible to go back in time and change any of that. I'm stuck with *Goodbye Yellow Brick Road*, with Candy and Ronnie, electric boots and mohair suits, and boys too young to be singing the blues. Maybe I'd have turned out to be a cooler person if my parents had turned me on to Dylan, the Stones, the Beatles, the Who, or whoever. But such was not to be my fate. And I've come to accept—even embrace— that accident of expendable income.

If I'd been a little brighter, perhaps, or at least better schooled in the ways of the record business, then I probably could have just as easily purchased an Elton John "Greatest Hits" album. For my purposes, that certainly would have made more sense. But then I'd

be here extolling the virtues of *Exile on Main St.* for like the
30,147th time in the history of rock criticism. And why double albums to begin with? Is more really always better? Why not Bad
Brains' *Rock For Light*? In fact, if you slowed that album down, it
probably actually *is* a double album—only, like a neutron star, it's
packed so densely and spinning at such a high rate of speed that
it's over before you know it. We critics, I suppose, prefer to dig our
typing fingers into something as meaty as possible when it comes
time to pick albums of importance: it's like *Exile On Main St.* and
London Calling are the bookends of greatness. In between is plenty
of great stuff, no doubt. But if you're going to chose a truly tran-
scendent album, well, then it's gotta be a magnum opus, a work of
depth. And two discs always seem to look deeper and more important than one, right? Plus, those double albums worked really well
for deseeding the really bad marijuana that you used to have to
buy, back before gene therapy somehow removed those nasty
seeds from the buds.

But I digress. The truth is, if I'd had the guts, my first real double-
album love would have been *Kiss Alive II*. And, if I'd had any taste
or foresight, and sometimes the two really are the same, then I'd
have picked *Live At Budokan* by Cheap Trick, because Cheap Trick
are suddenly and irreversibly cool again, especially now that
they've got Steve Albini recording their albums. But *Goodbye Yellow
Brick Road*, in retrospect, allowed for more drama over the course
of my musical awakening. And, unwittingly, it opened my ears to
an enormous range of music, thanks to the determination on the
part of Elton and Bernie to be all things to all rock 'n' roll
people—to pilfer from whoever and wherever they damn well
pleased. So what if David Bowie was the first to have a hit with an

extraterrestrial adventure called "Space Oddity": Elton and Bernie were happy to respond with "Rocket Man" and to do so unabashedly, with no shame whatsoever. Chances are, the first time I heard "Space Oddity" I thought to myself "this guy is ripping off Elton John." And *Goodbye Yellow Brick Road* is built upon a foundation of this sort of hubris.

For example—and this probably isn't the best example, it just happens to be the first—consider the monstrosity that is "Funeral For A Friend/Love Lies Bleeding." The eerie sound of a church organ segues into one of those cheesy Emerson, Lake and Palmer–style synth lines before Elton takes over on piano, bringing a somber mood to the proceedings. But before long, swirling synths meet a grand guitar line that's part solo, part stand-in for the vocal that just isn't there. And then the tempo picks up. . . .

This is no longer music you might consider playing at an actual funeral. It's too rock, too hard, too fast, too loud. And, above all, it's too completely and utterly ridiculous. It's indulgent in a way that thinking punk rock kids like Johnny Lydon knew was bad for the soul of England. It's mostly just a display of the Elton John Band's solid musicianship—their "chops." And it goes on for six minutes before Elton's comforting voice finally makes its entrance for what must be the "Love Lies Bleeding" portion of the duality that has gotta be one of the worst album openers in history. The dense lyrics make little or no sense as far as I can tell. And I've been puzzling through "You're a bluebird on a telegraph line/I hope you're happy now/Well if the wind of change/Comes down your way girl/You'll make it back somehow" for a couple decades now and I'm still not sure what it means. It *sounds* important, like poetry is supposed to sound. But does Elton even know what he's singing about there? I really don't think so. He just likes digging into that line "Love lies bleeding in my hands." Now that's a good image.

And therein lies one element of what's kept me coming back to *Goodbye Yellow Brick Road*: the sheer absurdity of so much of it. I'll also confess to being a big fan of that desert-dry '70s production, that sound that mutes the drums and leaves everything out there in front to be picked apart. It's like nobody had really figured out how to layer and blend textures. So each instrument was given its own space in its own isolation booth and kept separate from every other instrument throughout the production process. Why anyone would want to do that, I've no idea except, perhaps, that this was considered high-fidelity at the time. It was the polar opposite of the reverbed mess that '60s garage rock had been. And only hard-rock renegades like Led Zep were even toying with the notion of getting back to that raw, reverbed garageland sound. Elton was a purebred product of the '70s, and as such he remained true to those studio values. *Goodbye Yellow Brick Road*, along with a couple of Lou Reed albums that I have in my collection, is a tour de force of '70s production.

But we should move on to the real meat on the bones of *GYBR*. Once they've done away with "Love Lies Bleeding," EJ and BT get down to business with a trio of blockbusters that offer the first signs that this could have been a flawless single album if they'd just tossed out some of the more indulgent and ridiculous songs. Then again, it wouldn't be *Goodbye Yellow Brick Road* without all that silliness, now would it? That "Candle In the Wind" could be as affecting as it was to a kid—again, that would be me—who didn't even know that Marilyn Monroe was dead, much less that her real name was actually Norma Jean, is a tribute to the song's inner power.

Sadly, Elton ruined it with the rewrite in tribute to Princess Di. And it may be the only track on *Goodbye Yellow Brick Road* that I occasionally skip over, though I've been trying of late to remedy that situation by karaoke-ing the song as often as possible, much to the chagrin of some of my closer friends. But in all its pomposity, "Candle In the Wind" remains yet another indelible Elton/Bernie creation. I mean, just listen to Elton try to fit the line "Hollywood created a superstar/And pain was the price you paid/Even when you died, the press still hounded you/All the papers had to say was that Marilyn was found in the nude." It's truly masterful.

But even that doesn't come close to the fatted calf they kill on "Bennie and the Jets." Now, this was my introduction to Ziggy Stardust and the Spiders from Mars. It's, once again, a pure and unabashed Bowie rip-off. And yet, to someone who didn't quite get Bowie at the time, it was a perfect introduction to the fantasy world of rock 'n' roll. As kids, we were convinced that Bennie had "electric boobs," which made things all the more exciting and confusing because Bennie's a boy's name. So here was androgyny presented as a playful tale of the greatest rock band in the world—and an imaginary one at that. The line of guys with flying-V guitars who stood behind the androgynous image of Bennie inside the sleeve only heightened the song's appealing sense of surrealism. I didn't quite want to be Bennie yet, but I would have happily joined the Jets.

And then, as the applause dies down—the fake applause, though I think I probably thought "Bennie and the Jets" was an actual live recording at the time—the title track in all its Beatles-esque splendor presents itself. Those lyrics were studied in late-night bedroom sessions as I imagined it being pure autobiography and created an image of Elton as a country boy who'd been plucked out of anonymity and turned into a star because he showed so much promise as a piano player. I started taking my piano lessons more seriously and became convinced, despite all of Elton's warnings about howling dogs of society, that I too could be placed in the mystical penthouse, and given the freedom to write songs with titles like "This Song Has No Title." Yeah, never really got that one until later in my musical development when I started to appreciate its simplicity, both in terms of its lyrics and its melody. This is Bernie as Dylan channeled through Elton, or something like that. It's nonsense as parable, with lyrics like "I was an artist who paints with his eye/I'd study my subject and silently cry/Cry for the darkness to come down on me/For confusion to carry on turning the wheel." Of course I would. Wouldn't you?

So we'll stipulate, as I think we've essentially already done, that not every song on *Goodbye Yellow Brick Road* is a gem. "Grey Seal": underrated. I mean, I'm not sure who the wise grey seal is supposed to be, and the whole thing is just silly as hell. But the melody's great, and the band really gets a chance to stretch out toward the end, which is nice because, remember, at that point I just wanted to be one of the Jets, not Bennie him/herself. On the other hand, Elton doing reggae is just a ridiculous proposition, and the picture of the nice Jamaican farmer guy standing next to the lyrics is one of those caricatures that makes me a little uncomfortable. But whatever. At least Elton and Bernie had the sense of humor to credit the tune to "Reggae Dwight & Toots Taupin." In other words, they were having fun taking their little musical tour of the world, and it comes through in the recording.

Unfortunately, *Goodbye Yellow Brick Road* simply didn't fit any-where into the new world of punk rock that I entered once I started "thinking for myself." I couldn't quite bring myself to actu-ally throw the album out, even though I spent a drunken evening with the guys from the first band I played in smashing most of my old records (ELO, *Frampton Comes Alive*, Chicago, etc.) in a base-ment room we'd converted into a practice space at my parents' house. So, somewhere in the recesses of my unconscious, I must have known that *Goodbye Yellow Brick Road* would come back to play a role in my life once again. But, for a time there, Elton John represented everything that had gone wrong with music and that had needed correction via punk rock. It all made sense and it led me on my own long and winding road back through the Velvet Un-derground and the Stooges to the Stones and the Beatles even. (I should, however, admit that my Beatles development was hindered by that damn *Yellow Submarine* movie, which I never liked and which somehow made them seem about as important as the Mon-kees to me. In fact, I think I liked the Monkees more than the Beat-les for quite some time.) It was really only a matter of time before Elton John and *Goodbye Yellow Brick Road* would once again appear on my rock 'n' roll roadmap. And I'll blame that on a combination of the Replacements and "Saturday Night's Alright For Fighting."

If there was one song on *Goodbye Yellow Brick Road* that had al-ways stood out to me as a kid, it was "Saturday Night's Alright For Fighting." Something about Elton's faux tough-guy delivery and the distorted Keith Richards–esque guitar just struck a chord, and I'm not the least bit ashamed to admit that I'd jump up on my bed and play the living hell out of a tennis racket for hours on end.

And that was when I was in college. No, it wasn't. But it might as well have been. Because by that point I owned a real guitar and amp, and a distortion pedal, and I was determined to learn everything I could about that instrument in as short a period as possible. No lessons. No time for that. I'd watch other people play, figure out what chords looked like, and then put on my favorite songs and learn them. When I first heard the Replacements butchering classic rock tunes, the idea of going back to my old record collection finally dawned on me. After all, the intro to the Boston song "More Than a Feeling" had more or less come to me by accident one day when I was messing around with a few chords. And, since "Saturday Night's Alright For Fighting" was the Elton/Bernie attempt at proto-punk glam-rock à la T. Rex and the Stones, it was the most obvious choice. Now I was jumping around my room and actually playing the song along with Dee, Davey, Nigel, and Elton. I had come full circle, as so many of us are bound to do. History repeats itself for a reason. And as soon as I figure out what that reason is, I promise to let everyone know.

So why, I'm still left asking. Why *Goodbye Yellow Brick Road*? Surely there are better albums out there to take on some imaginary desert island adventure, right? I mean, I could name a dozen right off the top of my head. But those are all records that I've gotten too far inside for my own good. They're records that I've analyzed, reanalyzed, and, in some cases, overanalyzed to death. I'll still love them, and they'll always be a part of what I am. But I just can't help feeling that somehow I'm always hearing them through the filter of *Goodbye Yellow Brick Road*. Because *Goodbye Yellow Brick Road* is the first album that I really did try to get inside. Only I didn't have any of the tools necessary to do so. As a result, I got everything wrong. Hell, I didn't even know what a social disease was when I first tried to figure out what that song was about. And so, every time I hear even just one song from *Goodbye Yellow Brick Road*, I hear something different about it. I don't just hear it the way I once did. I notice new things, some good, some bad, some just amusing. But it never fails to awaken something inside me that in a very basic way led me to embrace music as a way to both prolong my youth and grow up way too fast.

And *Goodbye Yellow Brick Road* really does contain the building blocks for so much of what became my own musical aesthetic. It's hardwired into my brain in a way that very few other records will ever be. We all go through formative stages in our lives when colors are just a bit brighter, emotions just a bit more extreme, sensations just a bit more intense, and our guards come down just a bit more than we'd normally allow. I think that's what people mean when they say, "This is our song." I'm not talking about people who just feel that they *have* to have their own song just to be romantic because, you know, being romantic means having your own song. I'm talking about that song that accidentally becomes an intangible but very real bond between two people, maybe because you were a little drunk one night and you got your wife to sing it with you while you played the guitar. And then, she cried when you thought to play it a year later at your own wedding. A song like that is just locked into place. There's no changing the role it's played in your life or the associations that will forever be attached to it. All you can hope is that it's not a crappy song.

Goodbye Yellow Brick Road is, very fortunately, not a crappy record. It's not perfect by any means. And that's really part of what's imbued it with a resonance that I just can't shake. I'm not sure what the perfect album sounds like. But I have a feeling I wouldn't like it very much. Because, somewhere in the grooves— and at one point there really were grooves in my copy of *Goodbye Yellow Brick Road*—of one silly little double album that I spent my mom's cash on as a kid, there are reflections and refractions of my own imperfections, my own overindulgences, and my own sense of amusement at the ways of our oh-so-fucked-up world. It's an album that's an escape back to the innocence of my childhood, but also a wake-up call to the realities of the moment. But, mostly, it's an escape—an escape into a place that's continued to evolve ever since I first heard "Goodbye Yellow Brick Road" or "Saturday Night's Alright For Fighting" on the radio. If that unreachable place ever loses its connection with *Goodbye Yellow Brick Road*, well, then I guess I'll be done with the record.

But the real beauty of finding an album that can follow you through life is that its meaning and relevance continue to evolve along with you, even as it remains locked in a time period that will always be part of you. You know, it's like the grey seal. You want his wisdom. You want to see the world through his eyes. And then you realize that seals really aren't all that bright. I've seen killer whales fool them into coming close enough to the water's edge to be eaten. And I've seen polar bears snack on unwitting seals more than a few times on the Discovery Channel. So, I doubt very much that there's a grey seal out there who's got much wisdom to offer. But there's always the song. And the song always seems to strike a chord no matter how many documentaries on seals I manage to see. So I'm sticking with my *Yellow Brick Road*.

14

DIO
Anthology
Connoisseur
Collection, 1997

BY ANTHONY MICCIO

FORGIVE ME IF I'M TAKING THIS ALL TOO LITERALLY, BUT THERE'S NO WAY I'D WANT TO HEAR MOST OF MY FAVORITE ALBUMS IF I WERE STUCK ON FARAWAY SAND for the rest of my life. I'm plucking coconuts, wondering if I'll ever see my friends or family again, let alone a Wawa's. So why would I want to hear "Answering Machine" by the Replacements? The emotional pop-metal peaks of the last four decades (Desaparecidos' *Read Music/Speak Spanish*, Weezer's *Pinkerton*, the Replacements' *Let It Be* and Neil Young's *Rust Never Sleeps*, in case you've forgotten) have gotten me through the highs and lows of human interaction, but they're just not suited for tropical isolation.

I'd need something long, so no thirty-minute bits of beauty I'll wear out in a week. No REM's *Reckoning* or *Zoso*. I also wouldn't want anything that would make me miss what I don't have— AC/DC or Electric Six full-lengths will just remind me of the

other classics left behind. If I had my unfettered druthers, I'd probably ask for *It's Hotter Than Hawaii*, a boxed set of over one hundred beach-ready ukulele-festooned standards I've never heard
before. But according to the editor, box sets are cheating, and besides, it'd be hard to wax poetic about unknown audio here. So
what's needed is a long compilation of music I'm familiar with
that's inspiring without being too connected to human life as I
know it.

So I guess I'll go with *Anthology* by Dio, which I found sans lin-
ers in a used CD store on South Street in Philly sometime in 2004.
It has SEE INLAY FOR DETAILS on the disc and a London address on the back, so I'm guessing it's a promo import. It covers
the first four albums, only sharing half of its tracks with *The Very
Beast Of Dio* (someday I'll download "Mystery," "King Of Rock &
Roll," "Sacred Heart," "Hungry For Heaven," "Rock & Roll Children," "Man On The Silver Mountain (live)," "Dream Evil," "Lock
Up The Wolves," and "Strange Highways") and five of its tracks
don't show up on the double disc *Stand Up And Shout: The Dio Anthology*, so I can say with fair certainty that *Anthology* is a unique
experience.

For those not in the know, Dio is the musical vessel on which
Ronnie James Dio, a decrepit, elfin wailer who replaced Ozzy Osbourne in Black Sabbath, has ridden for the last twenty-five years.
His operatic howl, crisp enunciation, dramatic flair, and penchant
for referencing rainbows (and this *after* he fronted a band *named*
Rainbow) would make him a metal legend even if he didn't resemble a stoner Gollum. While he's unafraid of the synth, and
made a few crossover attempts in his mid-80s heyday (he even
wrote "We Are All Rainbows" for Hear'N'Aid, metal's answer to

"We Are The World"), there's never been any fear that he won't be considered metal, even as acts before and after him shift into the market of "hard rock" and "true" metal becomes the sole property of jackhammers vomiting gravel. For, as I said, he looks like a stoner Gollum.

Frankly, metal-metal (as opposed to pop-metal) doesn't work for me much in the real world. Fewer girls, more references to tanks, more songs from the tank's point of view, more songs that sound like tanks, more vocals that sound like somebody flipping a trash compactor on and off, more guitarists playing intricate blitzes while the drummer either doesn't play or plays all parts of the kit at the same time. If you've got any boogie or melody, you're only as metal as you dress, and even then you're not "brutal" enough for diehards. John fucking Bonham, Led Zep's late tubthumper, a motorcycle enthusiast and unquestionable badass, found Deep Purple and Black Sabbath too monochromatic and plodding for his time, so jeez louise, you know he'd have zero interest in Cystic Whatthefuckever, no matter how many pimply longhairs young and old told him about how metal has "evolved." So why the hell should I worry about *my* willingness to appreciate the shit?

And while every genre has humorless, defensive guardians who wish everybody understood why their sound's profound, metal's are the most infuriating. They claim to be getting off on verbal violence, ear-splitting chaos—the most oppressive, the most *intentionally* oppressive music outside of *Artforum*—and you're bummed that people don't *respect* it? You should laugh in my face, firebomb the nearest car, stab and/or fuck some trailer trash, and invade Poland! What the fuck do you care if Rock Critic No. 3223 digs Slayer: The Pierced Generation? If you're going to dig metal, be a tank! Justify the audio beatdown as cathartic by not being such a lame-ass, self-pitying bitch. At least Morrissey takes it out on himself.

But alone on some godforsaken rock, far from the people that make life worth living and hit power ballads personally poignant, I think Dio's Viking style would take on an unprecedented power. One doesn't imagine oneself as a magical gremlin straight through middle age without suffering a certain degree of solitary anguish. As I wander throughout my island, searching for co-conuts and hoping to spot the distant lights of a passing barge, I'll want to hear—if anything—the sound of a man who deals in heroic grandiosities. Ain't no way "Sister Ray" is gonna mean shit when the typhoon comes and I'm clinging to a palm tree for dear life. I'll need something hardcore! But with a melody.

"Holy Diver" opens with ominous, whistling wind, something I'll be very familiar with, before the guitars slam to attention, sig-nifying the arrival of the lone warrior, the solitary knight, aka *me.* "Holy Diver, you've been out too long in the midnight sea. Oh, what's becoming of me?" (Unless I've been able to make a knife out of flint rock, I'll probably have some scraggly long-ass beard and quickly discover just how long the hair on the back of my head can grow. Not only am I balding at the front, but the surviv-ing remnants of my once-glorious mop have a tendency to stick straight out, so I'll probably wind up with some hideous, post-electrocution Art Garfunkel 'do.)

"Ride the tiger! You can see his stripes but you know he's clean. Oh, can't you see what I mean?" While the presence of a tiger on the island would be frightening, if I survived our initial encounters, I'd desire to befriend the proud beast, and as we became comfortable with each other's presence, I would take advantage of his domestication by attempting to ride him. There probably wouldn't be much else to do.

"Between the velvet lies, there's a truth that's hard as steel. The vision never dies; life's a never ending wheel." One of the few benefits of this extremely solitary life would be the opportunity to experience a life free of the decadent and stultifying aspects of capitalist society. I would learn to survive *with* nature, rather than benefiting from its slow destruction at the hands of those who govern and provide for me, and neither would I have to passively abstain from the looting of Gaia, like some bookstore vegan—the offending culture would simply fail to exist. "Holy Diver" would ring of truth rather than ridiculous fantasy.

But with adventure comes danger, and "Rainbow In The Dark" delves into the emotional taxation that would follow. "When there's lightning, it always bring me down. 'Cause it's free and I see that it's me who's lost and never found." I wonder at what point the marveling at and fearing of nature would turn into envy. I never saw the movie *Cast Away*, but supposedly Tom Hanks starts treating a volleyball like a human companion. While my current life is fairly humble and bohemian, I've got enough imperialist drive in me that, when placed in a more primal terrain, I'd like to think I'd aim higher than Hanks did, imagining myself as an imprisoned God who must subjugate nature, though with Ted Nugent–like respect and communion. I'd rather do that than anthropomorphize a piece of sports equipment.

"I cry for magic! I feel it dancing in the light. But it was cold; I lost my hold to the shadows of the night." Though I lack the scientific

knowledge to craft a working sundial, I assume I'd begin to inter-
nalize the length of a day, and that the arrival of night wouldn't
surprise me. But what if I awoke at night, cold and afraid? Would
there be any way to tell when the sun would rise again? "There's
no sign of the morning coming. You've been left on your own, like
a rainbow in the dark."

While I like to think I'd abandon the regrets and memories that
I occasionally dwell on before sleep (if you've accepted your time
on the island as permanent, the past is of little importance), it's
possible that, in a pique of self-pity and mourning for my former
life, I would obsess about earlier failings. "Do your demons . . . do
they ever let you go? When you've tried, do they hide deep inside?
Is it someone that you know?" And even if I realize the worthless-
ness of this agonizing, hours of extreme darkness may lead to a
deep, almost suicidal sense of futility.

"You're a picture—just an image caught in time. We're a lie,
you and I. We're words without a rhyme." "Rainbow In The
Dark" may be a midget's metaphor for a life of D&D fantasy he'll
never achieve despite his vocal chops and leprechaunish stature,
but the existential pleas for freedom would be comforting and
cathartic as I try to sleep through a lonely night. Plus, unlike most
songs about long nights, he doesn't bring up girls. I'll be pining for
sexual companionship plenty without musical encouragement.

The inspirational kabooms of "Stand Up And Shout" should
prove a handy reminder that I need never follow rules again, but
its true value comes from Dio's almost orgasmic urgings: "You've
got desire—so let it out! You are the fire! Go on, explode!" Those
will help when I'm feeling skittish about humping trees or deciding which flora-derived faux-orifice feels best when squooshed

against my erogenous zones. (I refuse to believe I'll ever be reduced to bestiality, but I'll have no qualms about creating some sort of a banana-skin pump.)

I probably won't play "Straight Through The Heart" much, as it's not only a bit draggy beatwise, but I'm also not even sure what he's singing about. Something about how you should never tell the truth with your eyes because then it gets you straight through the heart. Even if the message became clear under further scrutiny, I doubt it would be worth applying in any *Marooned* scenario. The proud, apocalyptic metaphors of "The Last In Line" seem handier, but couplets like "We're all born upon the cross— the throw before the toss. You can release yourself, but the only way you go is down" are too Biblical for my tastes. Unless the Gideons get to the island first and leave me some reading material under a palm tree, I won't have much desire to think of my situation in that context.

Naturalistic spirituality seems more appealing for island meditation than the Judeo-Christian brand, so it's a shame that English-language rock music doesn't provide quality script of that fashion. The voices of neither Jim Morrison nor Ian Astbury, despite their aspirations for shamanhood, would be appreciated, aside from maybe "Fire Woman" and "She Sells Sanctuary" for spirit-restoring dance and maybe a few extended jams from a Doors live album as soundtrack during an unseemly binge of grapefruit fucking. It'd be a more erotic background than Dio's "One Night In The City," which starts out promisingly with Johnny the Dark Child meeting Sally the Princess during "one night in the city, one night looking pretty," but the song climaxes with an awkward "the children shared the wonder of the leather and the lace, but one child went away and one child stayed to play." Morrison's poetry isn't any less awkward, but at least you get endless blurts of Ray Manzarek's baby-elephant organ in between.

At first "We Rock," with its us vs. them triumphalism, may seem a little trite and gratuitous, but try reading up on Alexander Serkirk, the castaway who inspired Robert Louis Stevenson's *Robinson Crusoe*. This guy had to domesticate and sleep beside feral cats to keep rats from feeding on him at night. "They come for killing. They leave and still it seems, the cloud that's left behind, oh, can penetrate your mind. But sail on! Sing a song! Carry on! We Rock! We Rock! We Rock! We Rock!" Sounds like the perfect theme song for a night of watching my feisty felines pounce on vermin. A lot of people think they rock just because they bought the T-shirt, watch *Headbanger's Ball,* and occasionally piss on a wall, but it won't be until I've trained wild animals to be my guardians in the dark that I'll identify with this song in the truest, most fulfilling sense. There's no question that those cats will rock, too. Selkirk read the Bible to help keep his sanity, but even if I was doing likewise, I doubt I'd want to listen to Dio sing about Moses and "Egypt (The Chains Are On)" over a turgid, metronomic "Holy Diver" rewrite. Plus there are lyrics about people walking on the sea and sailing away as "each day you hear the sand as it moves and whispers." That imagery would probably inspire me to do something stupid like tie some branches together and see how far a shitty raft could take me. Even then, I'd probably turn the song off and start making that raft well before the gradual fade-out at six minutes thirty.

"Shoot Shoot" is probably swinging enough for Paul Stanley to do his foxy strut to, which in Dio's world makes the song "Jungle

Boogie." The message of being "free forever—I don't care! Anywhere!" is fine, but it's the modicum of shuffle that I'll appreciate,
giving me something to practice my calisthenics to, as I imagine
the montage in which my weak, doughy body takes on a svelte,
perhaps even buff form through weeks of jogging, crunches,
push-ups, rat hockey, and starvation.

Of all the tracks on *Anthology*, "Time to Burn" is the one most
worthy of being My Jam. Triumphant in a manner that's less Wag-
nerian and more Loverboyish, Dio recorded the track on a live EP
to represent his new band between albums, and you can hear the
pride. "Someone told me I would never be free—the way you are
is the way you'll always be. But it's all wrong, there's time to burn.
Hurt is on the pleasure wheel, but you can't hurt if you can't feel.
And you can feel! You've got something to learn. You've got time
to burn." True that! I'm looking at the most beautiful skylines of
my life, surrounded by nature, in great shape—I've got time to
burn! As long as I still giggle when he shouts "when the wolf is
loose in the city, the city will fight to survive," I'll know I haven't
lost my tether on reality. I'll go exploring! Try some amateur car-
tography! Learn how to whittle! I'll make clothes out of goatskin,
like Selkirk did! The chance to fashion a new life out of raw materials is one that should be appreciated with a flourish of power
chord and piercing shriek. Maybe I'll make myself a cape!

"All The Fools Sailed Away" is another sea-related track I'd be
wise to avoid, but "I Could Have Been A Dreamer," while equally
unhealthy, would qualify as a guilty pleasure. "Running with the
wolf pack, feels like I'm never coming back. And every time
there's sunshine, I'm blind. I am everybody, and everybody I know
is me. Everyone that I know won't see . . . I could have been a

dreamer. I could have been a shooting star. I could have been a dreamer." Deep shit. The wolf pack could apply to both the "real world" rat race and the attacking animals I have to bludgeon in order to survive on the island, so it's really a "grass is greener on the other side" plaint. I'll think of the women I could have touched, the movies I could have seen, the albums I could have written blurbs about, the catchphrases I could have heard, the friends I could have remembered the catchphrases with over alcohol, the headlines I could have been made nervous by, and all the other glories I won't get to enjoy now that it's only me, my goatskin loincloth, my pack of warrior cats, and Dio. It's possible I may not be sardonic about the routine of my bourgeois life if it was replaced by a primal environment. After all, I have a loving family, tasty food, and all sorts of toys. But I figure that if I don't conquer my newfound territory and learn to adapt to the situation, I'll probably die in extreme agony within the first week, probably from the rats or dehydration. So there's no point in crying for the populated world. But . . . but . . . "but maybe that was sunshine that I saw. . . . "

If I'm still feeling emo after "Dreamer," I can let the CD play on into "Sunset Superman," where the man who popularized throwing horns yells about a troubled dude who "moves in only places where the eyes can never be," "trying to hide his burning heart before somebody cuts it all away." It's an incoherent crock of bullshit, but the verses swarm as much as the chorus plods, with the drums shifting into a "We Will Rock You" break during the solo. Good music for when I've gone completely apeshit, throwing my cats against trees just to hear their cries, covering my face in blood, and dancing naked on the beach. As I moan to

God for relief and tear at my own skin, it will be good to have Dio drop some wicked self-mythology over brutal beats. I'll jack that shit up to ten on my magical CD player too, 'cause fuck if I care if the neighbors can hear. And if Dio is worried about the possibility that I'll get tinnitus, he can just send agents of Hear'N'Aid via Red Cross helicopter.

Hypothetically, despite my improved physique, oneness with the animal kingdom, and freedom from the confines of American society, I may grow tired of life, deciding to jump off a high cliff or throw rocks at the tigers and see how they react. If I do reach this dismal breaking point, "Shame On The Night" will be my closing volley before the jukebox reverts to pixie dust and flits back to Greil Marcus's bag of miracles. "Shame on the night: for places I've been and what I've seen, for giving me the strangest dreams, but you never really know just what they mean. So, oh, shame on the night." As I approach the precipice, no hope imaginable, wondering for what possible reason we're given intelligence if experience isn't reward enough, I'll stare straight into the worthless sun, spitefully cursing existence itself, as Dio cries "Shame on the sun: for the light you sold. I've lost my hold on the magic flame, but now I know your name. Oh lord, just go the way you came again. Oh, shame on the night!" You could say this is nothing but ersatz nihilism, but anything else from a rock critic stranded in the Pacific would be delusional.

15

THE METERS
The Meters
Josie, 1969

By Jeff Chang

HE THING ABOUT NEW ORLEANS MUSIC IS THAT AL-
MOST ANY CLAIM MADE ON ITS BEHALF COULD BE
TRUE. TAKE THIS ONE. JAZZ WAS MADE IN NEW OR-
leans," says hot-boy-turned-hip-hop-elder Juvenile. "Rap itself
started in New Orleans. People think it came from the East Coast
or the West Coast. But it didn't, it came from New Orleans. Everybody in New Orleans knows that."

Why not? The Mardi Gras Indians might have been the original
b-boys. They rode so deep they made you stare or follow. They
gave each other ill titles like Big Chief and Spyboy, called themselves names like Wild Tchoupitoulas, Wild Magnolias, and Co-
manche Hunters. They fussed year-round to make sure their gear
looked the flyest. They protected their flags like territory. And
they rolled block-to-block looking for other gangs to battle, spitting rhymes about how they'd never bow down.

The words were only half the story, or less. They needed a
beat to go. (And anyway, writing about music by obsessing over

lyrics is like talking rain and forgetting the clouds.) To flip Jay Cocks's script, rap was the magnetic part, the part that made somebody/anybody/everybody scream. The fun was all in the funk, the breaks that by themselves sounded calls and demanded responses. And in the beginning, down in New Orleans, they funked the finest.

Historians might date funk to the moment in 1967 when Los Angeles's Dyke and the Blazers syncopated down "Funky Broadway," or perhaps two years before that, when James Brown broke it down on "Papa's Got A Brand New Bag." Mid-60s Bronx-style *bugalu*—with its bang-bang horn stabs and exuberant dances bursting out of the wedding party of *montuno* and Memphis—was just as important. Funk came from both the sound of North American blues adapting to the herky-jerky pulse of the swelling cities, and the sound of Afro-Latin and Afro-Caribbean polyrhythms percolating up from the global South.

When the two came together, history shot forward. As 1977 was to punk and 1982 was to hip-hop, 1970 was to funk. Sly Stone's "Thank You Falettinme Be Mice Elf Agin" and "Everybody Is A Star." The Art Ensemble of Chicago's "Theme De Yo Yo" and "Bye Bye Baby." Rufus Thomas's "Funky Penguin" and "The Breakdown." King Floyd's "Groove Me." Donny Hathaway's "The Ghetto." Curtis Mayfield's "Move On Up." Funkadelic's self-titled album, and *Free Your Mind And Your Ass Will Follow*. David Axelrod's *Earth Rot*. Eddie Palmieri's *Harlem River Drive*. Santana's *Abraxas*. Jimi's *Band of Gypsys*. In the middle of it all, in hottest July, two monsters: James Brown with his precociously, ferociously talented new band, the JBs, cutting a new version of "Give It Up Or Turnit A Loose," cross-fading four-on-the-floor funk with three-two clavé, and Bootsy Collins, Johnny Griggs, and Clyde Stubblefield bridging North and South in the break. And the Meters' *second* paradigm-shattering album, *Look-Ka Py-Py*.

Funk picked up where *bugalu* and rhythm and blues left off. It was a recovery and visioning project. Rhythms locked away during the Middle Passage and isolated by slavery and racism across the diaspora were released for a reunion-turned-celebration: the pulse of the streets of Havana, San Juan, Sao Paolo, funky Nassau, Port-Au-Prince, Port of Spain, Santo Domingo, Kingston, San Francisco, the Bronx, Augusta, the clavé and the soul-beat coupling and layering at accelerating rates, reviving a carnival consciousness at the level of muscle memory and spirit dance. Funk was Black unity projected back into the global city.

But what the rest of the world caught up to in 1970 had been going on in New Orleans, a mainline vortex for the Africanized New World, for at least a century, where rhythms like calypso, rumba, junkanoo, mambo, samba, and reggae joined the blues. They all came together in the second line, the funeral march's second procession, with people singing and playing and drumming a passed soul's return home. The process was open, a foundational chant and meter at the center, everyone else getting in where they fit in, a dynamic, democratic architecture of rhythms providing as many ways to be inhabited as there were players to build it. On Mardi Gras Day, the liveliest of death's street pageants, the Indians led the most traditional of second-line parades. Dressed in boldly colored, hand-sewn costumes and masks, Mardi Gras Indian gangs brought lightning and thunder, shouted about how bad they were and the greatness of their fallen comrades. The world opened, and rhythms gathered like spirits.

"It was something you looked forward to seeing. Pan drums, tambourines, cowbells, and bottles. It's tribal in one way, but in another way, it's also pretty high-tech," said Meters drummer Joseph "Zigaboo" Modeliste. "It was definitely a percussive culture. Now I just happened to be born there." In 1965, the year that the 13th Ward boys who became Meters first began playing together, the Dixie Cups brought the second line, clavé and all, to the top of the pop charts with a sticks-and-chants version of Sugar Boy Crawford's Mardi Gras Indian adaptation, "Iko Iko." New Orleans music was South and North, tribal and futuristic, pop and vanguard, all at the same time. Small wonder that a half-decade later, Modeliste, Art Neville, George Porter Jr., and Leo Nocentelli, who had known nothing but this musical world, and so were worldly beyond all imagining, sounded like prophets.

In 1969, they recorded over a dozen three-minute marvels of rhythm and color, including all the songs on their self-titled debut and a handful more that would be released on *Look-Ka Py-Py*. The effect was immediate. Before the year was out, Motown's Funk Brothers cribbed Nocentelli and Porter's bottom lock for the Jackson 5's "I Want You Back," then took the sideways–Bo Diddley ride-or-die second line of "Here Comes The Meter Man" and the karate-kick intro from "Cissy Strut" to build a breakdown for "ABC." Legend has it that Pretty Purdie gave Miles Davis and his band copies of Meters records to study before they went in to record *Bitches Brew*. Even Booker T. & The MGs, once the Meters' model, tacked southward from orthodox bluesy funk to the wideopen Latinized groove of "Melting Pot," a vector continuing forward to Lonnie Liston Smith's "Expansions," Babe Ruth's "The

Mexican," and the Jimmy Castor Bunch's "It's Just Begun." The Meters didn't just create classic break records—a stunningly large portion of the breakbeat canon is unimaginable without them.

They must have sounded mysterious, uproarious, and seductive, all at the same time. When Jay Cocks wrote that Bobby Marchan's crazed chant on Huey "Piano" Smith's "Don't You Just Know It"—"Ah ha ha ha, hey-ey yo, gooba gooba gooba!"—sounds "like a gang of twisted Masons shouting a password," he might have also captured what the next generation of white musicians heard from Black NOLA musicians. The Who swiped the Dixie Cups for "Magic Bus," but the Meters would become the musical brown sugar for Paul McCartney, Lowell George, and especially Mick Jagger and Keith Richards. Connect the dots from "Meter Man" and "ABC" to "Sympathy For The Devil." Just maybe, the Meters kept all of rock from sucking in the '70s. In 1971, John Bonham put his drum kit into a deep stairwell to approximate Modeliste's lumberjack snare and canyon-sized kick for "When The Levee Breaks." With outsized world heroes like Jorge Ben, Juan Formell, Mulatu Astatqé, and Fela Anikulapo-Kuti, the funk went 360.

The cover of *The Meters* featured measuring devices—rulers, a barometer, a scale, a compass, a sextant, and at the center, a metronome and clocks, metaphors for the diversity and multidirectionality of their rhythms, and above all, a tribute to the musicians' extraordinarily complicated relationship to time. In a sense, the band's music embodied New Orleans in the last half of the twentieth century: time running out, a city declining through political abandonment, a singular cultural space so central in globalizing

America, in producing magnificent art beyond the constraints of time, and yet so valueless in the present that it would be forced into physical abandonment.

From the time of *Brown v. Board of Education* through the Civil Rights Act of 1964, the hits of Little Richard, Fats Domino, Lee Dorsey, Ernie K-Doe, and many more had helped bring down America's racial Jericho. But all the liberation they gave their fervent white fans couldn't save sweet Sugar Boy Crawford from being beaten like Bop on his way to a gig in Monroe, left paralyzed in a hospital bed, awaiting outrageous charges of drunk driving. The Meters were four children of segregation, alive in the rhythms of the secret old world. But they were also set free to hammer out the contours of a new one. Around them, the world would pivot from the American century into a global millennium.

The essence of New Orleans music has always been its private codes and languages, the inner worlds of sound that organized the villages of Africa, were dispersed in the Americas by the horrid strictures of slavery, and were once again available to Crescent City kids as a birth-inheritance. Art Neville, the founder of the Meters, was the eldest of the most famous Uptown musical family. At least a decade older than the other three band members, he came of age as New Orleans artists pulled North American pop south bar by bar, measure for measure, accent by accent, from the top of the charts. His first hit, 1954's "Mardi Gras Mambo" (its nod to Havana repaid decades later by Jesus Alemany's ¡Cubanismo!) simply made the shift explicit.

Around the time the Civil Rights Act was passed, Neville recruited three kids to back up himself, and his brothers, Aaron and Cyril. Guitarist Leo Nocentelli, bassist George Porter Jr., and Modeliste were each intimately familiar with the city's great musicians— life-guides through an Afrodiasporic universe of rhythm, melody, and sound—not to mention each other. Cyril's best friend was Modeliste. Modeliste and Porter were cousins, Nocentelli a childhood and family friend. When the band's gig stage literally shrunk, Art's brothers found themselves out of the band, and the Meters were suddenly a vocal-less unit.

In their intensely competitive high school music programs, the three teens had blossomed, and under Neville's tutelage, they entered the world of the city's working musicians. One day, Modeliste was studying Smokey Johnson's monstrous drumming on Professor Longhair's forty-five single, "Big Chief," the next he was by the bandstand, youth work permit in his pocket, studying his new mentor in action. Nocentelli was tapped by Allen Toussaint to back and write for Lee Dorsey before he was old enough to legally drink.

As the fires of 1968 began, the Meters were one of the only Black bands playing on Bourbon Street. But the scene was changing. Eight hours a night, six nights a week, they performed Booker T. & The MGs, Stax, and pop covers, oddball local hits like Roger and The Gypsies' "Pass The Hatchet," and sinewy originals at an integrated club called the Ivanhoe. They saw their audiences go from being all-white to mixed. If "rock" had by now, with perhaps the great exception of Jimi Hendrix, become rhetorically and socially white—"soul" its separate, sometimes equal counterpart— the Meters were in the first swell of the sea change that pulled American music back toward a global Blackness. They would anticipate the post-Motown racial crossover, the success of Santana, Bob Marley, and Run-D.M.C.

Those long, ecstatic nights at the Ivanhoe gave them an un-canny ability to read, even anticipate each other. They nurtured a bebop band's virtuosity, but balanced it with a dance band's func-tionality, and developed the kind of efficiency and chemistry that separates championship teams from the rest. "We thought as one person," says Porter. "We used to do things that were scary." On songs like "Cardova," they redefined The One, fitted together like pieces of a puzzle, complicated. Porter and Nocentelli doubled up on a dubwise throb. Modeliste scribbled percussive haiku. Neville added punctuation. Nocentelli's solos were both ornate and eco-nomic. With space, balance, and brevity, everyone shined in their own spotlight.

Unlike the MGs, which remained unquestionably Booker's band, the Meters sounded like—that is, through their first breakup in 1971—a leaderless crew, four the hard way. Nocentelli was the melodic engine, casually spinning out colorful bolts of ideas, hint-ing at the range of each song's latent possibilities. On their cover of Sly Stone's "Sing a Simple Song," his bracing licks in the bridge suggested something much more complicated. Neville, though ca-pable of a bold lead as on the galloping "Art," mainly added struc-ture and complementary colors.

Modeliste offered a propulsive, idiosyncratic minimalism. "A lot of times I was letting the music *breathe*, and just wasn't sticking to the same backbeat all the time like all the rest of the music was so uniformly put together," he said. On "6V6LA," he turned a mono-chromatic vamp into a jaw-dropping workout of cymbal and snare, with an eyebrow raise to Eddie Bo's drummer James Black and his sensational stickwork on "The Hook and Sling, Part 2." By contrast, Memphis drummers like Al Jackson Jr. and Willie Hall sounded rigid, even formal.

With characteristic humility, Porter once said, "I think my part in Zig's life is to get as close to his heartbeat as I can. That's my job as a bass player, I am supposed to make him make sense to everyone else." But his indispensable, endlessly inventive bottom sealed the Meters' funk. On "Livewire," the band's showcase tune, Modeliste recut Johnson's "Big Chief" beat like DJ Premier at an SP–1200, and with a succinct, meaty bassline, Porter converted the massive break into a vehicle for Nocentelli and Neville to drop explosive solos.

Toussaint signed them up as his house band, had them back Dorsey and Betty Harris, LaBelle, and himself, and brought them into bed with Sansu Enterprises's Marshall Sehorn, the start of another lost-royalty tragedy that ultimately sunk the band. (The game show–styled throwaway, "Sehorn's Farm," was a contract-slavery in-joke that quickly lost its humor.) But it became clear soon enough that what they were creating in their all-day-all-night sessions at Sea-Saint Studios wasn't just stuff for a singer to wail over. In 1969, Toussaint and Sehorn released "Sophisticated Cissy" and found themselves on a runaway train. They cut a deal with New York indie Josie Records to distribute the single and watched it reach *Billboard*'s R&B Top 10.

Written by Nocentelli, the song wasn't even a dance tune. It was a bluesy crawl turned into a display of purpose and control. It might have been a performance about setting up a performance, like a gentleman's club dancer primping before she goes onstage—Porter's bass rumbling like the diva to her makeup table, Modeliste's drums feeling every pimple and wrinkle, Neville's organ throwing strobes on her practiced, mirrored poses, Nocentelli's guitar commenting sarcastically on the whole scene. There was a sense of knowingness about it, almost an understanding that all the color, the masking, and the pomp exerted not a small cost.

New Orleans has always presented itself as being about taking care of the guest—"When you go to New Orleans," Professor Longhair sang, "you gotta go see the Mardi Gras," as if it were being staged only for the visitors' benefit—but "Sophisticated Cissy" seems instead to shift the spotlight to the dignity and pride of the host. This is the direction African American pop music has moved toward over the past century, the arc from Motown to Def Jam, the reversal of the crossover from Berry Gordy's Black-to-white to Rick Rubin's white-to-Black. Why wouldn't the hip-hop generation—with its first-person fixation and its personalized concerns with redress—be drawn to the Meters?

As punk exploded in London and hip-hop enjoyed its first (unrecorded) "golden era," the Meters split up, after transforming popular music as thoroughly as earlier generations of New Orleans musicians had. They expected not much more than to be forgotten, the fate of a cult band, a secret knowledge. When the clocks started showing up again—now around the necks of a new generation, stopped at 11:55, representing their urgent, combustible mix of apocalyptic pessimism and shut-'em-down idealism—it was time for the Meters to be rediscovered.

Modeliste was living in Los Angeles during the late '80s. One day, he turned on pioneering hip-hop radio station KDAY and was surprised to hear himself back on the radio. James Brown signified Black and proud and East Coast, not to mention generational difference, as in Stetsasonic's Daddy-O's pro-sampling manifesto, "Talking All That Jazz": "Tell the truth James Brown was old, 'til Eric and Ra came out with 'I Got Soul.'" But the Meters tended to inspire eccentric, liberating, often visionary performances.

Ultramagnetic MCs' "Ease Back," for instance, was driven by a reversed sample of Robert McCollough's famous whistling sax solo from The JBs' "The Grunt," DJ Moe Love's chopped, pitched-up break mimicking Modeliste's stop-and-go metronome, and Art Neville's money shot from *Look-Ka Py-Py*'s "Little Old Money-maker" inserted by producer Paul C., the John Bonham of his time, into the chorus. It was a no-gravity track, speeding in its orbit, perfect for Ced Gee and Kool Keith's abstract braggadocio. West Coast heads, from Dr. Dre to Cut Chemist and DJ Shadow, were particularly enamored of the Meters. The most loopy may have been DJ Pooh, who first added "Cissy Strut" to King Tee's 1987 single "The Coolest," and built much of his sound around the Meters aesthetic. Back then, using the Meters to ratify one's freshness was odd, but Tee and later Public Enemy (on "Timebomb," which sampled 1974's "Just Kissed My Baby") and Marley Marl (on Heavy D's "Gyrlz They Love Me," from *Look-Ka Py-Py*'s "Thinking") made it seem natural. As both Robert Farris Thompson and Fab Five Freddy have noted, the defining and redefining of coolness was itself an ancient Black art.

The Meters' music would, of course, eventually become raw material for hundreds, if not thousands, of hip-hop tracks. The band members, with the wounded humility of sidemen, still believe it was because the tracks seemed unfinished, grooves in search of a front person, a human voice to stamp them with capital-"I" importance. In fact, all of the songs on *The Meters*—not to mention most of the next two Josie albums—were entirely self-contained, didn't need anything else. They were coherent, pleasing, and nearly impossible to imitate. Like an Eames chair, not a line on a song like "Ease Back" was out of place. Another element might have tipped the whole thing over.

Modeliste once described the songs as "soundbites," as "entries of different grooves and different ideas about grooves." Indeed, they could fill a jam-band encyclopedia, hundreds of little ideas that could each be stretched out like twenty-minute rubber bands. From a hip-hop head's point of view, Meters songs were endlessly divisible. You could break them down to their most basic elements— filter in Porter's supple bass, capture Neville's splashy chords, wrangle a quivering Nocentelli line—and then break those pieces down again. They were as accessible and desirable to fakebook craftspeople possessed of artisan taste as untutored cut-and-stitch kids who had just come up on a little technology.

Way down below it all was Modeliste's crafty playing—unexpected, improvised doubled hits, crashes, and rolls, often not where they were supposed to be, but always where they needed to be, cool about getting back to the one, always on their own time, the sound of a thoroughly human heart thumping its uniquely strange rhythm. Following Modeliste through a song can make you hear the world differently, subtly reorient your entire personal sound-scape. But the truth is, each of us has grown up in a world like the Meters'—one large and rich in its sonic relations, one that awaits all the connections to be made. Too often, we just don't hear them yet. Maybe that's why Black music always tends to sound futuristic.

The older the Meters got, the more literally they sketched out their influences—calypso, high-life, reggae, mambo—unpacking on their Reprise albums all that they had done so instinctually on those first three Josie records. This is not to say—some have, but not me—that the albums they did after 1971 were the lesser for it. We should find virtue in exploring the roots and branches outward, diminishing false differences and divisions, and confronting a North American pop aesthetic that remains so jingoistic, devaluing, and destructive. Instead it is to say that sometimes the stuff that seems the simplest is really the most complex.

"Cissy Strut," the Meters' first big hit from that bright spring of 1969, is that simple song. But it's played for more than it's worth, with what Rufus Thomas called "the push and pull." Nocentelli, Neville, and Porter push the song forward. Modeliste does the pulling. Armed with a hurricane of hi-hat accents, he seems to be channeling an entire second line. At the center of the storm, you can hear him moaning like Monk and getting hit in his soul like Mingus. Generations of kids with their cheap samplers and freeware await over the horizon, to put that ghost in their machines, set it free in the circuitry. In New Orleans, old rhythms, like the funky old spirits, never die. They just keep on marching, all around the worlds we come to know and the others we may.

16

STEPHEN STILLS
Manassas
Atlantic, 1972

By Kandia Crazy Horse

For Craig Street

"More than even that of the American Indian, the consciousness of vast sections of our black women lies beyond the boundaries of the modern world, though they live and work in that world daily."
—Richard Wright

"Man is born free, and everywhere he is in chains."
—Jean-Jacques Rousseau

ELECTRIC PURGATORY: A PHONOGRAPHY IN FOUR PARTS

The Raven

America the Beautiful—thy true name is poison. So goes my belief, for I was born under a bad sign with the Bluenote in my veins. Emerging into a circle where the view prevailed that Africans existing on the verge of postmodernity were inherent enemies of the American Nation-State probably was to blame. Not to mention an inherited vernacular of rich, yearning avian imagery and an unshakeable will to flight. Sho'nuff I've always had the blues, praying for transcendence via the mysterious power of amplified sound, grasping for some utopian refuge like most outlaws and expatriates. Yet unlike my era's greatest Afrindian brave, Jimi Hendrix, I have more often than not been an armchair gypsy, the Ezy Rider of interiors.

I got the blues, sunrise, noon, and twilight, perpetually hoping against hope that the Black Ark has finally swung low enough to let me ride. Turbulent on the tightrope between the Red House and the Red Road, I have needed a native scout to navigate the nation's perilous highways and culture wars. That liminal creature is sometimes the Janus icon of Duane and Gregg Allman, but even more often it is Stephen Stills. To these ears, the ax ethics and inner clarity of Texan Stills's mid-Atlantic blues crown him tall in the saddle. Stills's 1972 double opus *Manassas* tells the tall tales. The African and the European meet in perfect rapport in Stephen Stills's aesthetic. And they could meet nowhere else but America, so I am grateful in my bitterness for some semblance of sonic wings. How else to embark for the distant shores where the war-ring selves are reconciled?

My friend Patterson calls it "the duality of the Southern Thang." That most eminent black intellectual W.E.B. DuBois called it "double consciousness." As a downlow Dixie queen, I am aware of Brother Hood's duality and embody it. As a twentieth century–born Negress and premillennial product of ruthless modernism, I kept DuBois's version too. Yet I am far more than two-headed: a proto-Virginian more fey and earthy than Terrence Malick's wet dreams; a sometime exile tethered to the American Southland by six-string belief; a prim Victorian ghost swaying through the Western twilight; and a glitter-glam, genderless nightbird resident in pleasure and pure sound. And don't forget the Funk, so richly documented by my friend and colleague Ned Sublette, another Texas-born singer-songwriter, who dismissed this project as my "love letter to Stephen Stills." But I cannot share the disdain of my folk for certain sacred cows from their '60s youth. Being now a twenty first–century Pale Fox, a trickster without nation and no blood but purple, my self was fashioned when Hendrix and Richie Havens and Carlos Santana and Sly and Stills took the stage at Woodstock. These brave souls' location of the most dangerous and complex space where East and West, cosmic and subterranean, interior and exterior, shadow and light meet created an illusory highway for my itinerant spirit to make its pilgrimages.

Thus I am helpless but to respond to the mythic in classic rock and roll, the dreams, hopes, and dystopian nightmares of its best artists being mine. *Manassas* is a vital cure for the Invisibility Blues.

They say rock and roll is the devil's music. But they forget that Lucifer is the morning star, the bringer of light. Stephen Stills, the Cosmic Fiddler and canyon crier of *Manassas*, is the morning star of my pilgrim's progress, my North on my metaphorical flight to Canada. Said Niggers can't make it on wings, wheels, or steel . . . but there is Stills, in cowboy boots, at the station just down the road from my hometown Chocolate City. He's summoning the Night Train carrying the cautionary "Jet Set (Sigh)," the reinvigorating "Cuban Bluegrass," and the long-hoped-for utopia of "Colorado." With ghostly blood on the tracks 'neath the blue light, Stills gets what it is to be a stranger in a strange land.

Blues may seem to have faded away underground since Muddy Waters gone to Glory. But the Bluenote has stealthily entered the digital age. Lewis Taylor knows I ain't lyin'. The very cover of the British singer-songwriter's U.S. debut, *Stoned*, has Taylor floating in the Red House. And venerating the blue-eyed, Afro-Atlantic soul of Stephen Stills across all divides. As the daughter of snakes, I ain't so afraid of this dark side. Thus I can appreciate the so-called black magik of Taylor's complicated, biracial response to the '60s psych-pop moment. For Taylor and me both, space is the place.

THE WILDERNESS. They say no man is an island. But I am woman and I know better, if no longer resident upon not-so-fair Manahatta and trapped for now in the Carolina Piedmont. I never aspired to rockcritdom, and yet it must be that I became a critic from a tacit need to bear witness for Les Mystères buried within the meshes of amplified Afro-Celt sound. I have never been an actor, but instead one who rests uneasily on the margins, seeking the bridge between foreign—often irreconcilable—elements. I was born and have always existed betwixt and between, in the aquatic washes of Stills's "Move Around." Neither fish nor flesh, I *can* hear Atlantis full of cheer. . . .

The view from Africa-on-the-Potomac, from Little-Africa-on-the-Hudson and the majestic banks of the mighty Niger somehow meshed for me with the new America reconstructed by Stills and his peers in the '60s. I have long reached for it and fallen short. And so I understand the singing cowboy Stills who aspires to Electric Ladyland and finds instead that his liberation machine, the white Gretsch Falcon he plays on the lone live Manassas DVD (*The Best of Musikladen Live*, 1972), still tethers him to Electric Purgatory, Rocky Mountain refuge or no. He is the Anglo-American heir, to the manner born, the Golden Child nonetheless struggling for freedom and transcendence in the shadow of Watergate and star shine. In *Cross the Border—Close the Gap*, a book that dropped the same year as *Manassas*—1972—mythographer/critic Leslie Fiedler declared that "to be an American (unlike being English or French or whatever) is precisely to *imagine* a destiny rather than to inherit one; since we have always been, insofar as we are Americans at all, inhabitants of myth rather than history. . . . " Above all, Fiedler should have been referring to those Africans in the West who were the human spoil of the Triangular Trade. We the people who are darker than blue have been ruthlessly modern since our arrival upon these shores, forced to imagine brand-new worlds due to a violent separation from history and roots. Unlike the exogamous groups who toil here, we have no other path than myth, and so there was no huge leap required for me to identify with the Voodoo Chile Hendrix, the Stone Flower Sly, the suicidal classicist

Arthur Lee, and with Stills, as little boys do with the X-Men. The limits this land imposes on our flesh are always apparent, along with the chaos and its betrayal and terrorism of colored bodies.

Yet the riot goin' on is also somewhat at a remove when the music plays, especially on *Manassas*, as Stills, the Captain Manyhands of open spaces and Love Gangster of amplified ecstasy, holds forth.

I also know that Lucifer's origin is Venus, the guiding planet of my soul. I ken the flesh and fantasy mysteries of the complete Passion Play that is Stills's *Manassas* and the fragmented, resequenced one of Taylor's *Stoned*. Stills and Taylor are both small but never quite Napoleonic. They lead because they have no other choice; few others come forward to skip the breach. These high lonesome, singing Sons of the Morning Star bear the burden of keeping the torches lit all along the western front.

Manassas is the ultimate in canyon rock; it is old-timey, folk, proto-ambient, chillout, gospel, country and western, *descarga*, metal, raga, bluegrass, swing, R&B, and funk. But above all, this double LP is blues, aptly released on the Atlantic label founded by another of my childhood heroes, Turkish émigré Ahmet Ertegun, who was catalyzed to enterprise by a youthful romance with R&B and jazz across the hurdle of cultural difference. *Manassas* is a multilayered and masterful narrative of a soul in torment that happens to rock and roll, which is key to understanding the aesthetic of Stephen Stills—just as the inchoate, cradle-era discovery of his music has been central to my love of every other style of music and acts that came after. Stills, my all-time favorite singer, gets no credit for his prescient experiments in Afropop and Latin hybrids; for some reason, the literal relation of his turbulent experiences in the jet set garner no sympathy and none of the praise that con-

temporaneous works by his peers do. Yet I am descendant from
the O.G. Jet Set that emigrated from Central Asia and met its
other half on the sea-girt shores of the original colonies, where
they've done that rag ever since. Listen to Stills's Funk if you have
ears to hear. I *know* that Lewis Taylor has long been keenly digging what our shining prince Hendrix referred to as "twinkling,
Western sky music."

Peep the connect between these lyrics, from Stills's "Both of Us
(Bound to Lose)" and Taylor's "Lovelight":

> *Why can't you hear me*
> *Why can't you see me*
> *How can you be so blind to this feelin' in my heart*
> *Now can you hear me*
> *Now can you see me*
> *How do you like the fool when he's down*
> *Is that really how you see me*
> *Just a statue making sounds*

and

> *Out of the darkness*
> *Your little light starts shining*
> *Just when I feel so sure*
> *You turn your lovelight down again*
> *Baby when you're with me*
> *Who do you think you're fooling?*
> *Just when I feel so sure*
> *You turn your lovelight down again*

Sure, it must be self-absorption that spurs my devotion to Stills. His itinerant childhood (as a military brat), immersion in other cultures abroad (Central America), foreign education, use of Spanish in composition, and musical apprenticeship served in the once most African of North American cities, New Orleans, effectively mirror the experiences of my own youth on both sides of the Atlantic. Some of the attraction to Stills's oeuvre is just the result of relief at finding some other being who articulates one's concerns, inner strivings, and worldview. As a Dixie fellow traveler—perceived as wholly southern amongst his L.A. rock milieu—Stills seems to be singing on *Manassas* (a work titled after a Civil War battlefield) about "my angels, my devils, the thorn in my pride . . ." twenty-odd years before the Black Crowes' Chris Robinson penned the thought, if only on the down low. On the surface, yes, the long-player *Manassas* is simply a masterpiece of so-called country-rock.

It's fitting to mention Robinson here, for all of my most favorite artists of European descent—Gram Parsons, Gene Clark, Eddie Hinton, Galt MacDermot, The Band (especially the late, great Richard Manuel), Daryl Hall—like the aforementioned Brothers Allman, Lewis Taylor, and Stills himself, share a primal moment of recognition/reckoning with Africana. And every time these artists perform, there is a sonic Nubian shadowing their act. If the Civil War remains the defining theatre of American history, then the great significance of Stills and his "cultural mulatto" peers is that they practice ongoing reconciliation beneath the American proscenium. And so *Stoned* is perfectly pitched to the altar of the Electric Sky Church, where identities and possibilities are infinite.

So imagine my relief when first youngish folk rocker Ray Lamontagne and then Lewis Taylor emerged in the critical purview last year to not only justify my veneration of Stills but to carry on this important cultural work of recovery from the primordial disconnect of the mid–nineteenth century uncivil war. (And erstwhile Byrd/Burrito Brother/Manassas member Chris Hillman surprised us with a left-field encore of "It Doesn't Matter" when he played Charlotte last autumn.) Someone has to be heroic enough to make us whole. I am duality in motion: the "dark-eyed country girl/tears in her eyes/needs the music of the wind in the pines . . ." of Stills's "Colorado" but also the red-eyed urban viper that thrives on looking at the stars from the gutter, framed by Manhattan chrome and steel. This is where Lewis Taylor comes in, surfing the Cool Jews zeitgeist and slaying identity politics in his electric blue wake.

Manassas opens with the frantic Delta slide-meets-Afro-Cuban rumble of "Song of Love," as my beloved "Both of Us" seamlessly moves from blue mysterious folk to churning Latin rock. "That's a lot of otherness to put on one child"—but I was never afraid. This Stills masterpiece, produced in tandem with Hillman and funky drummer Dallas Taylor, is most fitting to accompany any voyage to the outer limits for the monkeys and I will want to hear the fiddle strike and do-si-do. Simian/Sirian bred'ren and I won't be hung up on the bloated, coked-up Stills spectre of Boomer rockists' nightmares but the pure Stills who delivered the haunting solo piano demo of "Four Days Gone." Yet we'll also never wish to fake the Funk. So we'll pair Stills's soul yodel with Lewis Taylor's priapic praisesongs. Yodelay-ho-ho . . . stay on the One and a bottle of rum.

If *Manassas* is a meta-commentary on the exile's space-shifting subjectivity, on an alien state of being, then Taylor's *Stoned* is the microscopic slave narrative of the alien who's surrendered to the senses in a hermetically sealed cocoon. "I'm fascinated with the idea of art born of a disintegrated mind," Taylor has told the UK rock press. Like Stills, North London native Taylor hovers in his work somewhere in the mid-Atlantic skies, thrilling to the traditions of both sides of the Pond, resident of none. Stills's "Johnny's Garden" was also situated in Fair Albion, but Taylor eschews England's "green and pleasant land" for an illusory sonic netherworld where Sly Stone and Jeff Beck hold court. *Manassas* is divided into four parts: *The Raven* (allegedly about Stills's unrequited love for Rita Coolidge), *The Wilderness* (the site of the rugged, individualist western hero's retreat from society and human bonds), *Consider* (self-interrogation about possibilities and missteps), and *Rock & Roll Is Here To Stay*, wherein the hero emerges from the innermost cave to renew his spirit in the rock faith. *Stoned* shows Taylor as somewhat arrested at the Crossroads, still making his way along the perilous pathway and smarting from past paramours' arrows of desire (especially on the urgent, menacing "Lovelight" and the beautiful stylistic schizophrenia of "Shame"). However, the yearning breeze of "Send Me An Angel," with its superb nods to early '70s canyon rock, suggests Taylor's ultimate answer will also be— to quote Stills's longtime friend and greatest musical partner, Neil Young—"rock & roll will never die."

CONSIDER

Coming as I do from folk who rarely cop to their envy of Jews' maintenance of difference through faith and cultural tradition, the identity struggles of conflicted artists like Serge Gainsbourg have been somewhat opaque to me—as are the 1950s, when Jews attempted to negate their racial alien status by assimilating into that era's televised suburban whiteness. My brilliant colleague Josh Kun, soon to serve as professor at USC's Annenberg School of Communications, delves into that very complicated process of ethnic erasure in his recent University of California Press book *Audiotopia: Music, Race, and America.* Dr. Kun, whose Jewish father is the son of Hungarian émigrés who fled Hitler's march across Europe, could himself easily be an icon for the new generation of Jewish hip, between alienation from his own Jewishness and the tenets of Judaism, as well as pop boldface status from recurring appearances on AMC's *Movie Club* and multicultural savvy incisively applied to Americana in this tome. Yet neither Kun nor his masterwork—written as a result of his weariness from the 1980s and '90s culture wars—can be limited to faddishness. *Audiotopia's* scope is wide and eclectic, his scholarship on such important titans of black bohemia as gay author James Baldwin and graffiti-artist-turned-SoHo-titan Jean-Michel Basquiat, whose 1983 painting *Horn Players* adorns the cover, and radical L.A. fusionists Ozomatli is as rich and illuminating as his reading of Borscht Belt rebel Myron Meyer "Mickey" Katz and his "musical matzohpieces" mixing Yiddish-English wordplay with the klezmer's minor-key tones.

Audiotopia's most essential contribution to the current Cool Jews dialogue rests in Kun's sharp analysis of the threat Mickey Katz's "antic-Semitism"—Yinglish parodies on Capitol and ambivalence about assimilation—posed to postwar Jews attempting to expunge difference in the face of resurgent nativism, lingering Nazism, and any who considered Jews "probationary whites." Kun solidly makes the case for Katz being as much a forefather of the current cultural Judaism as the unequivocally hip comic martyr Lenny Bruce and white Negro apologist Norman Mailer. In addition to presaging the Jew-on-the-range shtick of Ramblin' Jack Elliott and Texan gubernatorial candidate Kinky Friedman (see "Borscht Riders in the Sky"), Katz looms large as the anti-Jolson, as one who started out as a straight jazz musician in Cleveland well-versed in African aesthetics yet neither masked his subjectivity in performative blackness (á la Sidney Bechet and Mezz Mezzrow) nor used black pop in the manner of minstrelsy tradition and vaudevillain Al Jolson, as a conduit for escape into whiteness.

Lewis Taylor, future soul artist extraordinaire and British Jew, is another rebellious anti-Jolson. But his media reticence and semi-seclusion in London beyond the stage makes it difficult to suss whether or not Taylor's swung the other way into donning an African mask. To be absolutely frank, upon first hearing of the singer-songwriter's magnificent disc Stoned (Hacktone), his blue tone and the album art's lack of images made it easy to assume Taylor was of African descent. Indeed, the two primary Taylor boosters of my acquaintance over the past seven years or so have been New York cultural scribes Greg Tate (the Village Voice's famed Bro-Ironman) and Amy Linden, a leading critic of contemporary R&B and hip-hop, a vital mentor, and the coolest Jew I know. So it followed, from listening to Stoned's Leon Ware–style chamber blues on "Positively Beautiful" and exquisite cover of "Stop, Look, Listen" by Philly Soul composers Bell-Taylor, that Lewis Taylor was indelibly putting the black in the Union Jack.

Professor Kun, owner of Taylor's self-titled debut and Lewis II on Island, is also a devoted fan. Yet the cultural critic in Kun cannot help but wonder how the specters of appropriation, identity, authenticity shadow Taylor's oeuvre. That Taylor is Jewish was a revelation to him but doesn't alter the nature of his fandom; Kun invoked black novelist Chester Himes's read of whiteness in *If He Hollers Let Him Go*—to paraphrase, Himes had no problem with whiteness per se but rather how it was "worn" and wielded.

Kun would doubtless agree that Lewis Taylor is probably the most important soul singer to emerge at the end of the twentieth century (aside from ATLien Donnie, I would add). Of course, as with most truly enduring musicians, Taylor is not a "new" artist. In the time-honored tradition of rock stars, Taylor is small, frail, and pale, a former North London greengrocer who served his apprenticeship in sex, drugs, and rock and roll as guitarist for '70s prog-rockers the Edgar Broughton Band. Then, in the later '80s, as his blue-devils and narco-romance with LSD and heroin threatened to render him a clone of his heroes Syd Barrett, Brian Wilson, and Marvin Gaye, Taylor was reincarnated as a straight psychedelic rocker, releasing two albums under the moniker Sheriff Jack (shades of Katz).

Taylor doesn't represent the cream of black British pop alone— Omar and Seal are also underrated geniuses of this scene (and please, y'all, pour some out for our late brotha Lynden David Hall). But Taylor is not black, and so loom the quoted words of white jazzman and star drug dealer Mezzrow from his white negro bible, *Really the Blues* (1946): "I not only loved those colored boys, but I was one of them. . . . I was going to be a musician, a Negro musician." However, Taylor resembles neither Mezzrow nor singer Joss Stone, Albion's most prominent urban contempo export of the 2000s. Stone overtly attempts to channel classic soul daughters past, surrounding herself with those artists as mentors.

Taylor eschews that route, making things much harder for himself (both as exogamous practitioner of soul and as a musician) by working in a psychedelic soul tradition that was already anathema to most diehards of the genre when it surfaced in the late '60s (ask Betty Davis and Edwin Birdsong, if not the Temptations and Sly Stone). Taylor is not a Mummer of Michael Bolton's ilk, over-souling his audiences to death; he most resembles his pioneering British Invasion forebear Steve Winwood, who, in the Spencer Davis Group and Traffic, expanded soul's vocabulary (and it was good enough for Hendrix). Most significant in Taylor's lineage is his foremother Laura Nyro, who also arrived at a legitimate form of soul that eclipsed her ethnicity, and, too, was broken on the altar of musical apartheid in her day.

Stoned seems to be effortlessly funky, but its exotic melodies and fuzzed-out romantic sweep, reminiscent of Shuggie Otis, have come at a high price, as the CD's best song shows. Musically sublime, "Lovelight" is a song so key for Taylor as to be recorded twice, its tentative and self-flagellating themes subsumed by a bittersweet, dirge-like twangy version and a more insistent, almost menacing mid-tempo one—the results rather like Otis in both L.A. rock and drum 'n' bass form. This delicate synthesis had its wages: Taylor had a personal and artistic crisis following the pair of Island Records releases that preceded the slate of self-released music Americans are just now discovering in the form of Stoned. The artist who, apocrypha has it, caused Marvin Gaye's producer Ware to weep upon hearing his album stopped aiming for the George Michael and Mick Hucknall crown in the late '90s, desiring in his depression to purge himself of all his black influences. In the wake of new demos shelved by Island, the dissolution of his contract and personal relationships, as well as another bout with heroin addiction, the Artist Formerly Known as Sheriff Jack carried over the inspired lunacy of his initial late-80s solo career to release Barrett and Wilson paeans on his own Slow Reality imprint (a cheeky anagram): *Stoned Pt. 1*, *Stoned Pt. 2*, *The Lost Album*, and *Limited Edition 2004*.

Taylor's racialized aesthetic crisis is provocative, for in attempting to slough off blackness, he still ran straight into the embrace of three blues-drenched L.A. rock icons that webbed most of America's regional sounds: Stills (the South), Gene Clark (the Midwest), David Crosby (the West, with New York Dutch aristo roots). *The Lost Album*—which includes California rock versions of some songs that eventually turned up in hardcore soul form on *Stoned*—particularly mines Taylor's love for the cool flip side of Wilson's surf anthems: see "Hide Your Heart Away," "Send Me An Angel," "Yeah," and "New Morning." The result is a great driving record that makes one feel as if one were listening to the greatest "Easy Rock" compilation ever.

Stills and Taylor share the aesthetic burden of being literal or figurative one-man bands, and thus prompt criticism that their work is overproduced and airless. This wrongheaded notion and hair-splitting accounts for ongoing crit worship of Neil Young, at Stills's expense. Taylor may yet escape this category, courtesy of his adherence to the Church of *Pet Sounds*. It's a canny moment to exult in Brian Wilson's failed mid-60s sonic experiments.

Of course, the visionary dementia of Wilson and Barrett puts them in hallowed company with Gaye. This twisted lineage has caused rock audiences to dismiss Taylor as another iteration of fellow British cool Jew, Jason Kay of Jamiroquai. (And for the record,

Taylor is the embodiment of everything we've always expected
from Lenny Kravitz.) Meanwhile, black soul fans that thrill to Taylor's Gaye-isms are thrown by his references to Tim Buckley and
Barrett. The Babel surrounding Taylor makes me ponder along
with Dr. Kun whether the artist's agenda is pan-racial unity? Or is
he an inveterate shedder of identities in the manner of Bob Dylan?

Certainly the armchair gypsy Taylor of this disc's stoned soul
picnic, obsessed with an emotive world in deep freeze, is virtually
indistinguishable from the archetypal blues spook Robert Johnson,
who sang this lyric in "Love in Vain":

> *When the train left the station*
> *It had two lights on behind*
> *Well, the blue light was my blues*
> *And the red light was my mind.*
> *All my love's*
> *In vain.*

Of course, the blue and red lights recombine for the purple of
rock royalty and Taylor's Lovelight questing vainly through London's urban jungle. As Stills is the "statue-making sound," Taylor
is the equally sensitive artist who pleads to be sent an angel lest he
fade away.

ROCK & ROLL IS HERE TO STAY

Taylor *can* groove like the best of Jamiroquai's digital disco—his
Mayfield-meets-Winwood acid vocals and Rhodes washes are con-
temporized by modern drum sounds and electronica effects—but

the Tim Buckley influence is more apt, since his strength is as an artist unafraid to explore the vulnerable side of the male psyche and he covered "Everybody Here Wants You" on *Lewis II*, honoring the '60s folk-funkateer's male songbird son, Jeff. Taylor can also wield rocker potency, as his albums are lyrically preoccupied with romantic angst and booty. They're wonderfully priapic and monomaniacal affairs akin to prime Prince, since our Lewis writes, produces, and plays everything too. Indeed, Lewis Taylor is today's foremost Sexy Motherfucker, although an erstwhile greengrocer from Barnet, North London. Taylor doesn't have to boast about being a babe magnet; he simply *does* his lovers, his all-encompassing, hush-sung odes to heartache certain to launch a million sperm, just like Isaac Hayes's epic early '70s soul. Besides the pent-up inferno of "Lovelight," "Til The Morning Light" and the exquisitely shape-shifting "Shame" affirm that Lewis Taylor's own private audiotopia is Electric Ladyland, a postmodern paradise of ecstatic shagging where he's so strung out on his lover that even his perennial studio woodshedding is disrupted.

We may never know exactly where Taylor is coming from, since Linden informed me that he's that rarest of exogamous rock-era artists who has no desire to conquer America, preferring instead to cocoon at his London home with his manager/ex-paramour, stirring only for the odd live date and appearances on Jools Holland's celebrated British music program *Later . . .*, which, in addition to Taylor's extant albums, have left David Bowie, Sir Elton John, Paul Weller, Daryl Hall (with whom he redid "She's Gone"), Q-Tip, and Angie Stone and her erstwhile baby daddy D'Angelo besotted with him (which led to the elusive Taylor being invited to Electric Lady Studios for the *Voodoo* sessions).

When still resident in Manhattan, Taylor attained the status of myth for me, his rumored comings and goings like a will o' the wisp passed via Tate's Grapevine, rendering his music akin to a holy sonic grail. *Stoned* is thus a revelation, but it does not disappoint. I emphatically declare Lewis Taylor's Stateside debut to be the album of 2005. While his politics, faith, and attitudes towards such movements as cultural Judaism may never be exposed, Taylor is a major artist who has finally arrived at pride of place in the American consciousness and pop prime time through his fearless and unique assimilation of Manifest Destiny's key California critics: Stills, Brian Wilson, and Sly Stone.

Aside from the acid doo-wop cover of "Melt Away" on *Stoned*, Taylor's growing American audience will have to await the artist's early 2006 tour and peep *Stoned II* (available online) to get the Wilson surf music flavor. The deified aural ancestor most prominently representing Taylor's identity dualism on *Stoned* itself are Texas-to-California-bred psych-soul icons Stills—twangy "Shame" uncannily resembling *Manassas's* opening Raven suite in dynamic and fluid hybridity—and Sly, a towering '60s social radical whose sonic sermons like "Stand!" and "Everyday People" inspired the previous generation of hip Jews and who proudly wore the golden Star of David gifted him by manager David Kapralik. The radio-ready cosmic soul of *Stoned* sees Taylor channeling Stone's highway rocker side and his pioneering trip-hop and ambient sounds as codified (especially) on side B of that dark masterpiece, *There's A Riot Goin' On*. For a brief shining time on the cusp of the '70s, Sly and his Family Stone band created one of the most enduring audiotopias America has ever seen, as the subsequent thirty-odd years of pop music attest from the funky pop of '70s Motown to the crossover hits of Taylor's better British soul forebears in the '80s like Human League and World Party's Karl Wallinger. Taylor is touched by genius, but he is still part of a tradition, one that somehow webs "Spaced Cowboy" Sly with Mickey "Bar Mitzvah Ranch" Katz to yield perfect Western pop for cruising either the 101 or the M1—whether or not the acolyte recognizes all of these forefathers in his own masks. Ultimately, what's most important is that Taylor's invisibility blues on *Stoned* never obscures that he, like Baldwin—whom Kun quotes in *Audiotopia*—would doubtless declare that "music was and is my salvation."

So *Stoned* is not mere pop fodder but a late, vital entry in the narrative of Black-Jewish relations. Lewis Taylor may be transgressing race and community with this document of sonic alliance building. Or else he's simply not interested in performing difference, as Katz did to keep body and soul together. Perhaps the result of Taylor not foregrounding his Jewish self in his work is that he is a postmodern Invisible Man who can seamlessly disappear in sound. The question is whether that impulse is tied to his roots. Ultimately, though, Taylor is just like his American brethren of rock reconstruction, exploring radical new ways to be Jewish (whether a conscious act or not)—and simply human.

"Lovelight" particularly, with its club-primed breakdowns, is the sound of postmillennial dystopia, an anthem for end times when cyber-innovations have taken crises of human voice and identity far beyond the moment of amped rupture that Hendrix's "Star-Spangled Banner" presented at Woodstock. The song seems an answer to "Both of Us (Bound to Lose)" across the subsequent thirty years, an attempt to grapple with not just the amorous plight of the song-and-dance man in the age of rock stardom but humankind's perpetual inability to connect and how that's complicated by the insistent static counterpoint to the track's more archaic bass drum. The synth-driven static and the primal drum hopscotch ominously in the song bed, with twangy acoustic guitar lines mediating, both competing to see which will win out as surrogate for the human heart.

Stoned proves Lewis Taylor will never be stone free, nor delivered from the electro-blues canyons of California-on-high. If Taylor can hang tight, he might emulate Stills's provocative example. There is a space where both coexist as authors of revolutionary cultural legacies, operating bold as love in the wake of Hendrix as they do. These times, when revolt is muted in sonic straitjackets, weren't made for them or me. *Terra incognita insulae* beckons.

But meanwhile, a revolution in the freeform of reenchantment is what we want. And rock and roll is still the key. How else to effect the rebirth of a nation? Reenchantment via the Bluenote. *It's nothing but dreaming anyhow.*

17

BRAND NUBIAN
One for All
Elektra, 1990

BY TOM BREIHAN

*"I do it good cuz I'm a positive black man/
Eating up suckers as if I was Pac-Man."*

THAT LINE COMES FROM ALL FOR ONE, THE FIRST
TRACK ON BRAND NUBIAN'S DEBUT ALBUM *ONE FOR
ALL*, AND IT'S A PRETTY GREAT ILLUSTRATION OF THE
album's dichotomous pleasures. The line comes from Lord Jamar,
whose warm, clunky monotone made him the least interesting of
the group's three rappers. But this is an impeccably constructed
punchline: the first half setup, the second half payoff. All of the
group's members, especially Jamar, were allied with the Five Percent Nation, a socioreligious group that teaches black pride and self-
reliance. So the "positive black man" part of the line is deeply
important to Jamar, but he's still not above using it to build up to a
ridiculously goofy joke about a video-game character. *One for All* is
full of moments like that. There's a lot of talk about the lingering
effects of slavery, and the black community's need for self-discipline,

and "production of black facts put onto black wax" (another Jamar quote), but it all coexists peacefully next to party-rhyme bravado and nasty sex talk and blendered pop-culture gibberish. Still, the album feels cohesive rather than conflicted—we never get the sense that there's any inherent contradiction between the group's tangled-up political rage and its endlessly infectious pleasure drive.

One for All came out in 1990, right in the midst of rap's so-called Golden Age. It was a curious and confused and fertile time for rap, a genre that was entering its second decade but still figuring out its own conflicted identity. Two years earlier, Public Enemy's It Takes a Nation of Millions to Hold Us Back had established rap's potential as a vehicle for righteous black-nationalist fury. Earlier that year, MC Hammer's Please Hammer Don't Hurt 'Em had established rap's potential as a cross-cultural commercial force. And an entire generation of New York rappers had spent years establishing rap's potential as a playground for any charismatic alpha dog with an outsized personality and an effortless command of rhythm and language.

Brand Nubian was a group of three rappers (Grand Puba, Sadat X, Lord Jamar) and one DJ (Alamo) from New Rochelle, New York, a Westchester County suburb of New York City. The group formed in 1989, and they signed with Elektra Records later that year. Pretty soon after the release of One for All, Puba left the group to go solo, and Alamo went with him. Brand Nubian's original lineup barely lasted long enough to release one album. In 1998 and then again in 2004, they'd get back together to release a couple of deeply forgettable reunion albums. After One for All, none of the group's members, together or on their own, would ever do anything with anything like that album's force and beauty and clarity. But for one brief, shining moment, they could do no wrong.

I was eleven years old when *One for All* came out, and I was barely aware of the group's existence; all I knew was that their name was sort of funny if you didn't think about it too much. I didn't hear the album until ten years later, after seeing it listed as 1990's number-two album in *Ego Trip's Big Book of Rap Lists* and fishing it out of a used-cassette rack. In the months after I first heard it, I didn't listen to a whole lot else. Maybe I was missing the fury and righteousness that was disappearing from commercial rap at the time, or maybe the Catholic in me needed to love an album from a group that made no bones about condemning white people. All the Five Percenter stuff tied the album in with the impenetrably dense cosmology of the Wu-Tang Clan, who were still putting out the occasional amazing record in 2000. And it was fun to rep for a largely forgotten rap record when all my friends were constantly jamming Modest Mouse. But I'm pretty sure what initially drew me to the album was its sound; I still haven't heard a rap record that comes anywhere near *One for All*'s joyous warmth.

The album was mostly produced by the group members themselves, and it nods to all the fads that were bouncing around in rap at the time: new jack swing, go-go, fake reggae. But nothing feels slapdash, and everything exists within the group's humid, organic sound. Sampling hadn't been *de facto* criminalized yet, so most of the tracks jack bits and pieces of old funk records, some obscure and some not. But everything fits together with an effortless ease: bubbling organs, chattering guitars, sweaty drumrolls, bright horn stabs. The vinyl crackles and sonar pings of "All For One" collapse together under the weight of a gloriously understated bassline and the elastic snap of the rappers' voices. "Dance to My Ministry" is a dense, hectic track, claustrophobically cluttering together fast breakbeats, moaning vocal samples, and squelchy guitars and horns, but it doesn't have the jarring urgency of a Bomb Squad production. Everything has a sweaty analog glow. And "Slow Down" famously swipes the amber-toned, loping guitar of Edie Brickell and the New Bohemians' neo-hippie jam "What I Am," transforming the original's lazy glide into hard funk. Every track is a small miracle, and *One for All* would be one of the most compulsively listenable rap albums of all time even if it didn't have any rapping.

But there is rapping: three huge personalities all competing for mic time. On some songs, there's a playful give-and-take. "Feels So Good" starts out with Puba, Sadat, and Jamar weaving in and out of each other, trading off lines and finishing each other's sentences, biting De La Soul's goofily good-natured style and maybe even improving on it. Then they start into their own verses, and Puba drops a great little nonsense brag-rap line: "I could get raw like a ancient dinosaur/Swing the microphone like the great Mighty Thor"; it's so good that Jamar steals the "ancient dinosaur" bit a minute or two later. When all three were on the same page, they needled each other toward greatness.

But they aren't on the same page all that often, and it's pretty obvious from a cursory glance at the album that the group's lineup wouldn't last long, not when one of its rappers so completely dwarfed the other two. That breakout star is Puba, who comes into this thing with such fierce charisma and big-hearted playfulness that it's a wonder he never places on top-five dead-or-alive lists. Just looking at the numbers, it's pretty obvious why Sadat and Jamar might've felt a bit overwhelmed. Sadat and Jamar both get one solo showcase track apiece over the album's sixteen tracks. Puba gets four, and then there's also a remix of one of those songs and another that features two of Puba's friends and neither of the other Nubian guys. *One for All* never comes across as a Puba solo album, but it's not exactly a unified group effort either, and it's easy to see how things might've gotten so tense in the group that Puba would've elected to part ways with the other two.

Part of it is that Puba was far and away the most versatile of the three. On "Wake Up," he talks about black self-actualization with the same fervor as Jamar. On the intro, a detractor is heard saying "Puba don't know nothing; he be talking about skins all the time." But pretty soon, Puba is talking about how white people pump crack into black ghettos and somehow sounding perfectly effort-less and alive: "Drugs in our community (that ain't right)/Can't even get a job (that ain't right)/Poisoning our babies/Lying who is God." It's gripping stuff, seething with paranoid fury, but one track later he's back to euphoric bragging, playing with words like a cat with string: "Puba ain't game for the shit chit chatter/Puba's in town, oh shit, let's scatter."

"Try to Do Me," maybe the most dated song on the album, is pure cheesed-out new jack swing, complete with synth-bass and histrionic male R&B singers, but Puba still manages to sound great on it, wrapping his warm, elastic voice around the trebly drum hits and figuring out some truly ridiculous ways to break up with a girl: "I think the best thing for you and me/Is to play like John Lennon and let it be." "Who Can Get Busy Like This Man," with sweltering bassline and echoing whistle, is an absolutely fuck-ing great take on late-80s Jamaican dancehall. At the time, damn near every rap album had an utterly lame fake reggae song, but Puba never takes the easy way out: no fake Jamaican accent, no slang-jacking about licking shots or whatever. Instead, he just slides a musical lope into his voice and keeps delivering great little sex-rap gems: "See, I'm the type of brother who likes to have fun/She said sixty-nine; I said sixty-eight and I owe you one." And "Dedication," the album's closer, is a ridiculous idea with an inspired execution. Puba recites the album's thank-you list in rap form, weaving in and out of nonsense battle-rap lines and a laundry list of name-drops. It shouldn't work, but Puba's on such a ridiculous roll that's he's basically incapable of saying anything that doesn't sound great.

In fact, the extent to which Puba dominates the album is pretty amazing. The liner notes say that the album was produced by "Brand Nubian and Grand Puba Maxwell." I don't know if that means he made most of the beats himself or what, but it reads like he's already distancing himself from the other two, getting ready to leave the others behind. The chemistry is always there, but it's still pretty obvious that the group made the album when they were just getting together and figuring out their roles. Nothing's written in stone yet; there's no talk about "Brand Nubian for life" or anything like that. It's a bit like *Straight Outta Compton*, where all the rappers were great but Ice Cube immediately jumped out as the guy who was going to leave the group and become a star on his own. Except Puba never became huge. Ice Cube is now a second-tier movie star who never has to rap again unless he feels like it, but Puba's working the nostalgia-rap circuit. Life isn't fair.

As for Sadat and Jamar, they're both stuck in the shadows, but they still have great moments. They're both still finding their feet.

Sadat spells his name as "Saddat" in the liner notes, and he keeps referring to himself as "Derek X" on the record; maybe he didn't even
decide what his name was until after the record was out. His voice is
a weirdly grizzled singsong growl-wheeze, the same sort of stoner
blur Dave Chappelle has—an expressive instrument. He can rap
fast, but when he does, a couple of syllables always come out gar-
bled and just slightly off the beat. But all his imperfections just serve
to set him a little further apart. He can't outrap Puba, so he doesn't
try. Even if he doesn't share Puba's technical dexterity or goofy un-
predictability, his weird mixture of unselfconscious generosity of
spirit and seething rage sort of make him the soul of the group.
He's funny and weirdly self-effacing: "I took the time to delete all
the curses / So moms, reach deep in your purses." And he's not
above kicking likeable gibberish: "I had a Royce, traded it in for a
horse / It died, I made glue; it's no loss." But he's quicker than his
comrades to talk no-nonsense racial politics. "Concerto in X Minor," his solo track, is all about how "New York's a powder keg, did
I forget to mention?," at least before he reverts right back to brag-
rap formalism near the end of the song. And on "Drop the Bomb,"
he gets right to the heart of the group's wounded pride: "What I
provide will collide with devilish ways of thinking / Erasing false
facts that started with Abe Lincoln / Being great, used his weight
and freed the slaves, but did he free us? / Take a look around at the
black man, see us."

If Sadat is the heart of the group, Jamar is the fist. With his
blunt, nasal declamations, he's nowhere near as nimble as Puba or
even Sadat. But he's more steeped in politics than the others;
nearly everything he says is some sort of ranted militant slogan:
"We've been enslaved for the longest / Time to rise up and gather

our strongest." But he's also the most esoteric member of the group, the one most focused on near-impenetrable Five Percenter theology. When he does indulge in the bread-and-butter battle-rap that Puba and Sadat love so much, he's vaguely uncomfortable, like he's itching to get this stock stuff out of the way so he can get back to recruiting more black militants. And so he leans back on Puba, stealing punchlines from him more than once and doing it right out in the open, using those lines on the same songs that Puba used the originals. And he's at his itchiest when he's talking about women: raining judgment on a prostitute on "Slow Down," talking about *running away* from imaginary mobs of female fans on "To the Right," presumably because "I didn't want to scuff up my brand new Ballys." And then there's this riff from "All for One": "Girls try to turn my knob cuz I'm a heartthrob / I guess it's just a hazard that comes with the job / Cuz every time I rock a rhyme and show Jamar's intellectual / Girls wanna get *sexual*." He clamps down on that last word, so it just drips with consternation. But he's bragging at the same time. I doubt there were really hordes of groupies doing everything they could to get into Lord Jamar's drawers, but he wanted us to think there were, and he further wanted us to think that he was turning them down, a bizarrely complex and guilt-ridden approach to standard-issue battle-rap. And let's not forget that Jamar is the guy responsible for the Pac-Man line, my favorite lyric on the entire album.

When any of the three is talking about politics, there's a palpable sense of profound disappointment, like they could see that things were bad and not getting better and that they didn't know what to do besides talk religion and revolution. MTV rejected the video for "Wake Up" because of the black actor in whiteface who plays the devil, horns and all, laughing as he hands off bags of coke to black dealers and trying to convince kids to eat pork. On "Slow Down," Sadat doesn't sound angry when he's addressing an addict. He just sounds sad: "Used to walk with a swagger/Now you simply stagger." When they *do* talk about revolution, about organizing armies, they aren't calling us to arms the way Public Enemy would. It's more like they'd love to see it happen, but they know it won't.

Or at least I think that's what they mean, but I'm obviously not the group's target audience. As a white suburban listener, listening to *One for All* feels like eavesdropping even a decade-plus after the album's release. In fact, it feels even more like eavesdropping now, since a lot of the lyrics make reference to stuff I wasn't around for. Here's Sadat on "Symphony in X Minor": "Case in point, y'all remember that Brooklyn Bridge joint when things got wild and wooly?" No. No, I don't remember that Brooklyn Bridge joint, and I don't have any idea what he's talking about. The Five Percenter stuff is also totally opaque in a way that's become almost comforting. I know that Yacub is the evil scientist who invented white people, but I don't know what Jamar is talking about when he says, "The body of the snake, that's fake." What's the snake? And why is its body fake? Does that even mean anything, or did he just say it because it sounds cool? And would I know all this stuff if I studied Five Percenter scripture?

I don't know how scary it was for white people to hear this stuff in 1990, but it's hard to imagine anyone being truly, deeply offended when Puba says that he's going to drop the bomb on the Yacub crew, not when the history of racial relationships in the United States put all their anger in a real and tragic context. I can't even get why MTV wouldn't accept the "Wake Up" video, since its white devil is more cartoonish than anything. Dante Ross, the guy who signed the group to Elektra and who served as the album's executive producer, is white, and they never talk shit about him the way the white rap group 3rd Bass did on "The Gas Face."

It does get a bit uncomfortable, though, when Puba uses weird homophobic digs as simple asides in his otherwise lighthearted battle-raps: "Brother, you're wrong if you think crime pays/Don't like gays and take vacations on the holidays." This isn't like talking about how you don't eat pork. The anti-white sentiments make sense coming from a group of young black men talking about institutional racism. The anti-gay stuff doesn't make sense coming from a young black guy just talking about how great he is. What did gay people ever do to Grand Puba?

But then, the opacities on *One for All* are what make it great. Without all its weird internal dynamics and tangled-up religious sloganeering and deeply felt sadness at the plight of America's black underclass, *One for All* would be one of the best party-rap records of all time and nothing more. But all that other stuff is what makes it such a fascinating and frustrating listen, a record to love and a record to pick apart.

18

THE CARS
The Cars
Elektra, 1978

BY ROB HARVILLA

THE FIRST SIXTY SECONDS OF JUST WHAT I NEEDED.
NO, SERIOUSLY, THAT'S ENOUGH. IT'S FINE. KEEP THE
REST. THE FIRST MINUTE OF JUST WHAT I NEEDED.
That's all I'll be needin'. Seeing as how I possess the forty-four seconds preceding *the greatest drumroll ever recorded*. The sixteen seconds immediately following *the greatest drumroll ever recorded*. And the two seconds during which transpires *the greatest drumroll ever recorded* itself. B.C. (Before Christ). A.D. (*Anno Domini*).[1] And in between, C.H. (Christ Himself).

Christ Himself, written phonetically, reads as follows:

Badadarumpbumpbumpbump.

It's a bit alarming—embarrassing? horrifying?—that nearly a decade into a preposterous career Writing About Music For Money, dispensing dubious insight and alleged humor to the faceless, perhaps entirely nonexistent masses one thousand words at a time—the fascination, obsession, and euphoria that drives this absurdity, distilled to its essence and written phonetically, reads as follows:

Badadarumpbumpbumpbump.

The greatest drum fill ever recorded was executed by Cars drummer David Robinson. I had to look that up, and did not particularly enjoy doing so. This is not a work of scholarship, nor does it provide, at least intentionally, any historical insight beyond my personal recollections regarding the first minute of "Just What I Needed" and its specific impact on me personally. You may find this approach narcissistic. I do not disagree. And yet, *dude, I'm on a deserted fucking island.* This lends itself to introspection, and furthermore, impedes access to AllMusic.com. Which frees me, happily, to fixate entirely on the sixty seconds of recorded sound I have granted myself.

B.C.

Initially just that iconic rhythm guitar, naked and robotic and unblinking—*chik chik chik chik chik chik chik*—interrupted periodically by a guitar and a drum striking a single beat that, written phonetically, reads as follows: WHUMP.

Full figure: *Chik chik chik chik chik chik WHUMP. Chik chik chik chik chik chik chik WHUMP.* Two more of these, and then, more urgently, and with a bit of bass on the *WHUMPs* now, *Chik chik chik chik chik chik WHUMP WHUMP. Chik chik chik chik chik chik WHUMP WHUMP.* Two more of those, and then, in a stoic, laconic, dismissive near-deadpan, a grudging confession of romantic longing veiled in feigned apathy: "I don't mind you comin' here / Wastin' all my time / 'Cause when you're standin' oh so near / I kinda lose my mind / It's not the perfume that you wear[2]/It's not the ribbons in your hair[3]/I don't mind you comin' here/And wastin' all my time."

Badadarumpbumpbumpbump.

Yeah, Catholic elementary school babes. You're cool. Stand there if you want. I don't care. Whatever. (Resumes serving as goalie in recess soccer game. Hopes for opposing team to launch a dramatic breakaway, five on one, hell, *eight* on one, maybe even *sixteen* on one, your own team turning against you for some reason, what the hell, guys, and barreling toward you now with nefarious grins and grunts of rage and ardor, a Normandy asphalt beachhead bum rush, until the biggest, baddest of them all takes control of the ball, amps up to ramming speed, legs temporarily an oscillating Roadrunner blur, and he kicks the crap outta the ball, *boods*[4] it, in the parlance of Sacred Heart Catholic elementary school recess soccer. The ball's whizzing toward a far-off corner of the goal, say the right-hand-side dull orange traffic cone, velocity impossibly fast, trajectory a deadly and precise angle, and you dive[5] at the last possible second, a graceful slo-mo arc, perhaps twisting in mid-air for visual effect, and you brush the ball with your fingertips, and it careens off the right-hand-side dull orange traffic cone, *no good*, bouncing down the hill and toward the highway leading out of Eureka, Missouri, *save!* And the babes who've watched this happen, at least those who have not fainted on account of the heartstopping melodrama, they cheer giddily, the ribbons in their hair bobbing ecstatically as they pick you up and carry you off, down to the tree-lined gully behind the swings, and. And. And?[6])

Badadarumpbumpbumpbump.

The music facilitating and slowly goosing this lyrical sentiment at first echoes that nonchalance. As "I don't mind you coming here" unfurls, the drummer (his name, incidentally, is David Robinson) does nothing but smack the snare drum on a lazy quarter-note *WHUMP*, regarding the *chik chik chik chik* rhythm guitar underpinning almost sarcastically. Perhaps he is guzzling a can of Tab with his free hand. The bassist (his name is lost to history) slides in sheepishly, late as usual, on "coming," aligning with the guitarist on a looping four-chord vista. "I kinda lose my mind." And now the intensity intensifies, the Cars—look, this is corny, I apologize in advance, but it's really the only appropriate metaphor here—*shifting into second gear* as our singer negates the effect of your perfume; David has drained his Tab and will condescend to provide *pish pish* hi-hat and *oomph* kick-drum now, a simple but exhilarating tectonic shift, and now there's a *second* guitar, not handcuffed to the *chik chik* downstroke, clipping jauntily, "It's not the ribbons in (where'd that second *voice* come from?) *yourrrr haaaair*," and now—third gear—flaring brashly as our singer grits his teeth and reiterates, "*I don't mind you coming here*," crescendoing and accelerating emotionally if not literally—fourth gear—"*And wasting all my time.*"

Then it shifts into reverse.

Badadarumpbumpbumpbump.

If I had Google on this island I would research what exactly occurs when a motorist traveling at, say, eighty miles an hour accidentally shifts into reverse.[7] Instant bloody carnage, or something less brutal and cinematic? Perhaps, like a Spinal Tap drummer, your vehicle simply explodes, and the smoke dissipates and reveals its instant replacement. But David Robinson, architect of the greatest drumroll ever recorded, cannot be so easily duplicated. Besides, this is a lousy metaphor,[8] because said drumroll's detonation isn't an unwelcome, destructive, quite possibly fatal catastrophe—your vomited transmission bouncing violently down the freeway—but a welcome epiphany, a rebirth, a two-second Tearing Down and Building Back Up, and now you're a completely different person. *Better.* Born again. Your inferior B.C. brain catapulting helplessly off a cliff like a deflected soccer ball, leaving a glorious void yearning to be filled. Ben Orr abhors a vacuum. His band has sixteen seconds to reprogram you. Their primary tool for this crucial job is perhaps unconventional—not a guitar solo, not another clattering drumroll (David's genius is defined by how rarely he employs it), not a human voice.

A.D.

It's a synthesizer. Keyboard. Whatever. The melody it describes, written phonetically, reads as follows: *Weeeuuu. Ooh-weeeuuu. A-WIEEE-eeeeee-uuuuu-ooooh-weeeuuu.* An extraterrestrial hum from what in 1978 portended the future but now reeks of the past, vintage new wave synths being a little dated lately maybe, but in this instance dated The First Day of The Rest of Your Suddenly Sweet-Ass Life. Drums, bass, and both guitars deferential, Best Supporting Actors, rumbling across that four-chord blacktop, the leading-man synth melody playfully bending above that fourth one the first time around, an insouciant half-step climb on the . . .

ooooh-weeeuuu, defiant and unresolved. Curling like a question mark as a *third* guitar—the lead guitar, finally—fires off a brash one-second vamp, notes tumbling down like a honky-tonk hotshot fretting with a beer bottle. The melody swings around for another pass, the synth ducking its head low and nearly inaudible on the fourth chord this time as the guitar slashes in again, slower but more dominant, one pigeon menacing another off its perch atop a telephone pole. Ain't big enough for the both of us.

David Robinson hits a cymbal. *Pssssh*. Minute over. Brick wall. Shifting into reverse for real. This is all I want—sixty seconds. A fraction, a microcosm. It seems cruel to deny myself the remaining 2:34 of "Just What I Needed." Some fascinating ephemera here. The second verse abandons chaste, awkward schoolyard flirtation-through-disinterest for images a bit more intimate ("Talking in your sleep"), not to mention goofier ("You look so fancy I can tell"). Fancy. Also: "It doesn't matter where you've been/As long as it was deep, *yeah*." Deep. Yeah. Let's just leave that alone. Focus on the euphoric video arcade symphony this tune becomes, that *weeeuuu* melody line picked up by ebullient keyboards of different dispositions and genders, the telephone pole–perched guitarist ripping an ecstatic solo over dainty (fancy?) staccato synth chords, a torrent precise but still brilliant and brawling, as though still fretted with a beer bottle, but this time a full one burping rivers of life-affirming Busch[9] as he shreds. More lyrical idiosyncrasy ("Wasting all my time *time*," adorable, like a Catholic grade school crush with the hiccups) and a bitchin' outro, another vicious synth hook just in case you thought they just had one—*we can do this all night, suckers*, boast the power- and Busch-drunk Cars, drinking and driving and dominating.

I'll (mostly) spare you even purpler prose in praise of *the chorus, JESUS CHRIST*[10] *THE CHORUS*, like a gas explosion at one of the barely legal fireworks stores lining the highway exits for several miles in either direction beyond Sacred Heart Catholic elementary school. Roman candles saluting everywhere. *Just what I need-ed.* A panorama thousands of times more vivid and monolithic and mesmerizing than the big-screen TVs the tune now helps hawk via Circuit City ads, and more boisterously American than the playoff football games you watch on 'em.

If you conjured up the first sixty seconds of "Just What I Needed" in one hundred parallel universes, each one then required to invent its own distinct 2:37 middle and ending, the full version of "Just What I Needed" available in this universe would still reign supreme, the Best Possible Outcome. It can quite simply not improve. But I'd rather have the intro alone, the hypothetical launching point for those one thousand lives of possibility, a fertile field of anticipation and especially hope—a deserted island's most valuable commodity.[11] This is a pattern with me and the Cars. As a soon-to-be-Nintendo-obsessed lad,[12] I gravitated toward the band's quirkier Arcade Symphony intros, eagerly cueing up "Since You're Gone" and marveling at its mind-boggling jumble of synthesized hand claps, Texas Instruments–worthy bleeps, sinister guitar, and equally doomy bass, a vivid but hopelessly jumbled Rubik's Cube that slowly shifts from total randomness to checkerboard to plaid to triumphant solid color in twenty-two seconds. Truly awesome. I'd yank up the needle and start over as soon as it resolved—the mid-80s hip-hop-deprived Midwestern white kid's wide-eyed conception of a "break." The Best Possible Outcome in this instance is that intro repeated on a loop for fifteen minutes.

My impatient seven-year-old self fixated on multiple tunes this way, almost all of them by the Cars.[13] Even dorky filler like "Think It Over" held me transfixed for thirty seconds or less, like a computer powered entirely by ping-pong balls noisily booting up. "Heartbeat City" is the most poignant example probably, a mournful arpeggiated synth pattern spiraling out into empty space—a creepy faux-NASA echo effect chasing after it—creating a sublime feeling of utter loneliness. The new wave equivalent to the deserted island.

The "Just What I Needed" intro is longer, more conventional, less gimmicky. But lest you've forgotten, it has one supremely important thing going for it: Christ Himself.

C.H.

Badadarumpbumpbumpbump.

For more than half of the '80s,[14] I would stomp down my Eureka, Missouri, house's basement stairs to the exact rhythm of the drum breakdown in John Cougar Mellencamp's "Jack and Diane." *Boo-doo. Boo-doo. Boo-doo. Boo-doo. Boo boom boomp BOOMP.* It very nearly challenges David Robinson's finest hour for overall drum-roll supremacy. Very nearly. The setup saves him. The first forty-four seconds of "Just What I Needed" are a perfect specimen of joyful momentum, everything building calmly but forcibly to that shocking moment when David unleashes euphoria, an ice cream truck flipping over and crashing on your front lawn, the driver unhurt and in a charitable mood, delectable treats[15] suddenly littering the driveway and hanging from the trees like glistening, melting Christmas ornaments.

Badadarumpbumpbumpbump.

At twenty-eight years old, jaded and beleagured, I am still *anni-hilated* by joy at that moment, my favorite two seconds of recorded sound for all eternity. I'll be wandering aimlessly through New York City, earbuds dug deep into my head to exacerbate the power of those *WHUMPs*, my pace subconsciously accelerating as the Cars shift into second/third/fourth/reverse. And when C.H. detonates, I literally break into a run, a lumbering jog at times wildly inappropriate given the real-word circumstances—amid a crowd of folks halted by a "Don't Walk" sign, for example—and I sense the amused/bemused/confused looks of passersby as I skip past, but for oftentimes a full minute or so I absolutely don't care, and even when the giddiness subsides and maybe I do, I often keep jogging anyway, maybe providing weak cover by lifting my gaze and pretending to spot some quickly receding spot in the distance that requires I race toward it. A bus, maybe, back to Eureka, or a helicopter to a deserted island, where I'll absorb the first sixty seconds of "Just What I Needed" on an endless summer loop, imagining something better even as I know that's not possible, and waiting to be rescued even as I know I already have been.

NOTES

1. Or, as my Latin-averse classmates at Sacred Heart Catholic elementary school in mid-80s Eureka, Missouri, preferred it, After Death.
2. A sensory presence not applicable among the girls at Sacred Heart Catholic elementary school.
3. Definitely applicable.

4. Not making this up.

5. Stoically.

6. And knowledge as to what might next transpire between mutually attracted boys and girls completely
   lacking until parents permit me to watch MTV starting in roughly 1985.

7. Almost done with this image, sorry.

8. Will being stranded on a desert island, with literally no
   one to judge or even observe me, make me *less* self-
   conscious and critical and prone to second-guessing,
   or paradoxically *more so*? If a chump self-loathes in a
   forest and no one is around to agree with him, does it
   make a sound?

9. One thing AllMusic.com won't tell you is that the Cars
   preferred the exact same brand of beer as my dad.

10. Sincere apologies to Sister Anna-Mary for breaking the
    Second Commandment. Ring me up, I'll play it for
    you, you'll understand.

11. Second, perhaps, to fire.

12. Along with MTV lust, the other profound cultural
    phenomenon to slap me upside the head circa 1985. I
    can't decide which is worse.

13. Notable exception: the Doobie Brothers' "Real Love."

14. For the remaining part of the decade, I either couldn't
    walk yet or didn't live there.

15. Most coveted item: the sherbet foot with a gumball in
    the big toe.

19

SONNY ROLLINS
A Night at the Village
Vanguard
Blue Note, 1957

By Derek Taylor

An intrinsic part of a music critic's job entails coming up with lists. Year-end tallies of new releases and reissues, vanity-fueled inventories of favorite recordings, even monthly mock-ups organizing writing assignments—all feed into the census-taking impulse. When it comes to jazz, these exercises often read like indexes of esoterica, at least when considered within the context of a larger pop milieu. Most entries on a jazz critic's lists hold only the faintest probability of ever cracking the *Billboard* Top 100, much less earning a laudable mention on MTV.

Polls and tabulations are such regular pursuits that any attempt at distilling a list down to a single item is bound to suggest a no-win proposition. This sort of antipathy to extreme reductionism runs directly contrary to the "desert island" conceit of this book: a mandate for the self-professed music maven to accomplish the impossible, to winnow his or her encyclopedic appetites down to a single lonely representative, one containing enough aural manna to properly nourish the faculties and soul in perpetuity. From a purely logical standpoint, it simply cannot be done.

Determined to meet the challenge directly, I first set about the task by referencing my past lists, specifically the slew of tabulations that litter the hard drive of my laptop. My safe presumption that the majority if not all of my fellow authors would avoid the genre of jazz entirely made it a sensible pick. But a music genre with nearly one hundred years of recorded history still leaves a daunting legion of possibilities.

First, there is the issue of practical playing value. Alone on an island with only coconuts and palm fronds for company, a typical forty-minute LP-length disc would leave me boxing my ears and howling at the moon in exasperation for more within a fortnight. Then there is the logic that suggests newness and novelty as advantages in the selection process. Who wants to be stuck sequestered with an album that they have listened to countless times already, especially when coping with the sobering reality of indefinite isolation?

To confront the selection process from a different angle, I turned to technology, transferring my top five contenders to a portable digital player, with the intention of immersing myself in each one individually for the span of several days. This earnestly executed exercise removed a few more runners-up before imploding completely upon the arrival of another package of must-hear promotional discs. A critic's mailbox is rarely a fallow place. In the anticlimactic end, my decision came down mostly to whim.

Before I justify my pick, a bit of backstory is in order. My first concrete memory relating to jazz ties to an ill-conceived epithet

uttered in a classical music appreciation class during my sophomore year of high school. We were knee-deep in Mozart, and had
just watched the film *Amadeus*. During a break, a friend asked me
if I had ever heard jazz. I had heard the word, but couldn't yet at-
tach its meaning to a specific musical style. The majority of my listening up until that point had centered on the folk-rock of my
parents' vinyl and tape collection and my own tentative forays into
'80s pop and alternative. Not wanting to seem stupid, and hoping
to appear aloofly cool, I replied: "jazz, oh yeah, I hate jazz." My
friend gawked back, incredulous. I knew then that in spinning my
little white lie I had gambled on the wrong uneducated guess.
Class concluded, and I headed home possessed by the desire to ed-
ify and redeem myself.

I found ingress through the remains of my mother's college
record collection, a modest cache of vintage Blue Note, Riverside,
and Prestige vinyl with bent corners and smudgy signs of ring
wear shelved in with the latest albums by George Winston, Anita
Baker, and other early '80s easy-listening staples. A scuffed copy of
Lee Morgan's *The Sidewinder* served as my gateway platter. On
first sampling, it sounded like game-show music to my pop- and
rock-weaned ears. But there was something about the title tune's
slinky, bass-driven groove and punchy horn chart that stuck in my
head. Several days later, on a trip down to a local brick and mortar,
I made a beeline for the jazz racks in search of more. Most of the
names on the bin cards drew blanks, but I found the sparely populated Morgan section and pulled a recently released *Best of the Blue
Note Years* compilation. Sonny Rollins's name rang a cerebral bell,
too, and I grabbed his like-titled single-disc collection along with
the Morgan.

The look and layout of these discs were instantly appealing, especially the Rollins edition. The cover featured a noirish black-and-white Francis Wolff photograph of a sharp-suited and cherub-cheeked Sonny standing beside his shadow-shrouded colleague, trumpeter Donald Byrd, both set against a spare mint green backdrop. The tray card not only specified tracks, but also identified personnel for each selection. I remember being impressed by the attention to detail paid to the musicians and their instruments, a custom that I would come to learn was routinely reflected in the music itself as a collaborative improvisatory art. All of the information was described in a neat miniature script and I made a mental note of the art designer, one Franco Caliguri, and his design company Inkwell, Inc. The Rollins and the Morgan entered steady rotation in my listening diet for the next several weeks. Seventeen years and thousands of albums later, I still have those two compilations. I have not listened to either one in quite a while, having long since acquired all of the individual albums from which their contents were extracted, but there is nostalgic comfort in knowing they are both within reach.

Spending initial time with the Rollins disc, I noticed that three cuts, a full one-third of the collection, were lifted from a date taped toward the end of his association with Blue Note at a tiny New York club called the Village Vanguard. Rollins released only four albums during his tenure with the label: the mundanely titled *Volume 1* and *Volume 2*, *Newk's Time*, and *A Night at the Village Vanguard*. The emphasis granted this last date by the disc's compilers piqued my interest, and the curiosity escalated exponentially upon auditioning the tracks. "Striver's Row" and "Sonnymoon for Two" were exciting, even revelatory, but the epochal rendering of

"Softly as in a Morning Sunrise" stupefied my ears and sensibilities completely.

The track started out innocuously with one of Rollins's congenial spoken non sequiturs to the audience: "We'd like to fix your rowboat right now with a little thing we hope you'll all be familiar with. . . . " and a whispered count-off right into the sequoia-wide sound of Wilbur Ware's double bass, plucking a line that was rhythmic and melodic in equal parts. Those opening bass notes knocked me for an instant loop. Rollins's tenor fluttered in, sounding more like Lester Young than Coleman Hawkins, who he claimed to idolize as a boy. He spooled out a succession of porous melodic ribbons across a chain of choruses, his tenor running through a consonant array of inflections while drummer Elvin Jones, grunting behind his kit and sounding as if he was using industrial-sized paint brushes on his skins, kept a sagaciously fluid time. Ware's spotlight solo commenced with little warning, precipitating an even more momentous epiphany for me. His stout fingers articulated each note with precision and prescience, drawing an ad-lib map that completely subverted the tune's core melody while simultaneously offering constant consideration of it. His improvisation instantly and permanently enamored me of the bass. It's a singular performance on the instrument that I've since come to place on the highest pedestal in my personal musical pedagogy.

Just as miraculous was the way Ware's sound was captured and preserved. His solo occupies a rare segment of near-pristine clarity, at odds with the murkier fidelity of much of the rest of the set. Engineer Rudy Van Gelder's mobile recording equipment, while state of the art for 1957, wasn't exactly up to space-age standards.

Add to that the generally problematic acoustics of the Vanguard itself, a narrow, bunker-like basement space with a pocket-sized stage and cramped seating, and it's a minor miracle that the music was documented with the degree of presence and depth that it has. Somehow, Van Gelder came up aces on this cut. And the visceral dynamics point to another enticing aspect of the music. Like few other live jazz recordings I can think of, the environment of the club seeps into the recording. The clink of glassware, the prattling of patrons, and the band's proximity to it all give the illusion of a spot at a table directly adjacent to the stage.

Ware's improvisation bled directly into Jones's solo. Still on brushes, the drummer was a model of marshaled energy. There were points where he struck his kit with such force that it sounded like he was playing with sticks, his stridency suggesting the imminent danger of puncturing the tautly stretched surfaces of snare and tom-tom. Rollins hung back through most of the piece, interjecting, between the statements of his sidemen, low-key, almost melancholy phrasings that perfectly suited the overarching smoky-hued mood of the performance. It's a track I've played countless times and one I never grow weary of hearing.

The complete *Vanguard* set includes another version of the tune. It's about a minute shorter, slower and more dolorous without compromising the romantic sentiment that fuels the core. Rollins's tone is velvety, a lush rasp texturing the edges of his opening theme statement. Ware once again tugs at and transposes time, his solo here broken into two halves by a speech-like Rollins declaration. Jones patters away on brushes casting a rhythmic shadow beneath the bassist and adding the occasional creaky mutter. Sliced into a pair of parts, the solo doesn't contain quite the

same degree of grandeur and cohesive presence, but Ware's closing pizzicato harmonics deliver a superlative coda to marvel at
ceaselessly just the same. Rollins tapers his tone into the near-alto
range at the track's close, once again signing the action off with an
autograph of inexorable cool.

Individual reissues of the Vanguard material hadn't made it to
compact disc when I first encountered the music, and my fickle
tastes quickly dragged me in other directions. I finally got around
to picking them up about five years after my first exposure, but
the turbid sound was still an issue. When the remastered version,
labeled shrewdly as the "Rudy Van Gelder Edition," came out in
'99, I jumped on it and quickly pawned my earlier editions. Marketing ploy or not, the idea of the original engineer (and Blue
Note's chief sonic chronicler) going back to the source tapes and
giving them a fresh scrub was just too appealing to pass up.

A peripheral part of the mystique of *A Night at the Village Vanguard*, and there are many, is the number of incarnations it's un-
dergone since its original vinyl pressing back in the '50s.
Subsequent tints to the strikingly simple Frank Wolff cover photo
range from the turquoise green of an early Japanese edition to
the current patina of cloudy fuchsia that graces the RVG release.
The image itself is an instant classic and a colophon of jazz
charisma: a murky close-up of Rollins' youthful mug captured in
mid-utterance, a pair of sunglasses obscuring the expression of his
eyes and lending his countenance a *Mona Lisa*–like mystery.

The track list is another mutable quantity, expanding gradually
over the years. Averred as complete, the RVG edition gathers
eighteen tracks (two consisting solely of brief introductory ban-
ter). The November 3, 1957, recording was actually part of a

larger sojourn at the club. On the particular date captured on tape, Rollins played afternoon and evening gigs with two different rhythm sections. I have long pondered the perplexing parameters of the earlier set. It's represented by only two surviving performances, though the afternoon trio undoubtedly played more music than that if the evening gig is any point of comparison. Fortunately, under the desert island circumstances of this essay, the pangs surrounding the respective paucity are easier to assuage, as the presence of additional extant tracks would probably necessitate a third disc and thus disqualify the set as a viable pick in my editor's eyes.

Conventional wisdom contends that their evening counterparts outgunned afternoon bassist Donald Bailey and drummer Pete La Roca, and I tend to agree. Even so, both men turn in exciting work on the two tracks on which they're featured, particularly La Roca, whose Art Blakey–influenced approach behind the kit prod Rollins into some seriously galvanizing improvisatory action. The trio's takedown of Cole Porter's aged "I've Got You Under My Skin" completely refurbishes the tune for modernist sensibilities. Rollins's horn sounds slightly fuzzy in the mix, but cedes nothing in the way of speed or agility. Bailey is prominent, fashioning a robust walking line punctuated by La Roca's cantering hi-hat. What follows is an ingenious extended interpolation of the theme, a melodic punch card packed with perfectly placed notes that beautifully illustrates Rollins's storytelling abilities with his horn. A predictable succession of drum breaks finds La Roca scaring up a series of rims-driven responses to Rollins's rapacious calls. Bailey moves out front, but squanders his solo space on a speed-walking solo as Rollins murmurs low phrases as his flank. Sensing that Bailey is coasting, Rollins reasserts himself, opening the piece up to an incredible series of closing choruses where his creativity refuses to flag, quoting freely and giving both his colleagues an invaluable lesson in improvisatory brinksmanship.

The afternoon and evening versions of "A Night In Tunisia" offer clear points of comparison between Rollins's two rhythm sections. On the former, the saxophonist wastes no time in diving right into the serpentine, exotic theme with brusque and staccato phrasing. La Roca keeps up an effervescing beat with frothing cymbals and choppy snare, as Rollins devises rhythmically pregnant permutations on the fly. He segues to a series of explosive breaks with the drummer, La Roca's growls of exertion and exaltation clearly audible as authoritative press rolls ricochet off his drums before subsiding with surprising deliquescence. Rollins's reentry is less urgent, too, his tone softened and phrases channeled through a higher register of his horn. The percussive click of his saxophone key pads, and a final arching wail, lead to broad applause.

The evening version follows a general schematic not far removed from the earlier reading, but from the onset Ware and Jones feel more measured and relaxed than their afternoon precursors. Rollins once again arrives with a singing vocalized tone, negotiating the theme with another note-packed sortie that consumes ample choruses without appearing the least bit gluttonous. Ware acts as anchor, stretching his notes to cover the harmonic spaces. Declamatory tenor cries mid-piece uncannily presage the tonal experiments that would rock jazz to its foundations a decade or so later with the ascendance of Albert Ayler. The urgency builds almost imperceptibly, until a string of explosive breaks and a monumental solo from Jones. His sticks skitter across the surfaces of his kit, birthing beats that lock together and create the feeling of rolling thunder. Floating Latin polyrhythms coalesce and recede. Rollins reconvenes for an a cappella cadenza that contorts into an almost primal cry at the track's close, arcing above a sizzling spray of cymbals. Stacked together, the two renderings of the tune reveal the obvious winner.

While undeniably a decent accompanist, Bailey's walking patterns are for the most part much more workmanlike than Ware's, lacking the latter man's harmonic cunning and eccentric sense of time. Similarly, La Roca was just getting his style together, and while he has energy and brio to spare, the adventurous, go-for-broke flavor of Jones's percussion provides a palpable advantage. Ware and Jones were the main event, and Rollins was understandably elated to have them both in the band.

For a musician of his stature, Ware recorded comparably little. His work on "Softly As In A Morning Sunrise" precipitated a search on my part to find all of his recordings and learn as much about him as I could. Unfortunately, anecdotal information is as sparse as his discography. References to drug abuse, an openly gay lifestyle, a later marriage, and a prison hitch all contribute to a nebulous portrait of the man. Rollins's Vanguard set remains the most copious place to hear him solo. Along with his outstanding work for Thelonious Monk, it comprises the cornerstone of his surviving musical legacy. Jones enjoyed something of an antipodal experience, recording often over the next half century as both sideman and leader. The advances he made as a member of John Coltrane's classic quartet have their genesis here.

Much has been made of the pianolessness of Rollins's Vanguard bands and their subsequent influence within and without jazz. By the late 1950s, like many of his peers, he was embroiled in a relent-less search to extend and hone his personal sound. Experiments with groups of varying sizes and combinations of instruments were continuous, but Rollins's residence at the Vanguard allowed him the special latitude to explore a trio format, free of a strict chordal voice. His recordings at the club weren't the first made by a saxophone, bass, and drums ensemble, nor were they even his own debut in that format. That distinction goes to *Way Out West*, recorded for the Contemporary label roughly six months earlier in Los Angeles, accompanied by bassist Ray Brown and drummer Shelly Manne. The loose, playful swing that predominates that date is sharpened and in some cases hardened in the context of the Vanguard material. But Rollins's humor and obvious joy for play-ing is common to both sessions. It's a durable draw to his music, regardless of vintage.

Six months after the Vanguard, he returned to the trio format for the Riverside label, waxing the seminal *Freedom Suite* with bassist Oscar Pettiford and drummer Max Roach. That date drew appreciably on the advancements honed during his Vanguard as-signment, attaching a political subtext to the emancipated inter-play of the title piece, in tune with the developing civil rights movement. Still, Rollins couldn't help but indulge the whimsical side of his personality by filling out the program out with a hand-ful of cleverly reconstituted standards.

Rollins had, and still harbors, an unabashed affection for pop, show tunes, and Tin Pan Alley songs. Under his clever, sponta-neous modifications, tunes considered irredeemably saccharine and genteel by the average jazz aficionado were revamped into fer-tile vehicles for genuine and extended extemporaneous expression.

Rollins received his share of static for mining such supposedly "square" fare, but the results were usually hard to argue against. Any specific correlation is undocumented, to my knowledge, but I like to think Coltrane's decision to retool tunes like "My Favorite Things" and "Greensleeves" into masterpieces of modal improvisation had some precedence in the earlier forays of his longtime friend.

On the Vanguard discs, Cole Porter songs like "I've Got You Under My Skin" and "What Is This Thing Called Love" alternate with reliable bop workhorses like Dizzy Gillespie's "Woody 'N' You" and Miles Davis's "Four." The bop tunes are Rollins's bread and butter, but his affection for the Porter songs seems to run equally deep. Stretching to fourteen minutes, "What Is . . ." is barely recognizable, its final third dominated by a discursive drum solo by Jones. Patterns become so abstracted and minimalist that it's almost as if the trio has jumped the track, but Rollins's rebound, precisely picking up the rhythm where Jones's statement leaves things hanging, immediately rights the listing locomotive and reestablishes the forward trajectory. It's that sort of split-second timing and consensus cementing that situates the trio in the top tier of jazz units.

"Four" finds the trio in a bright and ebullient mood. Rollins runs robustly through the theme, his tone strapping and muscular, his solo exuding concentrated creativity. Ware resides at center, striding with a pizzicato gait that continually responds to Rollins's improvisations, maintaining the limber pace while tossing in canny counterpoint. The expected drum break catches Jones burning with a volcanic vitality, venting energy with snare rolls and cymbal showers between Rollins's rhythmic paraphrases. The three reconvene for a rousing finale, punctuated by another geyser-like cry from the saxophone.

"Woody 'N' You" dates from slightly earlier, but its swinging bop architecture proves equally suited to high-velocity blowing. A laconic count-off and Rollins's tenor takes the lead, sharp-edged and surging into an extended solo that ebbs and flows on the back of Ware's jogging bass line. His lengthy extemporization is almost numbing in its detail, stocked as it is with so much information that it continually evades easy summation. Ware's swiftly executed solo comes out of nowhere, and it's one of his best of the entire date, traversing some of the same motivic terrain as the faultless "Softly as in a Morning Sunrise" improvisations. Exhibiting stunning incisiveness, it refocuses the trio and reins Rollins back into the fold. The leader responds with yet another speedy cadenza, signing off with a series of phrases that only peripherally orbit the core theme.

Standards vastly outnumber Rollins's originals in the *Vanguard's* set list, the two specimens from his songbook confined to the second disc. My preference of the pair is "Sonnymoon for Two," built from a repeating, swaggering blues riff that cuts like a Buck knife through sinewy venison. Rollins dominates the first five minutes of the piece, swinging one pugilistic phrase after another as Ware and Jones shape a perambulating bottom beneath him with bulbous string plucks and crackling cymbals. Temporal considerations drop away; it's so easy to become enthralled by the steady threading shapeliness of his tenor line. Sandwiched between two standards, Rollins's "Striver's Row" supplies another platform for extended and expressive blowing, saxophone lines spooling out with speed and symmetry across an undulating shuffle beat. The same is true for the trio's take on the Gershwin ballad "I Can't Get Started." Rollins once again softens his articulation with a rounded romanticism, his horn inhabiting, more accurately owning, the entire performance, start to finish. Ware and Jones wisely ease back. The drummer limits himself to barely perceptible brushes and hi-hat while the bassist fashions another skeletal pulse through string-torquing plucks. It's on pieces like this one where the sheer *joie de vivre* shared by the three shines most incandescently.

Rollins's indestructible jocularity extends to the extramusical aspects of the program. He sounds relaxed and in command, but is never openly ill-natured or condescending to either the audience or his sidemen. Instead, there's an air of equanimity to his musings and demeanor. The charismatic mantle of a young jazz hotshot sits well on his shoulders. He's a man aware of his own gargantuan talents, but one also constantly visited by the need to test and question them, never the sort to needlessly brag. His readiness to push the creative envelope arises not out of insecurity or worry that that he will be bested by a peer, but instead out of an internal desire to continuously stretch his parameters. In this sense, he stands apart from the stereotypical ace improvisers of earlier years, the Sonny Stitts and Roy Eldridges who made it their business to "cut" colleagues on the arena of battle that was the bandstand. Rollins's attitude was and remains conversely self-effacing and indicative of new directions and pursuits. It's a philosophy that would lead him down intriguing, and to my mind endlessly admirable, pathways of further self-discovery as his career progressed.

That particular night at the Vanguard, Rollins regularly addressed the crowd, joking and wisecracking like a stand-up comic in places, tossing off non sequiturs that instantly charmed with their peculiar reference points and sense of timing. During the spoken preface to "Old Devil Moon," he engages the audience in a debate as to the show tune's origins, querying whether it comes from *Finian's Rainbow* or *Kiss Me Kate*. The crowd answers with evenly divisive enthusiasm. Recognizing the time as ripe for another clever quip, Rollins settles the deadlock by crediting the song to the currently popular production of *Lil' Abner*.

The drollery permeates the music as well. Rollins regularly toys with the themes, parsing them, inverting them, and at times just plain discarding them. He's constantly on the move, and a sense of sharklike momentum maintains across the entire program. On "Moon," he sails through the mellow, effacing theme, his bell-clear horn traveling on another drum break–riddled journey with Ware vamping indomitably at his side. "Get Happy," a tune that carries a fair share of saccharine sweetness in so many other incarnations, gains weight and resonance, a genuine artistic depth under Rollins's impromptu ministrations.

Delving into the reasons why this set held such an enduring fascination for me was a difficult process. In the end, I think it comes down to its place as a harbinger of so much that came after. It's a convenient and comprehensive representation of the essence of what constitutes modern jazz in my mind. Such a large part of my listening diet over the last decade revolves around music made possible by these performances. So much Free Jazz and Fire Music past and present relies on the same configuration of instruments and the same general desire to push song forms to and past their limits.

In the many years since Rollins's Vanguard stand the numbers of fellow saxophonists who have experimented with a pianoless trio now far outweighs the numbers who haven't. The list is nearly

limitless, and runs a spectrum encompassing Ornette Coleman's
Golden Circle forays, also for Blue Note, through New Thing lead-
ers like Archie Shepp and Sam Rivers, to luminaries of other styles
of jazz like Warne Marsh and Lee Konitz. In recent years, newer
voices like James Finn and Stephen Gauci have fronted kindred
trios that are taking jazz in fresh directions. In a sense, the configuration has become almost as commonplace as the saxophone plus
piano-led rhythm section that preceded it. It's emblematic of the
idiom and shows no signs of settling into obsolescence. Perhaps
most directly indicative of the lineage, Joe Henderson, a Rollins
peer and a highly influential tenor saxophonist in his own right,
recorded his own set, *The State of the Tenor*, within the walls of the
Vanguard. Twenty-eight years to the month after Rollins's historic
stand, Henderson joined bassist Ron Carter and drummer Al Fos-
ter for another program of standards and originals in front of a
fortunate audience. The resultant two-disc set, also from Blue
Note, is a beautiful complement to Rollins's original run.

Sonny Rollins effectively bridges a divide between past and future with his Vanguard performances. The bop conventions of
theme statements, drum breaks, and exchanges of fours are present on many of the tracks. They're reliable signposts often used as
adhesive to connect the more discursive segments of the trio's
peregrinations, but they also give way to surprising passages that
presage the less-strictured jazz of later years. Rollins witnessed the
entire evolution of free jazz, from its nascent forms in the 1950s
through its solidification into the sometimes subtext-laden music
of the 1960s New Thing. He flirted periodically with it, most often
in live settings but also on pivotal recordings like *East Broadway
Run Down* for Impulse and *Our Man in Jazz* for RCA, but he never

fully abandoned form or custom. Just drop in on his closing send-off to the evening Vanguard take of "A Night in Tunisia," where he skirts the edges of tonality with braying honks and growling slurs. Listening to those vanguard voicings, it's not difficult to draw lines that lead to the iconoclastic work of later students like tenor saxophonist David S. Ware. That questing spirit and refusal to align with the status quo are virtues I repeatedly draw upon as inspiration for my own undertakings in life.

Longevity has proven an obvious blessing for Rollins, but also one plagued by predictable costs. He's lived many of the clichés of the jazz life, creating a few of his own along the way. Early on, he struggled through painful detours as drug addict and petty criminal, learning quickly from his mistakes made as both. His skills as an improviser were such that he rose to the top of his craft within a single short decade. At the close of the '60s, with his popularity at its zenith, he dropped out and devoted himself to other endeavors, a method of escape and renewal he would repeat periodically over the years. His place and popularity in jazz history are ironclad and unassailable, but there are still plenty of people who dismiss him on the dubious grounds of creative stagnation for his decisions to play with bands and material arguably far beneath his talent. To my mind, these charges are bogus and speak more to audience expectations and prejudices than any failings or faltering on Rollins's part.

Sure, he's gotten older. His age often precludes the sort of extended improvisatory flights that are on such ample and astounding display across the *Vanguard* discs. A comparison with his *Without a Song* concert recording, released in 2005, but taped just days after September 11, 2001, tellingly reveals the disparities between

Rollins the twentysomething heavyweight and Rollins the septuagenarian patriarch. He's also gotten comfortable, with himself and with his long-standing preferences. But his acumen and intelligence remain undiminished. Complacency doesn't seem a viable option for a man of his convictions and consistently inquisitive nature. More fundamentally, he's earned the inalienable right to play whatever he wants in whatever setting he likes. I've listened to *A Night At The Village Vanguard* in its entirety more times than I care to count. To me it fulfills the one fundamental requisite of a desert island pick: an album that yields new information and insight every time it's channeled through a set of speakers. If I have any say about it, and future progeny honor my will, this set will become a family heirloom on par with my great-great-uncle's bloodstained Civil War cutlass and my great-grandfather's complete first edition set of the works of Edgar Allan Poe. It holds commensurate significance to my personal history, and more importantly, belongs in the possession of anyone with even the passing interest in the American art form of jazz.

20

IRON MAIDEN
Killers
Capitol, 1981

BY IAN CHRISTE

LET'S BRIEFLY RECAP THE FAMILIAR SCENARIO: A MIGHTY VESSEL DEPOSITS ME ON A FARAWAY ISLAND, AND IN-STEAD OF FRIENDLY NATIVES THE FIRST BEING I EN-counter is a heavenly series producer who asks what one music selection I want delivered. Not a care for whether I'm hungry, hurt, or lonesome—he just needs a callous bit of music research for the desert island division. Sounds like a familiar parlor game, but I'm very glad somebody finally asked. A few years back I was actually stranded on a floating half-acre of useless land for an un-reasonable period of time. By a stroke of fate, I began my ordeal with a broad selection of music. Fortunately, I survived to tell the story exactly as it happened.

My nightmare began during an ill-fated transatlantic flight home from London after seeing Napalm Death and the Melvins. One of our tired jet engines exploded somewhere between Ire-land and Iceland. The pilot descended to just above water level, cruising above floating chunks of ice for more than an hour. I watched across the aisle as a priest tried to comfort a bored five-year-old girl, while on the movie screen Bette Midler was dancing a burlesque striptease in *The First Wives Club*. As I wiped her chubby fishnets clear from my eyes, our starboard wing dipped and collided with a large iceberg, sending the cabin into darkness and confusion.

When I became conscious, the airplane was half-submerged and bobbing in the Greenland Sea. I had been thrown clear of the wreckage, and my battered CD player swung from my neck skipping on a bluesy vocal roar from Carcass's "Keep on Rotting in the Free World." Voices all around cried for assistance, but in the twilight I could see nothing but faintly blinking lights as the aircraft's tail slipped into the ocean with a mighty dismal creak. Afterwards everything grew silent. Trembling, I tunneled into the snow, fashioning a crude igloo from my skimpy blanket and flotation device. I lay immobilized by shock, humming Bill Monroe's plaintive "Footprints in the Snow" until dawn.

The next morning I could only see smoke and litter. We had not eaten our meals before the catastrophe, so when I found a case of foil cartons I mixed the Kosher and vegetarian meals together with the sauced meat and prepared for a rough day. Also spilled from the flight cabin and now taunting me was a tape-loop cartridge used to feed low-level hum through the airplane armrests to cover up wing noise. When people who listen to in-flight music become wing mechanics, airplanes crash frequently, and I blamed their lazy incompetence for my plight. Raging, I reduced the smarmy U2 and the Black Eyed Peas's rock-soul-pop mix to a copyright-free heap of sharp plastic shards.

I stood alone on my ice flotilla—the other survivors must have tumbled to a separate island. Voices were yelling nearby—I could tell it wasn't the wind. Stumbling across my iceberg towards panicked voices, I heard the hovering roar of seaplanes. An olive drab military plane was evacuating men in robes and women wearing headgear. Soldiers pushed outstretched arms away as they helped the VIP families aboard the rescue craft. I was too delirious, and the weather too windy, to see any clearer. I could barely take twenty steps before I was forced to return to my snow hutch.

The weather gentled before gauzy midday. I regained my strength and ventured out again to find my entire landscape cluttered with the innards of several flight cases packed with CDs and vinyl records and tagged with orange stickers promoting "DJ F8— Freeform Fatwa UK." I hurled the first batch of twelve-inchers into the ocean in frustration, stupidly wasting my precious resources. Like so many distraught refugees before me, music would save my life. Breaking open a box of Smithsonian Folkways CDs, I studied the anthropological notes for survival details, then burned the thick booklets for heat and light. The discs themselves I dangled in prismatic constellations, hoping to catch the fading sunlight and signal someone.

I seemed to be floating in the wrong direction, as sounds grew more faint. Resigned to a slow rescue, I made my improvised nest into a fully insulated winter fortress. Carefully, I flipped through discs for an early '70s pressing of Amon Düül II's *Yeti*, and used the thick vinyl to shovel a more protective alcove for myself in the snowdrift. The K Records collection held back the snow, and the vintage pastel patterns on Softies and Beat Happening albums made soothing wallpaper. I heard the records snapping against the weight of the snow, but they held. Finally I opened the gatefold sleeve of Venom's *At War With Satan* and rubbed my hands together wishfully over the orange flames of the burning crucifix.

When I grew tired of eating airplane food, I shattered a Raymond Scott "Powerhouse" seventy-eight, and lashed together a crude spear using some tubing from the plane's fuselage. Aiming the reflections of my dangling CD signal toward the sea, I hunted young harbor seals. Burning more CD booklets, I sucked seal fat from the bone and added their furs to my increasingly swank bachelor's lair. Feeling a little like Boz Scaggs, I rolled up and smoked the swollen cardboard of his pimping *Middle Man* LP—enough pot smoke permeated my musty secondhand copy that I got a little high. I propped up a couple of glitter blizzards, Miss Broadway's *Belle Epoque* and Liquid Gold's *My Baby's Baby*, to liven up the scene. In this freezing temperature, the thrift store smell didn't bother me at all.

At least I was alive, if only barely. Thanks to the frigid air, my CD player's batteries enjoyed a long productive life, but eventually they were spent. Noting the slight powdery glint of the frozen earth, I received the inspiration that makes the rest of this story even possible. Sparing the usual scientific details, I was able to isolate enough zinc and carbon from the soil to create a rudimentary battery cell. This power source was nothing too elaborate, but with the help of some tangled cockpit wire it sparked the insides of the CD player. Glad I paid attention in seventh-grade science.

With my situation somewhat stabilized, I took stock. Here I was on a deserted slab of ice, surrounded by most of the decent recorded music in recent memory. Was I living in a cartoon in an old issue of Tower Records's *Pulse*? I started to daydream about the soundtracks to all the possible islands in the world. I've heard of a Boney M cover band that performs in a hotel lobby on the Canary Islands. You have to swim to your room, and every suite has its own waterfall. Then there are the cold mossy cliff islands outside the Isle of Man, where anything louder than the sheep and goats gets a standing ovation. On this cold polar drift I was overjoyed to have all 237 volumes of *Now That's What I Call Music*. I burned them to survive, and my conscience is clear.

Like a bad smell at a convention of rock critics, the desert island record question lingered. The *Blue Lagoon* soundtrack I used as an ashtray, and it reminded me of the original Italian film *Swept Away*. Forget about weedy Madonna. If only I was stuck with a porcine upper-class Mediteranean goddess like Mariangela Melato, I'd be compelled for political reasons to ravage her frequently to the tune of something from a Jess Franco soundtrack, or James Horner's excellent score from *Aliens*. Ejaculating during the violin stabs subverts the misogynist patriarchy. It really does. But ultimately sex about politics is worse than dancing about architecture.

Back home in New York, I could blank out for hours with a great mid-90s drum 'n' bass compilation like *Jungle Massive* or *History of Our World Part I*. I could start a new Arctic civilization with a few good dance records—same goes for Black Oak Arkansas's first album, Parliament's *Chocolate City*, or two copies of Kraftwerk's *Computer World*. But my island didn't have a mixer, let alone an optical cross-fader, let alone any women of breeding age.

I lost interest in Sigur Rós quickly. What's the point of music that emulates isolation and nature when isolation and nature are all I have? If I dropped it in the snow, I'd never find it. The opposite

was true for Oval's *Diskont*. I didn't want to drone out on cold office machine glitches. I couldn't help feeling that electronic ambient music was progressing swiftly without me back on the
mainland. Even alone on an island the best music of 1995 sounded
dated. Even the best club music of last week would sound hopelessly retro by the time it floated out to me.

Time stretched; summer came. I was accustomed to my fate
and practically enjoying myself. I used Sonic Youth's *Sister* as a dinner plate for steamed sea urchin and young walrus steak. Every
time I heard "Stereo Sanctity" I became royally pissed at all the for-
mulaic, unadventurous albums that band made afterward. For different reasons, *Scott Walker Sings Jacques Brel* became a fishing lure.
Despite the great associations, I was afraid of the effects of his
craven voice on my mental well-being. I was already starting to believe that the BBC was secretly filming me. I hoped the program-
ming department found my antics entertaining. I made a point of
flashing the covers to the most hated albums I used every morning
in my latrine trench. Take that, Kula Shaker.

One morning after unwinding Southern rap cassingles to use as
fishing line, I discovered I had eliminated, broken, or put to better
use every last note of recorded music on my island except for Iron
Maiden's second album, *Killers*. I jump-started the Discman and let
the flowery warning storm of "Ides of March" pollinate my numb
head. After a hanging pause, "Wrathchild" stormed down its
warpath. I agreed with each well-orchestrated flourish, the guitar
trills and drumrolls locked onto busy bass notes. I reflected that
this was what British punk could have sounded like with lots of
well-designed machinery instead of clever T-shirts. On that clear

morning, the scents of Thin Lizzy, Judas Priest, and bluegrass flew from *Killers* like primary colors on an elementary school mural.

I let the album play, ignoring the lazy gull waddling nearby and the potential lunch it presented. (Gull stomachs contain the most exquisite seafood terrine.) *Killers* astonished me anew—a majestic old-world terminal of an album that shrouds its destinations in heavy metal revolution. "Murders in the Rue Morgue" brings on Edgar Allan Poe-try. When Paul Di'Anno blurts "I was strolling through the streets of *Par-ee*/It was cold, it was starting to rain," he might as well be Serge Gainsbourg. The song's protagonist is accused of butchering two girls, yet he doesn't remember how he came to be standing in a back alley. His voice is so unencumbered by manners he seems to be thinking aloud. Absorbing the meticulous humanity of Iron Maiden, I started to forget I'd been sleeping in a 40-degree Fahrenheit hole in the ground for months.

I clutched the album, glad I had protected this one and its secrets until last. *Killers* is the music of captured civilization, a labyrinth of back alleys and secret passages. Each musical part is stacked to cooperate. Though the insistent bass of Steve Harris guides the ensemble, no simple-minded groove dominates its logic. Each player performs a separate integral role. Even the album cover, with its savage, grisly axe murder, is loaded with little jokes and gimmicks. The background presents a gritty European utopia populated by black cats, concerned citizens peering through window blinds, and red light district exhibitionists like the buxom flight attendant grappling with a nude man in her shower. The apartment buildings with their upright maze of television aerials are a contorted technological mess. I missed that patched-together grid we call modernity. And of course, always at the foreground, a truly frightening early painting of Eddie, raising a hatchet dripping with thick viscous blood while a pair of weak hands plead for mercy by clawing at the ghoul's white T-shirt. Who is being killed in the picture? Probably just some elderly hypocrite. Examining the image, I saw I'd remembered correctly—

Eddie wears Wrangler jeans.

After setting out a few fresh seal pelts to cure, I thought of all these details while the sky above my isle turned gray with foreboding clouds—just like the ceiling of smog and London fog on the album cover. At the time of *Killers's* release, Iron Maiden wasn't shooting for fourteen-year-olds yet. They already had a rapt urban audience of restless young adults ready to drink and shake the night away, educated enough to require substance in their newbreed metal deluge. *Killers* dealt with moral conflict like the plight of the Keats-inspired "Prodigal Son." Since I had no books to occupy my time, the simple words set to fluid, horror-inspired heavy metal grappled my imagination like the tentacles of the large inky squids I had caught using hooks baited with MIA "Sunshowers" radio promo discs.

One difference from the first Iron Maiden album is the addition of Urchin guitarist Adrian Smith, whose sharper style cut sharp melodic arcs through the long fluid lines of Dave Murray. The singer Paul Di'Anno was replaced before the next album, *The Number of the Beast,* and the band's international success, but in my predicament I didn't need Bruce Dickinson's stadium-sized air-raid siren of a voice. I wanted to hear a real human being. Likewise, drummer Clive Burr beats a stepping-stone path through the stories like a guide, not a tower of thunder. *Killers* heightened the mental and emotional experience of floating around the dull white sea. Even if all roads on *Killers* lead back to Iron Maiden mascot Eddie's skinny yellow cartoon arms on the record jacket, this record made my forced vacation three-dimensional.

A mid-level regional sales manager in Medina, Ohio, might listen to Jimmy Buffett for a cheap desert island vacation. When you are in fact on a desert island, the meditative onslaught of "Killers" does just fine. The line Paul Di'Anno snarls about his eyes burning a hole through the back of an innocent commuter walking through subway tunnels is supremely vicious, summoning the tube chase sequences in *An American Werewolf in London*. That's what I'm looking for in desert isle isolation—music about subway tunnels. Not inspired by subway tunnels, or Brian Eno–style *Music for Subways*—I want to imagine the great engineering ingenuity submerged beneath large cities, where trains filled with people zoom over and under sewage pipes, secret electrical conduits, and undiscovered Roman cemeteries. The fact that the song is a first-person boast by a Jack the Ripper–style killer, well—that bloodlust is the cracks in the sidewalk of humanity that make cities hum with anxious energy.

All the songs except for the brief subway sequence in "Killers" seem to take place outside. As the sole inhabitant of a wee island, I could relate to that. Don't tell me I should be listening to Steely Dan's *Aja* or Fleetwood Mac's *Rumours*—that's indoor music! On days when it was too bright to even read the lyrics to Voivod's *Dimension Hatross*, I could burrow in the snow and venture forth on Iron Maiden's lurid journeys.

The Western world could rebuild itself pretty well on the blueprint of Iron Maiden's second album. Sure, you could say there's
too great an emphasis on *killing*, but what's so unusual about that?
The trundling rhythms emulate just about every mode of trans-
portation and machinery in human history. If we can't recreate
civilization on the galloping acoustic guitar, ever-pumping bass,
and spectral vocals of the love song "Another Life" then we suck at
emotional archaeology and have no business sending hieroglyphic
codes into deep space for hapless aliens to decipher. My mind felt
almost overpopulated.

Ultimately, I could live with *Killers* for a long time—even back
on dry land, a cassette dupe of the album was always close to my
Walkman or car stereo. I had probably passed years alone with
this record already. Incredibly, at least three songs on the album
specifically deal with extended isolation: "Innocent Exile," "Purgatory," and "Prodigal Son." Thank God I got the American edition of the album including "Twilight Zone"—the track is
practically a desert island training manual, discussing how the
memory of a person missing for three years fades over time like a
phantom. Sadly, every castaway has to learn to deal with that. It's
a desert island thang.

With Iron Maiden doing arpeggio runs on my moral fiber, I became filled with thoughts of vengeance. I realized I wasn't passively stranded out on the ice. I had been actively *marooned*,
intentionally set aside like so many protagonists of Iron Maiden
songs. That hurt me. I'm really glad I made snowshoes out of
Gary Numan's anesthetic *Tubeway Army* album. *Killers* was actually preparing me psychologically for reentry. Fuckers wanted to

leave me for dead? After listening to *Killers* enough, I was ready to wreak massive havoc.

While I rocked back and forth, the perimeter of my floe raft was melting throughout the so-called summer. My world physically shrank, and I dreaded the coming cold. The Inuits break our calendar year into eight seasons, the warmest one a mere three-week summer hiatus between "later-late spring" and "pre-early winter." Plus the sea lions were starting to sniff around my pungent environment. I took down a beloved Mariah Carey pinup fearing it would attract horny two-ton sea lion bulls. I grew a little morose. I considered using the *Killers* sleeve as my headstone. Maybe I deserved to grow a beard and turn half-mad, then die alone in a cold, quiet place while listening to Iron Maiden.

Alone with my thoughts, I spent a final sleepless night gazing at the dancing lights and mucus-like array of stellar constellations visible only from the far North. A family of orca whales circled, perhaps like vultures knowing my time was short. They certainly could have swallowed my encampment whole if they wished—not before swallowing the shattered scraps of the entire Matador catalog. Choke on this Chavez joint, Shamu!

Knowing that I would never escape if I let another day pass, the next morning I began to dig deep down, using empty record jackets to keep the mossy earth from falling down and burying me alive. The sounds of *Killers* faded behind me, the makeshift battery wires unable to reach deep enough into the shaft. About thirty feet down, I reached a stopping point, a hard edge against which I could dig no more. Oddly, Steve Harris's directive bass lines were much louder at the bottom of the hole. I was exhausted and finally demoralized, convinced that I had already reached the Earth's extending crust. No way I could persevere through two miles of rock into the molten core of our planet, into hell's very fire—wrong Iron Maiden album, anyway.

As I collapsed on the floor of my tunnel, my hand hit something cold and brassy—a doorknob. I panicked, realizing I was atop a thick wooden door. This could not be. I clawed the wet dirt away from the knob, turned and pushed downward. As the latch unclasped I fell, hurtling wet, hairy, hungry, and delirious into an unkempt bedroom, and hit my head hard against a nightstand before falling onto the floor. Iron Maiden's "Drifter" blasted from a small compact stereo, the final song on *Killers*.

After a moment I reoriented, blinking my eyes. Down had become sideways, and I couldn't tell which end was up. I realized I was in a junior high school bedroom, a generic but immaculate simulacrum of a place I'd left behind over a decade ago. This impossible turn of events made perfect sense. The adolescent cave of eighth grade is the ultimate desert island in which lifelong musical biases are carved into the mind like hashmarks on a palm's trunk. I need the panic of "Killers" and "Wrathchild," and the seamless orchestration of "Genghis Khan" and "Another Life," just like the true grit of Motörhead's *On Parole*, the crystalline coldness of Judas Priest's *Stained Class*, and the inspired amateurism of Venom's *Welcome to Hell*. I see so much music through this lens. The quickening pace of "Innocent Exile" punctuated by drum blasts preceded the later breakbeat era. A favorite album is a choice of a desert island, not the other way around. To endorse Pavement's *Crooked Rain, Crooked Rain* is to lock into pre-skyscraper Williamsburg, Brooklyn, and suffer for the past. I guess the cult of dead musicians explains why so many people die when stranded on desert islands.

Walking through the bedroom door opposite I emerged onto a crowded subway platform. I felt free for the first time in months, and not the least bit surprised. Though everything felt vividly unnatural, following the trials of survival anything seemed acceptable. I recognized the train station as being nearly underneath Ground Zero in lower Manhattan. One of the first posters I saw on the wall advertised something called an iPod, a device that would radically change the future of desert island castaway music. Although my wet, worn outfit did not seem out of place, the scent of the ocean lingered. I was aware of eyes looking at me—lots of uptight Republican closet cases and the casual quick eye contact of curious females. I realized Iron Maiden couldn't help me any longer. My eyes burned holes through a few backs, sure, but I had not taken the lyrics of *Killers* too literally. I forgave the sloppy mechanics whose mind-numbing music made them too stupid to keep a plane in the air.

Hurtling home on the express, though, I was grateful that I had dug through all the drivel and found something to help me survive. I found a home in *Killers*. And now once again I can have all music, or I can choose nothing. Being freed from the island means being a citizen of the world again, a traveler across all recorded terrains. *Killers* taught me to experience all of it more richly. Now I believe we all spend much of our lives on desert islands, so the moral of the story is: pick your fucking records well.

21

RETURN TO TREASURE ISLAND

The final section of *Stranded* was Greil Marcus's attempt to answer the "martian question"—how do you define rock 'n' roll to a total stranger? And he did a pretty good job, albeit one that didn't mention Aerosmith or Black Sabbath or Van Halen, even though the first of those had beaten the Stones at their own game for five straight years, the second created a whole genre in its image (but who saw that coming, right?), and the third were secretly the Beach Boys' younger, meaner brothers. But I'm not gonna go backward and try to fix his errors in judgment here, in this space. This book isn't a rebuttal; it's a sequel. Thus, here in the back pages of *Marooned*, I will attempt to answer the martian who's asking me, "What's been going on with music since 1979?" For every album or song listed here, there are a dozen equally worthy candidates I omitted, but each one of these says something important about the state of music since 1979—how venerable forms have changed, how new ones have sprung up, etc. Some are just great songs the listener would have been poorer for having missed.

THE 5.6.7.8'S, *Bomb the Rocks: Early Days Singles 1989 to 1996* (Time Bomb). Three Japanese girls with more edge than the over-cutesy Shonen Knife. They weren't interested in pretending to be children; as they put it on a track not included here, they walked like Jayne Mansfield. A little surf, a little garage, a whole lot of throbbing jungle rhythm, and the occasional scream. 2003.

AC/DC, "You Shook Me All Night Long" (Atlantic). Their boogie died with Bon Scott, but this song had enough sex to overcome the martial stomping that was the rhythm section's near-exclusive purview from here on out. 1980.

————, "Thunderstruck" (Epic). Another exception to the rule. 1990.

ALICE IN CHAINS, "Would" (Epic). 1992.

ANAAL NATHRAKH, *The Codex Necro* (Mordgrimm). Black metal, a howl from the windblown Scandinavian tundra (or anyway, the basements of urban twentysomethings who wished they lived there), here adapted and run through the industrial noise-grinder by two nerds from England. A sustained, bilious shriek from hell's hard drive. 2003.

LAURIE ANDERSON, "O Superman" (Warner Bros.). 1981.

ANGRY SAMOANS, *The Unboxed Set* (Triple X). A hilarious first-wave L.A. punk outfit, pretending (quite convincingly at times) to be dumbasses. This single CD has everything (an ill-advised '90s reunion album aside), because why choose when any likely candidate is over in ninety seconds anyway? 1995.

APHEX TWIN, *Selected Ambient Works II* (Sire). Untitled pieces that drift like the lucid dreams he says he has. 1994.

FIONA APPLE, "Sleep To Dream" (Sony). 1996.

————, "Extraordinary Machine" (Sony). 2005.

THE ART OF NOISE, *(Who's Afraid Of?)* (ZTT). Early adopters, they knew everything in the world was fuel for the sampler. Three white people from England to whom hip-hop owes a mostly unacknowledged debt. 1984.

ATERCIOPELADOS, *Evolucion: Grandes Exitos* (BMG). A sometime couple from Colombia. She's a hippie poetess, he's the construction chief who builds albums around her. Solo discs have only served to prove how much they need each other, and this compilation's title is revealing—from punky beginnings they got a little more electronic and a lot prettier over the years. 2002.

ATHEIST, *Piece Of Time* (Relapse). Death metal was a raw-throated, blues-bereft roar from the Florida swamps when this was recorded. Lead guitarist Kelly Shaefer and bassist/partner Roger Patterson pushed the genre toward something more like amped-up jazz fusion, with lyrics that explored rote rage on this album, but on (Patterson-less) sequels turned philosophical and ecological by turns. 1990/2006.

AUTECHRE, *LP5* (Warp). This is the kind of music computers would make if the only listeners were other computers. 1998.

————, *EP7* (Warp). 1999.

————, *Confield* (Warp). 2001.

THE B-52's, *The B-52's* (Island). Herky-jerky funk that shouldn't work but does, with atonal screeching and gay-redneck yawping on top. They pretend they're only kidding around, but you can't get to a place like this by accident. 1979.

————, *Wild Planet* (Island). 1980.

BAD BRAINS, *Bad Brains* (ROIR). Four black guys from D.C. who discovered Rasta right around the time they gave up jazz fusion for nine hundred mph punk. They beat the white skinheads at their own game for several years, and pretty much invented funk-metal on their fourth album before burning out in 1989. 1982.

————, *Rock For Light* (PVC). The reggae is better on this follow-up, and the original mix, by producer Ric Ocasek, was fuller and more listener-friendly than hardcore had offered before. Later remixed, poorly, and reissued on Caroline with a different running order. Track down the original. 1983.

AFRIKA BAMBAATA & SOULSONIC FORCE, "Looking for the Perfect Beat" (Tommy Boy). 1982.

BAUHAUS, "Bela Lugosi's Dead" (Small Wonder). The song that started Goth. Turns out one song was enough. 1979.

BEASTIE BOYS, *Paul's Boutique* (Capitol). For one album, they weren't smarmy or sanctimonious. They built a wall of samples, and behind it took off their masks, revealing three thoughtful observers of an adopted Los Angeles. 1989.

BEAT HAPPENING, *You Turn Me On* (K). Instrumental incompetence and faux-naïveté by and for college students. Included lest we forget. 1992.

BEBE, "Malo" (EMI). An angry dismantling of machismo from a Spanish singer-songwriter. 2004.

BELLE AND SEBASTIAN, *If You're Feeling Sinister* (Matador). 1996.

BIG BLACK, *Atomizer* (Homestead). A drum machine set on "pile driver," guitars set on "jigsaw" and "pavement saw," respectively, and lyrics about how much everything sucks. 1986.

BIG DADDY KANE, "Raw" (Cold Chillin'). 1986.

BIKINI KILL, *The CD Version Of The First Two Records* (Kill Rock Stars). Entirely legitimate female anger channeled into punk that plays by the sonic rules of the boys' club scene it decries. 1992.

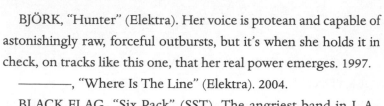

BJÖRK, "Hunter" (Elektra). Her voice is protean and capable of astonishingly raw, forceful outbursts, but it's when she holds it in check, on tracks like this one, that her real power emerges. 1997.

————, "Where Is The Line" (Elektra). 2004.

BLACK FLAG, "Six Pack" (SST). The angriest band in L.A., they rarely let their funny side show, but this single is a sneering classic. 1980.

————, *My War* (SST). On this album they kept their grimaces screwed on airtight. The fast side's brilliant, but the slow side allowed vocalist Henry Rollins to hammer home the real message— that punk and metal were blood brothers. 1984.

————, *Slip It In* (SST). There's even more metal in guitarist/ leader Greg Ginn's cranked-up, contorted riffs, and better drumming, especially on "The Bars," a heart-burster. 1984.

————, *Live '84* (SST). A gig so furious you're glad it's safely contained on CD—the idea of being there while it happened all around you is terrifying. 1985.

THE BLASTERS, *The Blasters* (Slash). Rockabilly, country, and the blues fueled by the energy that punk floated into L.A.'s air in the late '70s and early '80s—plus, of course, the combustible relationship between vocalist Phil Alvin and his guitarist brother Dave. 1981.

————, *Over There: Live At The Venue, London* (Slash). A blazing batch of covers with even more energy than their debut. 1982.

————, *Non Fiction* (Slash). Dave Alvin blossoms as a songwriter, and their music begins to become their own, rather than a pastiche of their influences. 1983.

BLONDIE, "Heart Of Glass" (Chrysalis). 1978.

KURTIS BLOW, "The Breaks" (Sugar Hill). 1980

BLUR, "Girls & Boys" (Food/SBK). 1994.

——— "Song 2" (Food/Virgin). 1997.

BORBETOMAGUS, *Barbed Wire Maggots* (Agaric). 1982.

BRATMOBILE, *Pottymouth* (Lookout!). 1993.

BURNT SUGAR, *Black Sex Yall: Liberation & Bloody Random Violets* (Trugroid). Contributor Greg Tate's amorphous ensemble treats the history of African American music as a vast river, coming up with something new every time they dip into it. This album encompasses metal, drum 'n' bass, jazz, and whatever Miles Davis was doing in 1974 (they cover his "Mtume"). 2003.

BURZUM, *Filosofem* (Misanthropic). Recorded in solitude by the former bassist for Norwegian black metal band Mayhem, this is cold, alienating music. The guitar riffs loop slowly, the programmed rhythms never erupting into catharsis. A good soundtrack to six months of northern darkness. 1996.

BUTTHOLE SURFERS, *Psychic . . . Powerless . . . Another Man's Sac* (Touch & Go). Texas punks who took impossible amounts of hallucinogenics to help them push punk's confrontationalism beyond mere anger at straight society into the realm of total sensory overload and disorientation. 1983.

———, *Rembrandt Pussyhorse* (Touch & Go). 1986.

———, *Cream Corn from the Socket of Davis* (Touch & Go). This album, and its predecessor immediately above, expand the band's sound into the realm of tape loops, unsettling demolitions of Grand Funk Railroad and the Guess Who, and much more. 1986.

———, *Hairway to Steven* (Touch & Go). Big riff-rock, a ballad that could have been a single if it wasn't for the lyrics, and some of vocalist Gibby Haynes's most surreal poetry. 1987.

DAVID BYRNE/BRIAN ENO, *My Life in the Bush of Ghosts* (EG). Tapes of preachers, looped rhythms, fragments of groove— more important for what it inspired than what it actually sounds like. 1981.

CAFÉ TACUBA, *Avalancha de Exitos* (WEA Latina). Before they made their masterpiece, this Mexican art-pop quartet acknowledged their roots with a batch of cover tunes. 1996.

————, *Reves/Yosoy* (WEA Latina). A two-CD set, one instrumental, the other a suite of melodic, occasionally psychedelic pop songs. On every level, a huge leap beyond everything their peers were doing. 1999.

CAMEO, "Word Up" (Mercury). 1986.

CASPAR BRÖTZMANN MASSAKER, *Home* (Thirsty Ear). The guitarist son of lung-busting tenor saxophonist Peter doesn't go for all-out assault like his dad. Instead, he lets his tracks burn slowly for ten or fifteen minutes at a stretch, the guitar intermittently exploding into Hendrixian power chords and walls of noise. 1995.

CARDINAL, *Cardinal* (Flydaddy). 1994.

KIM CARNES, "Bette Davis Eyes" (EMI America). 1981.

JOHNNY CASH, "Hurt" (American). 2004.

THE CHEMICAL BROTHERS, *Singles 1993–2003* (Astralwerks). This pair of Englishmen combined the thundering aggressiveness of Public Enemy's production team, the Bomb Squad, with an urge to fill the dance floor at any cost. 2005.

NENEH CHERRY, "Buffalo Stance" (Virgin). 1989.

THE CHILLS, *Submarine Bells* (Slash). They wrote a song called "Heavenly Pop Hit," but there was no way they were ever going to actually have one of their own. Groups that think too much about the meaning of pop never do. 1990.

ALEX CHILTON, "No Sex" (Big Time). 1986.

THE CIRCLE JERKS, *Group Sex* (Frontier). Recycled riffs and hilarious lyrics. They were pretty much a one-joke band, but fuck it, it was their debut album. 1980.

THE CLASH, "I Fought The Law" (Epic). 1979.

————, *London Calling* (Epic). Sprawling and overrated, but still good. 1979.

————, "Bankrobber" (Epic). 1980.

————, "Police On My Back" (Epic). 1980.

GEORGE CLINTON, "Atomic Dog" (Capitol). 1982.

LEONARD COHEN, "Closing Time" (Columbia). 1992.

————, "Democracy" (Columbia). 1992.

COLDPLAY, *Live 2003* (Capitol). All the best songs from their first two studio albums, heard in their proper context—they write minor-key balladry made for arenas. 2003.

CLAUDE COMA & THE IVs, *Art From Sin* (Government). Mordant humor ("Berserk On The Bus," "Child Molester") and upbeat, New Wave melody. A local band that should have gotten bigger. 1982.

THE CONTORTIONS, *Buy The Contortions* (ZE). James Chance took Robert "Chopper" McCullough's work with James Brown's 1969–70 band—skronking free sax over jagged funk—and assaulted New York's art-punk scenesters with it. In other words, it's not what you've got, but how well you can sell it that counts. 1979.

COOLIO, "Fantastic Voyage" (Tommy Boy). 1994.

————, "Gangsta's Paradise" (Tommy Boy). 1995.

CORNERSHOP, "Brimful of Asha" (Luaka Bop/Warner Bros.). 1997.

THE CRAMPS, *Gravest Hits* (IRS). Rockabilly at half-speed, throbbing like an undead heart. This five-song EP mixes originals with covers rendered almost unrecognizable. 1979.

————, *Songs The Lord Taught Us* (IRS). Same as the EP, but more so, and their black humor starts to come to the fore ("I was a teenage werewolf/Braces on my fangs"). 1980.

————, *Psychedelic Jungle* (IRS). A fuzzier, more echo-soaked album that finds them exploring garage rock. 1981.

————, *Bad Music For Bad People* (IRS). An odds-and-ends collection, occasionally so raw it sounds unearthed. 1982.

————, *Smell Of Female* (New Rose). A raucous EP of live versions of otherwise unreleased songs. 1983.

CRYPTOPSY, *Whisper Supremacy* (Century Media). Death metal is a music that attracts obsessives, willing to spend hours writing and rehearsing ultra-complex riff structures that owe absolutely nothing to the blues. These French Canadians are among the current masters of the form, and this album is more head-spinning than headbanging. 1998.

THE CURE, *Standing On A Beach: The Singles* (Elektra). Melancholy lyrics backed by surprisingly anthemic riffs and rhythms. 1986.

————, *Disintegration* (Elektra). 1988.

CYPRESS HILL, "How I Could Just Kill a Man" (Columbia). 1991.

DAFT PUNK, "Da Funk" (Virgin). 1996.

————, "Harder, Better, Faster, Stronger" (Virgin). 2001.

MILES DAVIS, *We Want Miles* (Columbia). Miles came back after five years of coke and paranoia with an airtight band more or less half his age, and drove them through slow sets of steaming street funk, his biting trumpet dueling for space with Mike Stern's screaming guitar leads. 1981.

————, *Tutu* (Warner Bros.). A line in the sand drawn to separate everything Miles had done in three decades at Columbia from his future work, it's an icy, mechanistic work of art, Miles playing against prerecorded backdrops set up by bassist Marcus Miller. As important, in its way, as his 1972 funk/noise masterpiece, *On The Corner*. 1986.

————, *The Complete Jack Johnson Sessions* (Sony). Searing blues-rock, with John McLaughlin's guitar as prominent as Miles' horn. 2005.

————, *The Cellar Door Sessions 1970* (Sony). An incredibly tight band kicking out an unholy racket for a week straight at a D.C. club. 2006.

dBs, "Amplifier" (IRS). 1982.

DEAD KENNEDYS, *Fresh Fruit For Rotting Vegetables* (Cherry Red). Political satire aimed at teenagers ("Kill The Poor," "Holiday In Cambodia," "Viva Las Vegas"), fueled by mechanistic surf-meets-No-Wave guitars. 1981.

DEATH, *Human* (Relativity). An early masterpiece of intricate, almost fusion-y death metal from Florida guitarist Chuck Schuldiner, who basically invented the form. 1986.

————, *Individual Thought Patterns* (Relativity). The sequel. A new rhythm section, and even more radical ideas. 1988.

DECAPITATED, *Nihility* (Earache). The future of death metal—raw and robotic at once, these Polish kids (all under twenty-one at the time of release) have assimilated everything their forefathers created and put their own twist on it. They're not innovators, but they're terrifyingly skilled. 2001.

DEFTONES, *White Pony* (Maverick). In the mid-to-late 1990s, the "nü-metal" movement married guitar crunch to hip-hop beats and teenage male angst. Deftones were the brainiest, artiest group in the bunch, and on this album they moved into atmospheric electronics, almost entirely abandoning catharsis; they'd rather brood and seethe. 2000.

DE LA SOUL, *3 Feet High and Rising* (Tommy Boy). The first suburban hip-hop album, steeped in the goofy side of pop culture and a general gentleness of spirit that wasn't as much an anomaly as a throwback to earlier pre-gangsta days. 1988.

DEPECHE MODE, *The Singles 81:85* (Mute). 1985.

————, *Music For The Masses* (Mute). 1985.

THE DESCENDENTS, *Milo Goes To College* (SST). They shared a drummer with Black Flag's best lineup, but they didn't share a worldview—where the Flag were pissed-off muscular metalheads disguised as punks, the Descendents were a power pop group playing too fast to catch the ear of the pop charts. 1982.

————, *Fat* (SST). 1983.

DEVO, *Pioneers Who Got Scalped: The Anthology* (Rhino). Devo's body of work may never be totally understood, because the people who love them most dearly often choose to emphasize their quirkiness and their perceptive social satire, and ignore the boiling rage at its core. This anthology covers all the major bases. 2000.

DIGITAL UNDERGROUND, "The Humpty Dance" (Tommy Boy). 1991.

DIMMU BORGIR, *Death Cult Armageddon* (Nuclear Blast). If John Williams started a black metal band, it would sound like this—epic, grandiose, theatrical, and ultimately meaningless, but a hell of a kick in the ass while it's blaring at you. 2003.

DISPOSABLE HEROES OF HIPHOPRISY, "Television, the Drug of the Nation" (4th & Broadway / Island). 1990.

DMX, . . . *And Then There Was X* (Def Jam). DMX always sounds weary, on the verge of a breakdown, like he regrets having been forced to kill all those people, sell all those drugs. Most of his songs are about sin or betrayal, whether by women or trusted subordinates. This is his most focused and pained effort—even more than the follow-up, which he called *The Great Depression*, giving away the game. 2003.

DRAMARAMA, *Hi-Fi Sci-Fi* (Chameleon). 1993.

EINSTÜRZENDE NEUBAUTEN, *Strategies Against Architecture* (Homestead). Junk percussion, Dada poetry, one-chord (and sometimes one-note) riffs—surrounded by technology, these Germans strip music down to its most tribal, pounding core. This anthology documents their early, writhing work. 1983.

————, *Strategies Against Architecture II* (Mute). The middle-period years, in which tape loops and an increased interest in melody turned them into something close to a rock band. 1991.

MISSY ELLIOTT, "The Rain" (Atlantic). 1997.

————, "Gossip Folks" (Atlantic). 2002.

EMINEM, *The Marshall Mathers LP* (Interscope). A white rapper with a witty take on pop culture, and some issues to work out with (or on) his ex-wife and his mother. He hadn't yet realized that critics have no sense of humor. 1996.

————, "Lose Yourself" (Interscope). 2004.

ERIC B. & RAKIM, "I Ain't No Joke" (4th & Broadway/Island). 1987.

————, "Paid In Full (Seven Minutes Of Madness—The Coldcut Remix)" (4th & Broadway/Island). 1987.

————, *Follow The Leader* (MCA). After the two epic singles above, and a few others like them, this duo released a miles-deep, rumbling masterpiece of a sophomore album. Rakim's lyrics and delivery, and Eric B.'s jazzy, haunted beats, set a standard that's kept a subset of fans disappointed by everyone who's come along since. 1988.

LOS FABULOSOS CADILLACS, "El Matador" (Sony). 1985.

DONALD FAGEN, *The Nightfly* (Warner Bros.). Steely Dan's coleader steps out on his own—veiled autobiography, childhood fantasies, and a sound that's immaculate but still human, a balance he never struck again. 1982

FAITH NO MORE, *Angel Dust* (Slash). They had a huge hit, then power-dived into the perverse with this disc. Styles collide, vocalist Mike Patton indulges all his scatological obsessions, and somehow it all comes together into a fistful of compelling, shouldn't-be-this-melodic art-rock anthems. 1991.

MARIANNE FAITHFULL, *Broken English* (Island). 1979.

THE FALL, *50,000 Fall Fans Can't Be Wrong: 39 Golden Greats* (Sanctuary). Mark E. Smith is a Northern England misanthrope and poet of the working class in a Beckettian way Springsteen could never conceive of. He's kicked a dozen bands' worth of sidemen to roadside over the last three decades, but the sound remains generally unchanged: a steady beat, rockabilly/garage guitars, occasional synth stabs, and always, always Smith's bilious, occasionally comprehensible tirades. They're one of the most polarizing bands on the planet; this compilation will either begin a lifelong obsession, or you'll never make it to track two. 2004.

FANTOMAS, *Suspended Animation* (Ipecac). An all-star team of late-twentieth-century art-metal: vocalist Mike Patton recruited Slayer drummer Dave Lombardo and Melvins guitarist Buzz Osbourne to make spastic, complex, and almost absurdly compressed music. On this record, they reach a natural conclusion and incorporate cartoon sound effects. 2005.

FATBOY SLIM, "Praise You" (Astralwerks). 1998.

FEAR, *The Record* (Slash). Frontman Lee Ving was the funniest and most hateful guy in L.A., but what made Fear great was the fact that the band could actually play. Local chauvinism ("New York's All Right If You Like Saxophones") meets fuck 'em all scorn ("Let's Have a War"). 1982.

THE FEELIES, *Crazy Rhythms* (A&M). Nerdy, jumpy, poppy guitar rock with an incredible sense of rhythm and an unshowy introspectiveness at its core. 1980.

————, *The Good Earth* (Twin/Tone). 1986.

THE FIERY FURNACES, *Blueberry Boat* (Rough Trade/Sanctuary). A brother and sister who write multifaceted, melodic songs about all kinds of weird shit. 2004.

FINE YOUNG CANNIBALS, "Good Thing" (IRS). 1988.

FISHBONE, *Truth And Soul* (Epic). Their convulsive live shows were always the real attraction, but on this album they gave their blend of funk, hard rock, soul, and righteous anger ("Slow Bus

Movin' [Howard Beach Party]") the coating of studio polish it needed, without sucking out a drop of vitality. 1986.

FLIPPER, *Generic* (Subterranean). San Francisco's greatest contribution to punk (and, indeed, the '80s), Flipper's innovation was to play slow when everyone else was playing fast. Their songs came at you like glaciers, the lyrics dripping with loathing for themselves and everyone around them. They could rave up when they wanted to ("Sex Bomb"), but were usually too drunk or pissed to bother. 1981.

FUGAZI, *13 Songs* (Dischord). Their first two EPs, combined. Dubby basslines, guitars that carve melodies out of sheet metal, and two vocalists—one a punk howler and the other a virtual basket case who aims for catharsis every time out and never quite makes it. 1990.

THE FUGEES, *The Score* (Columbia). 1994.

FUNKY FOUR PLUS ONE, "That's the Joint" (Sugar Hill). 1980.

FUSHITSUSHA, *Live II* (PSF). Japanese guitarist Keiji Haino creates a louder noise than almost anyone on the planet. With his power trio, he turns psychedelic rock into something genuinely unearthly. This was the album that brought them to the attention of a few hundred tastemakers, and it's a multifaceted symphony of emotions previously thought inexpressible. 1993.

——, *The Wound That Was Given Birth To Must Be Greater Than The Wound That Gave Birth* (Blast First). Another two-CD set, this one recorded in London and owing more to traditional notions of hard rock. 1996.

——, *Gold Blood* (Charnel Music). A San Francisco concert; the band delves into drone, with the same overwhelming power as ever. 1998.

WARREN G, "Regulate" (Def Jam). 1994.

GALAXIE 500, *On Fire* (Rykodisc). 1989.

GANG OF FOUR, *Entertainment!* (EMI). Marxist whiteboy funk with just enough anger to count as punk rock. The pleasures of rhythm never quite seduced them completely. 1979.

————, *Solid Gold* (EMI). The follow-up was slightly harder-edged and more metallic, just as angry but more tempered. 1980.

THE GERALDINE FIBBERS, *Lost Somewhere Between The Earth and My Home* (Virgin). 1995.

GENIUS / GZA, "4th Chamber" (Geffen). 1996.

GERMS, "Lexicon Devil" (Slash). 1981.

GETO BOYS, *Geto Boys* (American). The single below is their masterpiece, but this album sent a shiver through the hip-hop world, putting Texas on the map in the worst—and best—possible way. 1990.

————, "Mind Playing Tricks On Me" (Rap-A-Lot). 1992.

GHOSTFACE KILLAH, *Supreme Clientele* (Loud). The Wu-Tang Clan's most brilliant molder of language is also its most florid romantic, and on this, his second solo album, he covered all the bases: weepy childhood reminiscence, surreal braggadocio, tales of street violence. Somehow, it became a seamless whole. 2000.

————, "The Champ" (Def Jam). 2006.

GO-BETWEENS, *Before Hollywood* (Beggars Banquet). 1983.

————, *1978–1990* (Capitol). 1990.

GODFLESH, *Streetcleaner* (Earache). These two natives of Black Sabbath's hometown employed a drum machine just like Big Black had, but their rage was directed inward. Their music crawled in the muck at a time when all their label mates were addicted to velocity. 1989.

————, "Love Is A Dog From Hell" (Pathological). 1989.

————, *Pure* (Earache). Singer-guitarist Justin Broadrick expands his consciousness, and his sound—suddenly, melody glimmers atop the machine beats. 1992.

GORILLAZ, "Clint Eastwood" (Virgin). 2002.

GRANDMASTER FLASH AND THE FURIOUS FIVE, "The Message" (Sugar Hill). 1982.

————, "The Adventures of Grandmaster Flash on the Wheels of Steel" (Sugar Hill). 1982.

MACY GRAY, "I Try" (Epic). 1999.

GUIDED BY VOICES, *Alien Lanes* (Matador). Group leader Robert Pollard was a drunk worshipper of the Who and the Beatles who wrote about a thousand songs a year. This album had some good ones. 1995.

GUNS 'N' ROSES, *Appetite For Destruction* (Geffen). They had one album in 'em, though they wound up making four, including a set of cover tunes. This disc promised much more than any band could have been expected to deliver—truly menacing hard rock. 1987.

BERNHARD GÜNTER, *Univers Temporel Espoir* (Trente Oiseaux). Not rock in any sense; many would say not even music. But its tiny whispers, scrapes, hums, and clicks take ambient music into a realm of almost pure silence, making you hear everything else that much more clearly. 1991.

GUY, "Groove Me" (MCA). 1987.

HANDSOME FAMILY, *Twilight* (Carrot Top). 2001.

PJ HARVEY, "Down By The Water" (Island). 1995.

———— "A Perfect Day Elise" (Island). 1998.

JON HASSELL, *Dream Theory In Malaya: Fourth World Vol. 2* (EG). Like *My Life In The Bush Of Ghosts* (and, indeed, almost everything Brian Eno's ever been connected with), more important as a catalyst and an early exploration of promising ideas than as an actual piece of music, but this trumpet-plus-electronics-plus-world-music blend *is* pretty. 1981.

JON HASSELL/BRIAN ENO, *Fourth World Vol. I: Possible Musics* (EG). 1980.

HIGH ON FIRE, *Blessed Black Wings* (Relapse). This Bay Area trio blends Motörhead's greasy biker rock with Black Sabbath's mountain-moving throb. Guitarist Matt Pike, formerly of stoner metal cult fave Sleep, really can't sing, but the band is airtight the way only true road dogs ever become. On this, their third album, they replaced their original bassist with the Melvins' Joe Preston, and got Steve Albini to man the boards, winding up with an album that'll collapse the shelf holding your stereo. 2005.

HIGH RISE, *Durophet* (Fractal). Garage rock pushed straight into the red; Motörhead's motto "Everything Louder than Everything Else" (which they stole from Deep Purple anyway) has never been more militantly applied than here. 1999.

HÜSKER DÜ, *Land Speed Record* (SST). A minimalist, Minnesotan vision of hardcore as ritual purgation. 1981.

————, *Zen Arcade* (SST). A somewhat psychedelic expansion of their early sound, with added melody and some acoustic guitar just to show they weren't *entirely* dependent on their amps. 1984.

ICE CUBE, *AmeriKKKa's Most Wanted* (Profile). One year after leaving California's nihilistic cartoon monsters, N.W.A., he hooked up with Public Enemy's production team and cracked a few mordant smiles. He'd never be this funny, or perceptive, again. 1990.

————, "It Was A Good Day" (Profile). 1993.

ICE-T, *O.G. Original Gangsta* (Sire). A summing-up. His tales of gangsta venality always ended with nearly Old Testament visions of punishment, but by his fourth album, he'd seen enough of the world beyond California that the whole thing seemed to tire him out. These days, he's playing a cop on TV. 1991.

RYOJI IKEDA, +/- (Touch). Sine waves; sound stripped to its purest essence, and still somehow made to dance. 1996.

IMMORTAL, *At The Heart Of Winter* (Osmose). Immortal started life as just another Scandinavian black metal band, blasting away with no thought for melody or nuance. By this album, they'd decided maybe it was OK to shoot for rock dynamics from time to time, and had slowed down and become nearly anthemic. 2001.

INTERPOL, *Turn On The Bright Lights* (Matador). The comparisons to Joy Division were somewhat fair, but Ian Curtis never understood the visual side of being a rock band the way these guys did. 2002.

IRON MAIDEN, *The Number Of The Beast* (Capitol). The first album on which they truly became themselves, as much because of bassist Steve Harris's newly discovered talent for melding prog ambition with punk gallop and fist-pumping choruses as because of new vocalist Bruce Dickinson's ability to deliver same. 1983.

————, *Powerslave* (Capitol). Epic without bloating. 1985.

JAGUARES, *Cuando La Sangre Galopa* (BMG). Saul Hernandez formed this bluesy, hard-rocking trio when his earlier, artier band, Caifanes, imploded. The lyrics are still filled with florid imagery, but the riffs are as much Texas blues-rock as Mexican art-funk. 2001.

———— *Cronicas De Un Laberinto* (Sony). Guest guitarist Adrian Belew expands the group's sonic range, making them heavier at some points and more beautiful at others. 2005.

JANE'S ADDICTION, *Nothing's Shocking* (Warner Bros.). Junkie art-metal, the psychedelic, blissed-out ("Summertime Rolls") flip side of Guns 'n' Roses's angry hedonism. 1988.

————, *Ritual De Lo Habitual* (Warner Bros.). Five short, punchy songs and three long, proggy workouts. 1990.

THE JESUS AND MARY CHAIN, *Psychocandy* (Warner Bros.). The "Be My Baby" beat atop an ocean of feedback. They were never this noisy, or half this good, again. 1985.

JOY DIVISION, *Unknown Pleasures* (Factory). Punk the way Northern England factory townies envisioned it—punishing, bleak, driven by existential despair. 1979.

————, "Love Will Tear Us Apart" (Factory). 1988.

JUDAS PRIEST, "Breaking The Law" (Epic). 1980.

————, *Screaming For Vengeance* (Epic). Metal custom-built for arenas and so thoroughly buffed and gleaming, the blues are all but gone. 1982.

JUNGLE BROTHERS, "Straight Out The Jungle" (Warlock.) 1988.

KHANATE, *Things Viral* (Hydra Head). Lots of bands ripped off Black Sabbath, but only Khanate thought the original doom-mongers were playing too damned fast. Their music is pure dread, with beats spaced so far apart you could smoke a cigarette between them and more feedback than chords. 2002.

DJ KRUSH, *Kakusei* (Sony). Krush is a Japanese hip-hop DJ who's been laying down tracks for American rappers since the mid-90s.

This entirely instrumental album shows him at his best, though, sculpting drumbeats and space into a kind of Zen funk. 1999.

———, *Jaku* (Sony). His usual slow, contemplative beats supporting traditional Japanese instrumentalists (saxophone, piano, shakuhachi). Cinematic, sweeping, beautiful. 2004.

NATALIA LAFOURCADE, *Natalia Lafourcade* (Sony). A quirky little girl with an acoustic guitar and a feel for hip-hop, funk, samba, and rock, this debut sounded like she was skipping to the microphone to deliver every lyric with an ear-to-ear grin. 2003.

LAIBACH, "Life Is Life" (Mute). 1985.

———, "Across The Universe" (Mute). 1987.

———, *Kapital* (Mute). A Slovenian art project, masquerading as fascists and as a rock band. On early singles and full-length releases, their beats were martial and minimal; on this album, they embraced techno and the future (or Futurism, anyway). 1992.

LAMB, *Lamb* (Mercury). A trip-hop duo (female vocalist, male everything else) who were also an offstage couple. On this, their debut, he often seemed to be throwing drum breaks or sudden melodic stabs in her way, rather than supporting her. It created a fascinating tension the genre usually opted to avoid. 1996.

LAST EXIT, *Last Exit* (Enemy). A supergroup of sorts—saxophonist Peter Brötzmann, guitarist Sonny Sharrock, bassist Bill Laswell, and drummer Ronald Shannon Jackson. All their albums but one were recorded live, under less than optimum conditions (loud, drunk, and hostile was their style, both personally and musically). This debut sets the pattern. 1986.

———, *Cassette Recordings '87* (Celluloid). More raucous blowouts, this time including the marathon "Line Of Fire" and Shannon's vocals on a cover of "Big Boss Man." 1988.

————, *Headfirst Into The Flames* (Muworks). On their final tour, they became almost introspective. 1993.

CYNDI LAUPER, "Money Changes Everything" (Portrait). 1983.

————, "Girls Just Want to Have Fun" (Portrait). 1983.

LEFTFIELD, *Leftism* (Columbia). A dubby, African-funk-informed style of dance music—one of the rare albums appreciable as a cohesive work, rather than a collection of singles (though those were uniformly astonishing) and filler. 1995.

————, "Afrika Shox" (Columbia). Afrika Bambaataa provides vocals, the Leftfielders provide the ominous vibe and the irresistible beat. 1999.

LE TIGRE, *Le Tigre* (Mr. Lady). Kathleen Hanna's post–Bikini Kill project. Dance beats, sort of; lyrics as strident as ever; not as noisy, but just as polarizing as anything she'd done before. 1999.

MADNESS, *Complete Madness* (Virgin). Ska, retooled and sent up the UK pop charts. 1982.

MADONNA, *The Immaculate Collection* (Sire). All the songs you need, as decontextualized as possible. 1992.

MAGNETIC FIELDS, *69 Love Songs* (Merge). 1999.

MAIN, *Hz* (Beggars Banquet). The guitar as sound source rather than as instrument—Robert Hampson samples and collages, letting sounds echo and drift in loops that seem endless, but somehow wind up implying song structure. 1996.

MAINLINER, *Mellow Out* (Charnel Music). High Rise's heavier, more solo-happy cousin. 1996.

MALDITA VECINDAD Y LOS HIJOS DEL QUINTO PATIO, "Pachuco" (Sony). 1991.

AIMEE MANN, "Amateur" (Geffen). 1995.

THE MARS VOLTA, *De-Loused In The Comatorium* (Universal). Born out of the fragments of the overrated Texas band At The Drive-In, two Mexican-American prog-punks combine early '70s Santana and Led Zeppelin's "Achilles Last Stand" into a heady blend. 2003.

MAYHEM, *De Mysteriis Dom Sathanas* (Century Media). One of the sacred texts, if that's the phrase, of Norwegian black metal. Released in the wake of guitarist Euronymous's murder and founding vocalist Dead's shotgun suicide. Buzzsaw guitars, nihilistic shrieking, blasting drums—a music that concedes nothing to the unconverted. 1994.

MAZZY STAR, "Fade Into You" (Capitol). 1993.

MEAT PUPPETS, *Huevos* (SST). Texan punks with an appreciation for country, psychedelia, and Southern rock combine all those styles on this, a swirling and head-spinning album. 1984.

THE MEKONS, *Fear And Whiskey* (Sin). 1985.

————, *Edge Of The World* (Sin). 1986.

MEN AT WORK, "Down Under" (CBS). 1982.

METALLICA, *Ride The Lightning* (Elektra). Metallica combined the gallop of early '80s British metal (Motörhead, Iron Maiden, Diamond Head) and the repetitive, choppy riffing of hardcore punk and, along with a few peers (Anthrax, their former lead guitarist's band Megadeth, and Slayer), created the "thrash" style, which emphasized guttural, man-in-the-street vocals and guitar virtuosity over the theatrics of Judas Priest, et al. 1984.

————, *Master Of Puppets* (Elektra). A refinement of the previous album's somewhat shocking achievements. Harder, faster, meaner. 1986.

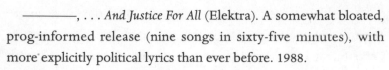

————, *... And Justice For All* (Elektra). A somewhat bloated, prog-informed release (nine songs in sixty-five minutes), with more explicitly political lyrics than ever before. 1988.

————, *Metallica* (Elektra). The album that made them megastars. Simpler, more fundamentally "rock" riffs, sing-along choruses . . . and a ballad. 1991.

MINISTRY, *The Land Of Rape And Honey* (Sire). Founder Al Jourgensen started out as a New Wave electro-disco boy, but quickly adopted (OK, stole) Big Black's mix of electronic rhythms and roaring guitars. He added cartoon rage and a dash of generic antiestablishment rabble-rousing and seemed like the future of rock for a few minutes. 1988.

————, *The Mind Is A Terrible Thing To Taste* (Sire). Samples (drills, movie dialogue, random noise) fly fast and thick, the only common factor amid a bunch of songs trying on styles from post-punk to thrash. 1989.

MINOR THREAT, *Complete Discography* (Dischord). They set the sonic and lyrical rules ("Straight Edge") for a huge swath of American hardcore bands in the mid-80s. Their vocalist cofounded Fugazi; their guitarist joined the Meatmen, then formed L.A. metallers Junkyard with a former member of Texan punk-funkers the Big Boys. 1988.

MINUTEMEN, *Paranoid Time* (SST). An early, frantic EP from this trio, who'd break just about every rule of punk, sometimes deliberately. 1980.

————, *What Makes A Man Start Fires?* (SST). Does twenty minutes or so count as a full-length album? When it contains nearly that many songs, and about a thousand ideas, it does. 1982.

————, *Double Nickels On The Dime* (SST). A sprawling master-piece—forty-five songs in just over an hour, including covers of

Steely Dan, Creedence Clearwater Revival, and Van Halen, instrumentals, homespun Beat-inspired poetry, and guitar solos almost as revolutionary as their politics. 1984.

THE MISFITS, *Walk Among Us* (Ruby). Melodic punk 'n' roll inspired by pulp horror and science fiction, with a vocalist somewhere between Elvis and Jim Morrison. 1982.

MOBY, *Play* (V2). Blues and gospel singers get hauled into the future. This album became omnipresent due to commercial licensing, but it's still a good, fun listen. 1999.

MORRISSEY, "Suedehead" (Sire). 1988.

————, *Your Arsenal* (Sire). Producer Mick Ronson and guitarist Boz Boorer force the mopemaster to actually rock. 1992.

MOTÖRHEAD, *Ace Of Spades* (Bronze). Probably the album with the best ratio of gold to lead—at least a half dozen of the tracks here are great, and the rest are tolerable while you're waiting for another classic. Fast, hard, uncompromising, and mordantly funny. 1980.

————, *Another Perfect Day* (Bronze). Lemmy briefly hired a guitar player who thought he was too good for the band. The resulting album had a couple of truly great moments, including some singles that could have been pop hits with a more conventional singer. 1983.

————, *Rock 'n' Roll* (GWR). After an experimental album that largely fell flat, the band returns to form with a stripped-down, raucous blast. 1987.

NAPALM DEATH, *Scum* (Earache). Combining thrash metal and the dirty, early '80s British punk bands (the Exploited, Crass), these UK howlers wrote ten-second songs, but even when they kept pummeling for a minute or even two their rage never flagged. 1987.

————, *Diatribes* (Earache). With all their original members gone, a more stable and more metallic lineup injected dub into their sound and created a weirdly noisy, Killing Joke–derived post-thrash. 1996.

NECROPHAGIST, *Onset Of Putrefaction* (Willowtip). Turkish guitarist Muhammed Suicmez taught himself the instrument in secret, to avoid pissing off his strict Muslim father. His music, entirely self-performed on this debut CD, is as ultra-complex as it can be when you don't have to teach it to anybody else, or play it live. 2004.

NEGATIVLAND, "U2" (SST). 1991.

THE NEGRO PROBLEM, *Welcome Black* (Smile). 2002.

NEURAXIS, *Trilateral Progression* (Willowtip). More technical death metal, this time with a frontman who doesn't play an instrument himself, so the airlessness is slightly relieved in favor of rock and groove. 2005.

NEUTRAL MILK HOTEL, *In The Aeroplane Over The Sea* (Merge). 1998.

NEW ORDER, *Substance 1987* (Qwest). These ex-members of Joy Division have never made a front-to-back great album. This collection of singles and reworked tracks contains almost all their triumphs. 1987.

NEW PORNOGRAPHERS, "Mass Romantic" (Matador). 2000.

NEW RADICALS, "You Get What You Give" (MCA). 1998.

NINE INCH NAILS, *The Downward Spiral* (Interscope). Trent Reznor figured industrial rock (cf. Ministry) needed sing-along choruses and Cure-esque lyrics about the pain of love. Millions of record buyers agreed. 1994.

NIRVANA, "Smells Like Teen Spirit" (DGC). 1991.

NORTT/XASTHUR, *Nortt/Xasthur* (Southern Lord). Some-time around the turn of the millennium, black metal went from an insurgent movement of bands to the province of loners with basement studios. Two of the best share space on this disc, though of course they don't collaborate. 2005.

GARY NUMAN, "Cars" (EMI). 1979.

THE OBSESSED, *Lunar Womb* (Meteor City). Scott "Wino" Weinrich has led several bands, all of which sound pretty much the same—Sabbathy biker-rock with guitar solos inspired by late Hendrix and Randy Holden (*Population II*). This album was the bluesiest and best one by his first group. 2006.

SINEAD O'CONNOR, "Nothing Compares 2 U" (Chrysalis). 1990.

OL' DIRTY BASTARD, *Return To The 36 Chambers: The Dirty Version* (Elektra). The Wu-Tang's id bursts out in every direction at once, on the funniest rap album since *AmeriKKKa's Most Wanted*. 1995.

OPETH, *Deliverance* (Koch). Singer-guitarist Mikael Akerfeldt is as inspired by early '70s progressive and symphonic rock as by his fellow Scandinavian metalheads. This leads to rifftastic songs that hover around the ten-minute mark and sometimes go flying well past it. This album was paired with *Damnation*, an almost-acoustic set of ballads. 2004.

———, *Ghost Reveries* (Roadrunner). A new label and a full-time keyboardist make the band a little more prog, and a little more rock. 2006.

ORTHRELM, *OV* (Ipecac). Early recordings by this instrumen-tal guitar-drums duo were ultra-compressed nuggets of gnarled metal riffing atop free-jazz rattle. On this disc, they went in exactly the opposite direction, pursuing a cyclical minimalism that flirted with and occasionally embraced an almost maddening monotony. 2005.

OVAL, *Systemisch* (Thrill Jockey). Soft, beautiful keyboard melodies interrupted, and shaped, by the sound of CDs skipping, sampled and used as percussion and alternate melody. A gentle hum that makes its stutter charming. 1996.

PANTERA, *Vulgar Display Of Power* (Atco). Texan metal obsessed with groove and rage. Vocalist Phil Anselmo was like Henry Rollins on steroids, and guitarist Dimebag Darrell made a sound like a jigsaw cutting through sheet steel. 1990.

PAVEMENT, *Slanted & Enchanted* (Matador). 1992.

———, *Crooked Rain, Crooked Rain* (Matador). 1994.

PERE UBU, *Terminal Tower* (Twin / Tone). Early singles, displaying all the bordering-on-hysterical poetry and scrape-and-thud melodicism of their later albums without the polish that sapped their strength later. 1991.

PET SHOP BOYS, *Pop Art: The Singles* (EMI). Like New Order, they never could hold it together over a whole album, but that's because their aesthetic owed as much to Cole Porter as to rock, or even disco. 2005.

TOM PETTY AND THE HEARTBREAKERS, "Refugee" (MCA). 1979.

LIZ PHAIR, *Exile In Guyville* (Matador). 1994.

PHOTEK, "Ni-Ten-Ichi-Ryu (Two Swords Technique)" (Astralwerks). 1996.

PIXIES, *Surfer Rosa* (4AD). 1988.

———, *Doolittle* (A&M). 1989.

PLACEBO, *Once More With Feeling: Singles 1996–2004* (Astralw-erks). 2006.

THE PLUGZ, *Electrify Me* (Enigma). Two Mexicans and a white guy make one of the great unsung L.A. punk albums. Bouncy, with a dash of fake reggae and a killer reclamation of "La Bamba." 1979.

P.M. DAWN, *The Bliss Album . . . ?* (Gee Street). 1993.

THE POGUES, *Red Roses For Me* (Restless). Play Celtic music fast and drunk enough and it turns into punk. 1984.

———, *Rum, Sodomy And The Lash* (MCA). More of the same, but they're coming into their own as lyricists. 1985.

PORTISHEAD, *Dummy* (Polygram). Vocalist Beth Gibbons was older than her trip-hop peers, and sounded it, mustering an almost Marianne Faithfull–esque world-weariness on these anthems of lost love. 1994.

———, *Portishead* (Polygram). A little slicker, with dashes of John Barry and minimal hip-hop. 1997.

PRETENDERS, "Brass in Pocket" (Sire). 1980.

PRIMAL SCREAM, *Screamadelica* (Creation). They started out as guitar-rock hippies, then surrendered to a dance producer and wound up something much better than themselves. This album should have been co-credited to Andrew Weatherall. 1993.

———, *XTRMNTR* (Creation). Mean, harsh, loud—turns dub and Krautrock into a platform for phony revolutionary posturing. 2000.

PRINCE, *Purple Rain* (Warner Bros.). Never mind the lyrics, which lay gender-bending hoo-ha over otherwise unsurprising love songs (except for "When Doves Cry," which gets to love via family drama). Pay attention to the guitar solos, and the astonish-ing number of pop hooks. 1984.

————, "Kiss" (Warner Bros.). 1985.

————, *Sign O'The Times* (Warner Bros.). Extremely multifaceted, and again, hooks everywhere. It's impossible to listen to this album and not like *something*. 1987.

————, *The Black Album* (Warner Bros.). Nasty, sexy funk, shelved by its creator only to be briefly released years later, when the label was mad at him for leaving. 1990.

PRINCE PAUL, *A Prince Among Thieves* (Tommy Boy). 1999.

PRONG, *Beg To Differ* (CBS). Ultradry, crisp thrash that made New York, a haven for knuckle-dragging hardcore at the time, realize there was room for real art in hard 'n' heavy music. 1990.

PUBLIC ENEMY, *It Takes A Nation Of Millions To Hold Us Back* (Def Jam). As important for what it sounds like as for what the lyrics—filled with righteous fury and reveling in contradiction—say. The Bomb Squad layered sirens, saxophones, speeches, and Slayer into collages that made urban chaos into arena-rocking anthems for pissed-off teenagers of all races. 1988.

————, *Fear Of A Black Planet* (Def Jam). An even more chaotic and confused follow-up, but it does have their two greatest singles ("Welcome To The Terrordome," "Fight The Power"). 1989.

PUBLIC IMAGE LTD., *Second Edition* (Warner Bros.). If you're an audiophile, get the UK import vinyl version. If you just want to hear John Lydon wail over dub basslines, this'll do fine. He never topped it, with the Sex Pistols or since. 1979.

PULP, "Common People" (Island). 1995.

PYLON, "Cool" (DB). 1980.

RADIOHEAD, *OK Computer* (Capitol). These art-school Brits rose out of the UK's indie scene and reinvented art-rock, taking bits of Pink Floyd and bolting them onto dissonant guitar rock for a country that kept trying to tell itself it'd outgrown such things. 1997.

———, *Amnesiac* (Capitol). On *Kid A*, they tried to shrug off everything they'd done before, but they couldn't quite manage to let go of melody. 2001.

RAMMSTEIN, "Du Hast" (Polygram). 1997.

THE RAMONES, "Bonzo Goes to Bitburg" (Sire). 1985.

THE RAPTURE, *Echoes* (Mercury). Disco, punk, and occasional Cure-esque electro-balladry. Every twenty years or so, white hipsters need to relearn rhythm: these guys and a few others picked up where Gang of Four, James Chance, and their fellows had left off in the early '80s. 2003.

LOU REED, *The Blue Mask* (RCA). In which the terrors of domesticity exert as powerful a grip on the critics' favorite rock poet as heroin ever did. 1983.

REM, "Tongue" (Warner Bros.). 1996.

THE REPLACEMENTS, *Pleased To Meet Me* (Sire). Their first major-label album, and their artistic peak—no jokey covers, no throwaways of any kind, just raw rock, occasional dashes of soul, and lyrics that mixed introspection and bravado. 1986.

THE RESIDENTS, *Commercial Album* (Ralph). Minute-long songs that claimed to cut the fat out of pop, and succeeded on that score—but that didn't make it exactly friendly stuff. 1980.

———, *The King And Eye* (Enigma). Mournful, suspicious, and paranoid takes on Elvis songs, as a way of explaining him to their fans—and to themselves. 1988.

ROCHES, "Maid of the Sea" (MCA). 1992.

ROCKET FROM THE TOMBS, *The Day The Earth Met The . . .* (Smog Veil). The folks who later formed Pere Ubu and the Dead Boys started out in this avant-garage ball of seething frustration. This disc compiles early demo recordings and live stuff, and since they never recorded a real album in their prime, you'll have to be satisfied with that. 2002.

ROMEO VOID, "Never Say Never" (Columbia). 1982.

RUN-D.M.C., *Greatest Hits* (Profile). They took hip-hop from post–P-Funk costumed superheroics to street-level tough-guy posturing, but at the same time created a model for fraternity and good humor that kids of all ages could love without their parents minding. It was a difficult balance to strike, as evidenced by how few have pulled it off since. 2002.

SAINT ETIENNE, *So Tough* (Warner Bros.). 1993.

SALT-N-PEPA, "Shoop" (London). 1993.

SCARFACE, "I Seen a Man Die" (Rap-A-Lot). 1994.

SCHOOLLY D, "Parkside 5–2" (Jive). An utterly nihilistic and hostile anthem, the drug dealer not as hero but as the only larger-than-life figure around. Schoolly shrugs off responsibility and owns his rage ("A little white kid called me a nigger/If I'd had a gun then I'd have pulled that trigger"). 1986.

————, *Smoke Some Kill* (Jive). His second full-length album contains a song called "No More Rock 'n' Roll" and one that revisits Dolemite's "Signifying Monkey" routine atop the riff from Led Zeppelin's "Kashmir." Out of print because Jimmy Page didn't crack a smile. 1988.

SCRAPING FOETUS OFF THE WHEEL, *Nail* (Self Immolation). 1985.

————, *Hole* (Self Immolation). 1988.

SCREAMING BLUE MESSIAHS, *Gun-Shy* (Elektra). Three Brits obsessed with Americana, whether it's rockabilly, the Kennedy assassination, or obscurities from Hank Williams's back catalog ("You're Gonna Change"). Lead guitarist and bawler Bill Carter churns the whole thing into the best rock his country mustered in all of the '80s. 1985.

————, *Bikini Red* (Elektra). The follow-up, recorded on the heels of a U.S. tour, was even more obsessed with America than the debut, and the riffs were faster and more ferocious ("I Can Speak American," "I Wanna Be A Flintstone," "Jesus Chrysler Drives A Dodge"). 1986.

SCRITTI POLITTI, "The 'Sweetest' Girl" (Rough Trade). 1982.

————, "The Perfect Way" (Warner Bros.). 1985.

SEBADOH, *Bakesale* (Sub Pop). 1994.

DJ SHADOW, *Endtroducing . . .* (Mo'Wax). A white kid from California, steeped in the culture of crate digging and tape trading, made this entirely instrumental, sample-stuffed soundtrack to the movies playing in his mind. He's worked with rappers before and since, of course, but on this landmark disc it was all about hip-hop as music, not a mere backdrop to braggadocio. 1996.

SONNY SHARROCK, *Ask The Ages* (Axiom). After producer Bill Laswell invited him back into the spotlight with Last Exit, this album as a leader allowed Sharrock to reassert his free jazz bona fides, putting saxophonist Pharoah Sanders, bassist Charnett Moffett, and drummer Elvin Jones through a polished set of melodic, swinging, ferocious tunes. 1991.

WILLIAM SHATNER, "Common People" (Shout! Factory). 2005.

SIGUR ROS, "Svefn-G-Englar" (Fat Cat). 1999.

————, ( ) (Fat Cat). A series of untitled tracks that blend into each other. Pet a baby seal and huddle around the stereo for warmth. 2002.

SIOUXSIE AND THE BANSHEES, *Once Upon A Time: The Singles* (Polydor). 1981.

SLAYER, *Reign In Blood* (Def Jam). The first of a trilogy of thrash triumphs. Ten songs, twenty-eight minutes, headlong fury and blood-soaked screaming. 1986.

————, *South Of Heaven* (American). They couldn't possibly go any faster (except on "Silent Scream"), so they decided to slow down and pay tribute to an earlier generation with a cover of Judas Priest's "Dissident Aggressor." 1988.

————, *Seasons in the Abyss* (American). The third and most melodic of their classic trilogy, including one misstep ("Dead Skin Mask") but outweighing it with a fistful of mosh-pit anthems ("War Ensemble," "Hallowed Point," the epic title track). 1990.

SOCIAL DISTORTION, *Social Distortion* (Epic). L.A. punks, thought second-rate for years because frontman Mike Ness couldn't clean up long enough to make a serious statement. He finally did with major-label money behind him, and emerged as a hard-rockabilly working-class poet whose version of "Ring Of Fire" was stronger than the original. 1990.

————, *Somewhere Between Heaven And Hell* (Epic). A little more feedback and fury, but the fundamental viewpoint is the same—country laments (including Kitty Wells's "Making Believe") with a stomping backbeat and power chords best played in steel-toed boots and cuffed black jeans. 1992.

SOFT CELL, "Tainted Love/Where Did Our Love Go" (Vertigo). 1981.

SONIC YOUTH, *Bad Moon Rising* (Homestead). The beginning of their artistic peak—an EP that goes from shrieking noisefest ("Death Valley '69") to the most beautiful ballad they'd ever record that bassist Kim Gordon didn't sing ("I Love Her All The Time"). 1986.

————, *EVOL* (SST). Poetry, dissonant guitars, throbbing beats, seething sexual tension. 1986.

————, *Sister* (SST). More of the same, but they still found a way to make it new, for almost the last time. 1987.

————, "Teen Age Riot" (Blast First). 1988.

SOUNDMURDERER, *Wired For Sound* (Violent Turd). Before it got self-consciously arty and started calling itself drum 'n' bass, the fastest and most furious music in England was jungle, a blend of dance-hall chanting and frenetic breakbeats. This compilation of obscure outside-the-scene twelve-inch singles, mixed for maximum assaultiveness into three epic explosions, makes the music seem even more insane than it was back then. 2003.

SPACEMEN 3, *Taking Drugs To Make Music To Take Drugs To* (Bomp!). 1990.

SPIRIT CARAVAN, *The Last Embrace* (Meteor City). Another Wino band (see entry on the Obsessed); this two-CD set compiles almost their entire discography. If biker-rock that teeters on the brink of being metal is your thing, he should already be your hero. 2004.

SQUAREPUSHER, "Come On My Selector" (Warp). 1997.

STEW, "The Naked Dutch Painter" (Smile). 2002.

SUGAR, *Copper Blue* (Rykodisc). Bob Mould made two solo albums after Hüsker Dü exploded, but exploring semi-acoustic singer-songwriterdom (*Workbook*) and roaring, doomy catharsis

(*Black Sheets Of Rain*) didn't work for him. So he started another band and made feedback-laced, melodic alternative rock for another decade or so. Whether that represents a retreat or a wise recognition of his own talent's scope depends on your outlook, but you can't deny the songs. 1992.

SUICIDAL TENDENCIES, "Institutionalized" (Frontier). Hilariously cynical take on teenaged angst, with a powerful blend of punk and metal backing it up. 1983.

——— "How Will I Laugh Tomorrow" (Epic). Full-on thrash, with lyrics more emotionally open than that genre ever got in anyone else's hands. 1988.

SWANS, *Cop / Young God / Greed / Holy Money* (Thirsty Ear). A compilation of their second, third, and fourth albums, and a stray EP. Punishing, doom-laced stuff, utterly misanthropic, so loud it'll make your brain feel stuck to the inside of your skull and so slow every line bites like a bear trap. 1999.

SYSTEM OF A DOWN, *Toxicity* (American). Armenians from L.A., drunk on Zappa and thrash, never content to put one musical idea into a song if they could cram in seventeen. 2001.

TALKING HEADS, *Remain In Light* (Sire). This collaboration with Brian Eno is their studio peak, full of trance grooves and lyrics expressing perspectives beyond the New York art ghetto. 1980.

———, *Speaking In Tongues* (Sire). A funk album, even getting them into go-go territory at times ("Burning Down The House"). 1982.

———, *Stop Making Sense* (Sire). They recruit a half dozen ringers, including former P-Funk member Bernie Worrell, and make one of the best live albums in rock history. 1984.

TEENA MARIE, "Square Biz" (Motown). 1981.

RICHARD & LINDA THOMPSON, *Shoot Out The Lights* (Hannibal). 1982.

TLC, "No Scrubs" (LaFace). 1999.

TOM TOM CLUB, "Genius Of Love" (Island). 1981.

TRICKY, "Hell Is Around The Corner" (Island). 1994.

———, *Pre-Millennium Tension* (Island). A dark, minimal album; his vocals have gone from evocatively raspy to an asthmatic wheeze. 1996.

TROUBLE FUNK, "Drop The Bomb" (Sugar Hill). 1983.

U2, *War* (Island). Earnest Irish Christians who took postpunk to the arenas of the world. Anthems of revolution vaguer than any that had come before, and love songs that weren't directed at a woman so much as at Woman. Somehow, they're not ridiculous. In fact, when nobody's looking, it's OK to think they're great. 1983.

———, *The Joshua Tree* (Island). A journey to America through a haze of reverb they carry with them like one of those cartoon characters with a perpetual rain cloud overhead. 1987.

———, *Achtung Baby* (Island). They discover irony, and the small gesture. It doesn't stick for long, but one or two songs on this album posit a whole alternate future for them. 1989.

UNCLE TUPELO, *Anodyne* (Sire). 1993.

UNDERWORLD, *1992–2002* (V2). The best of their trance-inducing, hypnotic singles. Nobody ever seems to notice Karl Hyde's incredible vocal similarity to the Fall's Mark E. Smith, but it's one of their most powerful tools—his incomprehensible incantations balance their gleaming techno grooves perfectly. 2002.

V/A, *My House in Montmartre* (Astralwerks). A collection of tracks by loosely affiliated French electronic musicians. They owe a lot to disco, but just as much to the overtly experimental side of electronic music—and there was plenty of experimentation going on in disco, anyway. 2002.

————, *This Are Two Tone* (Chrysalis). A compilation of U.K. ska revival acts, including Madness, the Specials, and the Selecter. Upbeat, occasionally political, and soaked in irresistible groove. 1983.

————, *Total 6* (Kompakt). Ultrasmooth German techno, perfect for soundtracking the Michael Mann movie in your head. 2005.

VAN HALEN, "Beautiful Girls" (Warner Bros.). 1979.

————, "And The Cradle Will Rock" (Warner Bros.). 1980.

————, "Everybody Wants Some!!" (Warner Bros.). 1980.

————, "Mean Street" (Warner Bros.). 1981.

————, "Panama" (Warner Bros.). 1984.

————, "Hot For Teacher" (Warner Bros.). 1984.

————, "I'll Wait" (Warner Bros.). 1984.

JULIETA VENEGAS, *Bueninvento* (BMG). A singer-songwriter (and accordion player) who's Mexican in that she was born in Tijuana, but American enough to want to reshape rock in her own image. On this album, Café Tacuba help her, but she doesn't really need them. 2000.

VENOM, *Welcome To Hell* (Neat). An absolute lack of a recording budget and ambitions beyond their technical capabilities wound up founding a genre—black metal. 1981.

TOM VERLAINE, *Dreamtime* (Warner Bros.). 1981.

TOM WAITS, *Rain Dogs* (Island). This album's predecessor, *Swordfishtrombones*, was the album on which the character of "Tom Waits" underwent a radical revision, the Beatnik piano-man of the '70s tossed into the junkyard to build a jazz combo. This album mixes talking blues, sardonic mythmaking from an alternate America, and weepy declarations of doomed love into a place you can fool yourself into thinking you'd really like to visit. 1985.

————, *Frank's Wild Years* (Island). Waits gives one of his typical characters a whole album to shamble around in. 1987.

————, *Bone Machine* (Island). Obsessed with death and destruction ("The Earth Died Screaming"), Waits builds rattletrap sculptures and beats on them until the demons come out to dance. 1992.

WEATHER GIRLS, "It's Raining Men" (Columbia). 1983.

KANYE WEST, "Gold Digger" (Roc-A-Fella). 2005.

WILCO, *Yankee Hotel Foxtrot* (Nonesuch). 2002.

LUCINDA WILLIAMS, "Passionate Kisses" (Rough Trade). 1989.

VICTORIA WILLIAMS, "You R Loved" (Atlantic/WEA). 1994.

WIRE, "A Serious of Snakes" (Mute). 1987.

WU-TANG CLAN, *36 Chambers: Enter The Wu-Tang* (Loud). A nine-man crew coming out of nowhere (OK, Staten Island) with heads full of kung-fu mythology and ideas of loyalty many had thought outmoded in the post-gangsta years. This album's brilliance and fluke success allowed for the release of some astonishing solo albums (Method Man's *Tical*, the Genius/GZA's *Liquid Swords*, the two mentioned above), but as a group they never pulled it together this way again. 1993.

————, "Hollow Bones" (Loud). This track, from their third album, a sort of comeback simply called *The W*, is actually a showcase for Ghostface at his most desperate and magisterial at once. 2000.

X, *Los Angeles* (Slash). 1980. Singers John Doe and Exene Cervenka were an emotional vortex, howling at and past each other and occasionally connecting in unexpectedly beautiful ways. Guitarist Billy Zoom knew his Chuck Berry, and saw how easily those ideas could be transformed into raucous punk rock, especially with a crushing drummer like DJ Bonebrake behind him. This album is ferocious from beginning to end, establishing a poetic but fierce style they'd almost immediately expand to the point that they might as well have abandoned it entirely.

————, *Wild Gift* (Slash). 1981. Their lyrics are more expansive, their range of tempos wider, and Zoom's guitar licks and Bonebrake's beats have more rockabilly and country to 'em. They even sound slightly less desperate.

————, *Under The Big Black Sun* (Slash). 1982. Their third disc, on which marimbas, gender-bending love ballads, and saxophones all turn up, all for the better. The last unambiguously great thing they'd ever do.

YEAH YEAH YEAHS, *Fever To Tell* (Interscope). 2004.

YO LA TENGO, *I Can Feel the Heart Beating as One* (Matador). If you must own a mid-90s indie rock album, this is probably the one to have. It's got a nice ballady single ("Autumn Sweater"), a semi-ironic but actually wistful Beach Boys cover ("Little Honda"), and pretty much everything else a highly educated rock critic could ever want. 1997.

NEIL YOUNG, *Eldorado* (Reprise). A five-song EP, never released in the United States, that absolutely smokes the album (*Freedom*) on which three of its songs—"Don't Cry," a crushing metal remake of "On Broadway," and "Eldorado"—were also placed, somewhat less comfortably. Fronting a shrieking, battering power trio, Young sounds angrier and more alive than at any other point in his discography, Crazy Horse live albums included. 1989.

ZZ TOP, *Degüello* (Warner Bros.). Their early '70s boogie days behind them, the gleaming wasteland of synths and MTV still unseen, this was the Texan trio's last truly great album. They kept their roots showing like always, reworking Sam & Dave's "I Thank You" and Elmore James's "Dust My Broom," and dipped into funk with "Cheap Sunglasses" and "Lowdown In The Street." But the anthems—"I'm Bad, I'm Nationwide" and "She Loves My Automobile"—are the tracks that'll make the hair on all the hidden parts of your body stand up. 1979.

———, "Gimme All Your Lovin'" (Warner Bros.). 1983.

ABOUT THE AUTHORS

MATT ASHARE is the music editor at the *Boston Phoenix*, where he's been writing about music and other cultural emissions for the past fifteen years. He's also written for numerous other publications, including *ArtForum* and *Penthouse*. He continues to dream of publishing his first book, and has fond recollections of the many bands he played in, especially his full-album cover band Squadcar. He loves his wife, family, and cat, as well as every one of his guitars.

TOM BREIHAN writes the Status Ain't Hood blog on the *Village Voice* website. He's also a staff writer for Pitchforkmedia.com, and he's written about music for *Spin*, *Blender*, *D.I.W.*, *Stuff*, *Seattle Weekly*, the Baltimore *City Paper*, and *Hit It or Quit It*. He lives in Brooklyn, and he's extraordinarily tall.

DAPHNE CARR is a music journalist, critic, and scholar pursuing a Ph.D. in ethnomusicology at Columbia University. She is the series editor of *Da Capo Best Music Writing* and author of *Pretty Hate*

Machine (Continuum). She lives between New York City and Ohio via the backroads.

JEFF CHANG wrote a book called *Can't Stop Won't Stop: A History of the Hip-Hop Generation* that won an American Book Award and put him in the hospital twice. He hopes his next book, *Total Chaos: The Art and Aesthetics of Hip-Hop*, treats him better.

IAN CHRISTE is the author of *Sound of The Beast: The Complete Headbanging History of Heavy Metal* (HarperCollins, 2003), the bible of heavy metal music and its culture, now available for burning in seven countries. He has been yelling fascinating things into a microphone on Sirius Satellite Radio's Hard Attack channel since 2004. His novel *Satan's Hollow* deals with a Satanic panic on a deserted island—er, in a suburban town in the American Midwest. He is currently learning to play "Eruption" and writing *Van Halen: A Love Story*—the first major history of the group, due in 2007 from Wiley & Sons.
http://www.soundofthebeast.com
http://www.myspace.com/ianchriste

KANDIA CRAZY HORSE is music editor at *Creative Loafing* in Charlotte, NC. She also edited *Rip It Up: The Black Experience in Rock & Roll*, a selective history of black rock artists, published in 2004 by Palgrave Macmillan. Her work has appeared in publications including the *Village Voice*, *Harp*, *Paste*, and the *Boston Phoenix*.

JOHN DARNIELLE, a longtime advocate of home cooking and champion of unremembered middleweights, sings for the Mountain Goats and maintains the website http://www.lastplaneto jakarta.com. He is convinced that smooth jazz is what's next and is willing to put his money where his mouth is on the question, should it come to that, which he hopes it doesn't.

LAINA DAWES is a freelance writer and music and cultural critic from Toronto, Canada. She is also the music editor for Suite101.com. Current projects include the recent completion of her first novel and attempting to start production for *What Are You Doing Here?*, a documentary on the history of black women in the rock and heavy metal scenes.

GEETA DAYAL has written for the *Village Voice*, the *New York Times*, *The Wire*, *Seattle Weekly*, *Publishers Weekly*, *Wired*, and other places, too. She travels a lot.

ROB HARVILLA is music editor of the *Village Voice*, after serving a similar function for the Oakland-area *East Bay Express* and Columbus, Ohio's *Other Paper*. He is tolerated by his sweetie Nicole, his cat Bumf, and, to a lesser extent, the *Voice*'s readership.

MICHAELANGELO MATOS is the author of *Sign 'O' the Times* (Continuum, 2004) and contributes to *Spin*, *City Pages*, *Nerve*, and *Seattle Weekly*.

ANTHONY MICCIO lives in Philadelphia. His blurbs about pop music have been published in *Blender*, the *Village Voice*, and beyond. He writes longer pieces on his blog, Anthony Is Right, with modest regularity. Mostly, he's just glad that he got through college loan-free.

DAVE QUEEN is an itinerant typist whose work has appeared in the *Village Voice*, the *Seattle Weekly*, and *Stylus*.

NED RAGGETT was once approached at an EMP Pop Music Conference and asked if he was "the king of ILXor.com." He's still thinking about the best possible answer. When he's not infesting said web-board, his various earnest typings are most usually found as a regular freelancer for the All Music Guide, as well as pieces for Freaky Trigger, *Careless Talk Costs Lives*, Plan B, *Loose Lips Sink Ships*, Stylus, Fake Jazz, *Dream* Magazine, the *Seattle Weekly*, Perfect Sound Forever and sundry other locales. He DJed via college radio for over a decade, recorded a spoken-word album of sorts on a dare (and a follow-up similarly), and has sometimes performed live with the Gang Wizard while reading from Petronius or Rabelais (or alternately, video-game manuals from 1984). When not doing any of this he works at a university library, figures out new places in the world to travel, and iscurrently trying to learn how to cook Persian cuisine. www.myspace.com/nedraggett is the best place to find him for now, as he's still not sure about a regular blog.

SIMON REYNOLDS, born in London but resident in New York since the mid-90s, is the author of four books, including *Rip It Up and Start Again: Postpunk 1978–84* (Penguin, 2006) and *Generation Ecstasy: Into the World of Techno and Rave Culture* (Little, Brown, 1998). His latest tome, *Bring the Noise: 20 Years of Writing About Hip Rock and Hip Hop* is due to be published in summer 2007 by Faber & Faber. A freelance contributor for magazines including Slate, *The Observer*, the *Village Voice*, *The Wire*, *Blender*, and *Uncut*,

Reynolds operates a blog at http://blissout.blogspot.com/ and a website at http://www.simonreynolds.net/.

SCOTT SEWARD single-handedly transformed and revolutionized the field of music criticism when he was asked by his boyhood idol, Chuck Eddy, to write for the *Village Voice* in 1999. Since then, he has spread joy and wisdom throughout the world via anarchy, peace, freedom, and unparalleled craftsmanship. Scott writes monthly about goregrind and corpsepaint for *Decibel Magazine*. He lives on an island with Maria, Rufus, Cyrus, and Catcher.

GREG TATE's books include *Flyboy in the Buttermilk, Midnight Lightning: Jimi Hendrix and the Black Experience*, and *Everything but the Burden—What White People Are Taking from Black Culture*. Slated for publication in 2007 are *Flyboy 2: The Greg Tate Reader* (Duke University Press) and *The 100 Best Lyrics of Hiphop* (Penguin). Tate is also the leader of Burnt Sugar The Arkestra Chamber, a twenty-member ensemble of improvisers who deploy Butch Morris's patented Conduction system and have released ten albums on their own truGROID label since 2000. www.burntsugarindex.com.

DEREK TAYLOR hails originally from the cedar-blanketed, ocean-scented environs of the Pacific Northwest. He has finally come to terms with the fact that the lion's share of his listening habits revolves around the discographies of dead guys. Whenever polled on the subject, he answers unequivocally (and with duly noted irony) that jazz is *not* dead.

DOUGLAS WOLK lives in Portland, Oregon, and writes about music and comic books for *Blender*, *Rolling Stone*, the *New York Times*, eMusic.com, Salon.com, and elsewhere. He is the author of *Live at the Apollo* (Continuum, 2004) and *Reading Comics* (Da Capo, 2007), and runs the tiny label Dark Beloved Cloud.

CREDITS

ACKNOWLEDGMENTS

Thanks to my agent, Andrew Stuart; my editor, Ben Schafer; and the project editor, Shana Murph; all the contributing writers; all the writers who expressed enthusiasm for the project, even if they weren't able to contribute themselves; all those who supported and/or ridiculed and/or debated the validity of the concept, the selected albums, and the list of contributors in various online fora; and all the artists whose music motivated this project, and are discussed herein.